Weaving the Strands of Sarayei

Channeled Wisdom
from the Ascended Master Sarah

Rachel Goodwin

'Rachel Goodwin's connection to Sarah in her new book 'Weaving the strands of Sarayei' is deeply moving and heart-warming! She brings her voice/energy alive in the richness of her storytelling! It is a must read for those who feel Sarayei beckoning their soul to return to love! I highly recommend it!'

— LEA CHAPIN, MS;ED. AUTHOR OF
DIVINE UNION: THE LOVE STORY OF JESUS AND MARY MAGDALENE

'I highly recommend this powerful light-encoded handbook of ascension processes that will activate and support you in navigating the current global paradigm shift. I found a deeper intimacy with Sarah who has recently more fully revealed herself as an Avatar of the Aquarian Age. She herself is the embodiment of the most sacred union, the alchemical marriage, and her profound teachings assist us to find balance, even amid the most extreme polarities that have been unleashed within ourselves and the outer world. She lovingly shows us that our times are truly ripe with opportunities for growth and expansion as we begin to see the world and ourselves through her divine perceptions that she so generously shares through her extraordinary channel, Rachel Goodwin.

During the reading of this book, I received deeper insight into what Sarah refers to as the "original wound." This wound is a deep-rooted, primal frequency of separation that occurs when our soul, that which is free and divinely innocent, chooses to individuate and incarnate into the body. The fragmentation that occurs is the birth of the ego, the belief that we are separate from our Creator, and this is the root of all human suffering. Engaging with Sarah's energy was so highly purifying that the honeymoon didn't last too long. I began to experience the most devastating frequencies of separation, horrific energies of abandonment and of being betrayed by my own God, accompanied by overwhelming emotions of grief. This was very unexpected! As I raged at the heavens, "how can you do this to me, I hate you, you're a liar," I had a sudden realization that this was my own self-hatred, my own self-abandonment projected onto an outer construct of what God is. My own deluded and unconscious perceptions were coming up to the surface of my awareness to be cleansed and purified by Sarah's Violet Flame. I had a visceral experience of Sarah being right by my side. "I'm here," she declared, "you're not abandoned, but infinitely loved no matter what, you are love." Her mantra, *Om Shri Sarayei Narayani Namostute*, began to gently repeat itself inside me. Now I felt relief for some moments, but then my mind again was seduced by my comfort zone of victimized thoughts, and once again Sarah made her presence known with the sacred sounds. So in this way, through this expansion followed by contraction…expansion… contraction…the frequencies of separation burn away, removing the obstructions to union through Sarah's grace and never-ending support. I can now see that I clearly have the capacity to choose my experience. One of the most basic teachings of Ascension, knowing that I am the creator of my reality, became authentic.'

– ANA ESTRADA, QUANTUM LIGHT PRACTICE, USA

www.quantumlightpractice.com

'Rachel Goodwin is a pure and loving channel for the wisdom and teachings of Sarah. Weaving the Strands of Sarayei is a divinely timed guidebook for anyone who is awakening to their truth, and seeking to be part of the co-creation of the New Earth. It really is wonderful! So needed and so grounded for day-to-day loving – but at the same time it builds the bridge to the 5th dimension. I loved it!!'

– MARY FARRELL TOBIN, SPIRITUAL TEACHER, MYSTIC AND AUTHOR OF

MAGDALENE: TEMPLE OF THE DIVINE FEMININE

'Rachel Goodwin's "Weaving the Strands of Sarayei" is a grace and a blessing – its reading has been so for me, and I believe shall be for others. The channeled wisdom received from a higher being called 'Sarah' brings comfort, guidance and insight. Sarah's messages gave me a new lens to perceive a divine grace, new to my consciousness.

Over the past years, I have come to believe that Jesus was married to Mary Magdalene, his beloved companion. While their sacred story is biblical, historical, and is celebrated often as the union of the Divine Masculine and Divine Feminine, the legendary existence of their child named Sarah Tamar has fascinated me. Imagine – a child born of this Sacred Union!

Rachel's publications have illuminated my imagination, and belief that such an enlightened, glorious being exists and is available to us now, revealing herself at a time when her message is so needed. Indeed, the overall message I perceive from Sarah is of Oneness. And of course, Love, in its many manifestations.

Rachel has dedicated herself to hearing and recording these words over the past decades, and we owe her so much gratitude for being the messenger of such grace. Indeed, the various threads of these messages weave a tapestry of beauty and hope, for those with "eyes to see" and "ears to hear".'

– **The Rev. Hollis Holder Galgano**
Deacon, The Episcopal Church

The contents of this book are for informational and educational purposes only. They are not intended as a replacement for diagnosis or treatment of any medical, emotional, psychological, spiritual or other issue. If medical or other professional assistance if needed, services of these kinds should be sought. The author disclaims any liability for individuals using information in this book.

Copyright © 2022 Rachel Goodwin
All rights reserved.

Illustration, Cover and Text Design by kozakura

Acknowledgements

I used to wonder why authors wrote acknowledgements, as surely – well, they'd written it? Aha, now I am on my fourth book, I am much wiser and realise that writing the actual book is just the first step of many for a book to be brought out into the world! So here we go… Firstly, I'd like to thank Sarah, without whom none of this would ever have happened! Secondly, I would like to thank all of you who have been part of this Sarah journey, in this life and others! Your love and dedication to Sarah and interest in my work has inspired me to keep working at it, as well as your companionship on Facebook and Instagram. And to all of you who have plunged into the unknown with me and taken the training courses as priest/esses and healers, so that we can emerge from the other end full of wonder, magick, delight and awe!! Thirdly I'd like to thank everyone who has helped me produce this book, and all of the proof readers and helpers who gave me valuable feedback - with especial thanks to Holly Galgano whose keen eye and dedicated editing turned up many a small detail. Lastly, I'd like to thank my family for having patience with me for the last year when I keep disappearing at inopportune moments to work on this book!

Thank you, all of you, without you, this book wouldn't be here!!
I AM IN GRATEFULNESS! Mahalo Nui! Blessed Be, Amen!

"We all should know that diversity makes for a rich tapestry, and we must understand that all the threads of the tapestry are equal in value no matter their color…" Maya Angelou.

"There is much that needs to be said about life as it is in this day and age.
Much that needs to be understood about the dynamics that are at play in the
society in which you live.

Much that when it is understood, and you see the truth
of what is really happening,

you will find that you naturally do something quite different!

…that your old behaviours, thoughts and feelings are no longer what they once
were and are irrevocably changed just from realising the conscious understandings
that I have come to give you.

There is a New way to live, a New way to be,
it is manifesting on the Earth now,

and the Earth is being made anew.

It is a new beginning!

It is the Age of Aquarius coming to pass,
and you are all instrumental in this occurrence.

It is why you are all here!!

Each of you has your perfect part to play, and these parts to be played are
hidden away in the desires of your hearts and souls.

I am the Key!

I can be the Key for you to unlock these mysteries,
finding the Divinity within you, and the magic of knowing these truths
of who you are, and what you are to do first hand,

experiencing them directly for yourselves.

Then you can know them.

Then you can manifest them.

Then you can be exactly as you are, the Divine's hands and feet
here on the earth!!

I am Sarah, come to teach you ways of being who you are!

May blessings come down upon you, each and every moment of your lives,
Blessed be, Amen."

— Ascended Master Sarah.

Contents

Acknowledgements vii

Contents xi

Preface 1
   The Red Thread 1

Introduction 7
   The Silver Thread 7

Chapter 1: About Sarah
   The Green Thread 11
      What should we call her?.. 11
      Sarayei... 14
      Sarah Tamar.. 15
      SaRa the Egyptian 15
      The Beginning. 17
      How Sarah came to me 18
      The very first Sarah channeling 'Love is the Key'................. 19
      Sarah's energy is pure, powerful and unique........................ 21
      Sarah is more than just a myth or a nice story 21
      Sarah holds the Christlight in Unity Consciousness 22
      Sarah is present in the Etheric... 23
      Sarah is an Ascended Master teacher for our time
      and for the New Age.. 24

Sarah has her own 5th dimensional vibration of the violet flame...............25

Sarah has a Host of Angels 25

More and more people are called to work with Sarah! 26

But Who is Sarah?...27

Sarah The Ascended Master 29

Sarah the Human & Healing the #Sarahwound.................................30

Sarah and Healing the Original Wound..31

Exploring our Connections to Sarah. 35

Has Sarah incarnated on the Earth?..36

Sarah the Black..38

Sarah's Twin Flame...39

Sarah the Forest Witch 40

Sarah as the Holy Grail 42

But what about the Merovingian Kings?!...44

Sarah shows us that 'she is us' and we are the Grail!.........................45

Sarah/ Solaris 47

Sarah Primal Earth Goddess!..47

How to build a practice with Sarah 48

Sarah doesn't belong to any religious hierarchy.................................50

Sarah the Star Elder 51

Sarah & the Lineage of the Blue Rose 53

Sarah and the Akashic Records..54

How we are connected to Sarah 55

Soul Fragments 55

Sarah, teacher, healer, sister, mentor.
An Ascended Master for our Time...57

Chapter 2: Gaia

The Blue Thread 59

Your body is the Earth...61

Living on the earth is a blessing 62

Healing of the Earth 64

A channeling from the time of Corona 67

Sarah's Violet Flame and how to live 5th dimensionally
in a 3D world 69

The time of Corona.. 74

CHAPTER THREE: HEALING & SARAH'S ANGELS

The White Thread 79

Calling Sarah in... 80

Sarah's energy can help repair your DNA 82

Calling on Sarah's Angels for healing help 82

Sarah's energies blends well with others 84

Sarah's Angels connect into Highness 85

You are Blooming into a New Era of Growth! 86

Description of Sarah's Angels... 88

How Sarah's Angels work with healing 91

The Great Angel Saraniel 93

The Work we have come to do! 95

Waiting in the Darkness 99

Sarah tells us how to experience a healing… 103

Sarah is here to help us bring our Divine Spark into consciousness 105

CHAPTER 4: THE FLAMES

The Violet Thread 109

What's the point Sarah of these flames'?!' 110

Sarah's Violet Flame... 112

Sarah has a Violet Flame Temple at Glastonbury, UK! 116

Sarah's Flame of Unity... 119

Inspiration through Sarah's Flame 121

    Sarah's flame is coming upon the Earth 122

Chapter 5: The New Age: New Earth, New Humanity

The Platinum Thread 125

    Sarah and Humanity's Evolutionary Journey 126

    Hi'iaka & the Light 128

    Priest/esses! The future is already there… 131

    Connecting to the Elohim 132

    Sarah's support with the evolution of our Lightbody 134

    An Evening with Sarah: 137

    How can you help us Sarah?' 138

    Sarah what is your mission here?' 139

    Why is this development, this work, important to humanity?' 140

    What do we need to know about our evolution and the earth's right now?' 142

    How are you connected to the Earth grid here in Roskilde?' 143

    To find the Source of all life 145

    Sarah through the Ages 146

    Sarah and the times of the year 147

    Channeling about Christmas 148

    Spring 150

    The Equinoxes 151

    Easter Channeling 153

    Sarah's Temple of the Sacred Flame 154

    Preparing for the way ahead… 154

Chapter 6: Sarah's Teachings

The Yellow Thread 157

    Be Happy & Full of Joy 158

What Can I do for Myself in Love? 159
Do the Things that You Love 160
Blessings Are Upon Us 163
God is bringing you home to yourSelf 165
Being Loved 170
All is Well 173
In Sarah's Presence 178
All is God/ Journey into darkness 179
Interdependency 181
Co-creating with the Divine 182
Be honest and true to yourself 184
Know YourSelf 185
You are a Brave Pioneer 188
We are Already Home 188
Dance with Life 190

Chapter 7: Weaving the Oneness
The Golden Thread 193
    Sarah Integrates! 195
    Sara-la-Kali 197
    Healing with Sarah & the Angels 200
    Sarah's Flame 202
    Ascended Master Sarah is a Wayshower 203
    Sarah's Evolutionary Blueprint embodied the male
    and the female in Oneness 206

Chapter 8: You Are The Power!!
The Pink Thread 211
    The Daughter Archetype 211
    Walking the path of Sarayei - Sarah by my side 213

I AM the Wake-up Call 216

Empowered to be YourSelf 218

Your True Self... 221

Believe in YourSelf 224

The Heart of Your Joy 228

Sarah is an Initiator for the New Age 230

Blessings from Sarah 231

Do it now! 232

Be positive & strong in times like these... 234

Your Emotions Are Your Power 236

The Way of the Heart 238

What Can I do Today..? 239

Seeking wisdom and acknowledging your self-worth
with Grandmother Anna 241

Freedom... 242

CHAPTER NINE: THE ANCESTORS & THE FUTURE

The Black Thread 245

Ancestral lines & DNA 247

The Importance of your Ancestral line 254

Sarah & the Star Babies 256

The Land where you Live 257

Earth Engineers from Atlantis and Lemuria are Awakening...... 259

There is a Light coming over the Earth................................... 263

What should you do?!.. 265

Blessings for the Sea 265

Afterword 271

The Orange Thread 271

Sarah's 12 Step Program to Ascension..................................... 271

Just Before You Go…	275
Glossary	277
Healing System with Sarah & the Angels	283
Links	285
Links to our online Sarah pages	287
Website:	287
Welcome newsletter:	287
Sarah & the Angels Healing System:	287
Sarah's Temple & Priest/ess Training	288
Facebook:	288
Sarah's Sacred Healing Circle FB Group:	288
Sarah's Temple of the Sacred Flame FB Group	288
Ascended Master Sarah Facebook Page	288
Instagram:	288
Online Classes	289
Bibliography	293
About the Author	295

Preface

The Red Thread

The red thread has become synonymous with Mary Magdalene, and many have come to Sarah through her. Red is the colour of fire and the passion that we have for life, as well as the colour of blood, which carries our life force – we could call it 'the blood of life'!

This book is about Sarah, daughter of the Magdalene and Yeshua, and the miracles she has come to share! As you will hear me say more than once, she is An Ascended Master for Our Time! She steps forward now, as sister, teacher, friend and mentor and offers to walk by our side as we go together into the New Age of Aquarius – but now let's start at the beginning…

Meggan Watterson writes 'The red thread.. is a symbol of the unbroken transmission of the spiritual legacy of the divine feminine – the spiritual teachings that are innate to us, that course through our blood, that stream out through us when we dare to love.' https://www.megganwatterson.com ' Sarah shares this thread, she is her Mother's daughter! She too is part of the legacy of the Divine Feminine, and her teachings are built upon the wisdom of her Ancestors; her Mother and Father, and those that came before…

I love this idea of a 'thread' running through our different stories, and through our different languages, cultures and spiritualities; it helps us to recognise that it is the same energy showing up again and again - even though the names that are used in different cultures are different. When I thought about Sarah's thread and what that could be, I had an immediate knowing that Sarah is limitless! Her archetypal energy is that of oneness, integration; she is in all of the Spheres. (meaning she can be energetically present at any vibrational level – not just the 'high' ones!) She cannot be defined, put into a box, and her essence cannot be described by only one colour!

One person I know, sees Sarah's energy as a rainbow of colours, which I think is a beautiful way to describe her energy. The rainbow also has a connection to Bi-Frost, the rainbow bridge of the Old Norse, that connects Earth to the realm of the gods. In the same way Sarah is a 'connector', she is in all of the Spheres. Through calling on her energy, we can much more easily and powerfully connect to higher or lower realms of vibration than otherwise we would be able to. This is why when we bring Sarah into Sacred Circle with us, she effortlessly expands and grounds our energy at the same time!

The rainbow has also become a symbol of the LGBTQ movement, and again, this strikes a chord with me for Sarah. For me, Sarah has a special connection with this aspect of our humanity. I can easily imagine Sarah as gender-neutral, or otherwise 'gender-bending'.

We are drawn to Sarah; those of us who live on the periphery of the society… Those of who just don't fit in with the 'norm'. The witches, psychics, shamans and healers, the unusual, the weird, the transgressive, the wonderful, the eccentric, the rebellious, the anarchic - the pioneers!! As Sarah Bollinger writes in her article about discovering Sarah in a church in Brazil, http://drsarahbollinger.com/blog/saintsarah

'Here was a saint, with my name, representing all misfits everywhere who love adventures and travel (and I LOVE adventures and travel), wrapped up in images of divinity. The underdog, minority, traveling, female saint who is a symbol of refuge to the persecuted and marginalized, shining in all her glory and whispering in my ear about all of the buried, hidden, sacred things that I wasn't suppose to know about growing up. Somehow the misfits and gypsies and travelers managed to keep this image alive in a world where men dominate the celestial scene. I was in love!'

And that is how the title 'Weaving the Strands of Sarayei' came about. Sarah is undefinable, ineffable, beyond the limitation of a single label or word. And so, we must make do with more than one! Living in Denmark as I do, I have come to study and become fascinated by the old Norse cosmology – especially the Norns. The Norns are the weavers; they watch over the Web of Wyrd - which we can imagine as the energetic equivalent of what has been, what is becoming, and what will be.

Weaving has long been associated with women's magick, and magickal mysteries and secrets! For me, Sarah too has an energy of being a weaver, expertly untangling something, adding a thread of life here, ending a thread there, carefully making good the weave in this place over here – all expertly woven and creating a new weave upon the web!! She is an overseer, keeping her careful gaze on how things are going! At the same time, she is willing to 'come down to Earth' and get her hands messy!!

'Weaving the Strands of Sarayei' is an attempt to show how the many different aspects of Sarah, (who is an archetype of the Divine, and mirroring to us what we too are capable of) are beautiful and multi-coloured threads that are helping to weave the tapestry of the New Earth, The New Humanity.

So, I hope you enjoy this book and receive inspiration from it! Maybe not everything in it is for you, but my sense is that there is something special in here for everybody! I have tried to include as many of the different views there are of her. Be discerning, take only what resonates with you! When I started working with Sarah in 2006, all I had to really start working with was a name! There were no pictures of her that I could find, and only small crumbs of myths here and there. Over the years this body of intuitive knowledge has grown and grown, as we have created together something out of the ethers! I experience Sarah as an energy, she's not someone that I 'believe' in – to me she's real! But I don't pretend to know all there is to know about Sarah, and I'm not supposed to! I am here as a wayshower, a bridge, a portal to Sarah….

One way to use the book, is to pick it up when you need… something – and open it randomly up at a page, and see what the words speak to you. Louise Keoghan, who has worked closely with me for many years with my Sarah work, loves to do this with the first book 'Sarah's little book of Healing', and she's received help and support numerous times when she's needed it. The channelings contain not just the words, but coded matrices of energy for you to receive; and that's why I say 'see what the words speak to YOU', because the same set of words can mean one thing one day, and then another thing another day – depending on the need of what you need to receive!

Sarah's energy is so grounding, and as the colour red can symbolise blood and our opportunity at having a manifested life here on the physical plane, so we start at the beginning of the book with that colour. Mary Magdalene, Sarah's mother, has prepared the way – she offers us the healing we need in order to move forward on our path. She holds us when we are broken and apparently lifeless.

In Glastonbury, by the side of the Tor, is Chalice Hill. Legend has it that Joseph of Arimathea brought the Holy Grail to England and that its final resting place was with Chalice Hill. Within Chalice Hill, there is an etheric Healing Temple, dedicated to the Magdalene, and in this place, Sarah is Handmaiden and assists her mother with her work. The Magdalene is the great healer, she heals our trauma and prepares the way for us to move onto the next stage of our evolution, with her daughter Sarah by her side. We can enter this Healing Temple when we need healing, and it will be given to us.

But there comes a time in our healing journey where we are ready to step out back into the world once again. Re-made, renewed, rejuvenated; ready for the next adventure! Then Sarah comes to us, ready with her bag of wonders. If you have picked up this book, then I suspect Sarah has managed to magically appear in your life in one way or another! As I talk about later in the book, she appeared in my life unexpectedly in the June of 2006, and I have never looked back!

I hope that your journey brings you the many blessings that I have received, (often in the hidden form of unwanted challenges!) But in whatever way you have received Sarah onto your path, the different aspects of Sarah weave a rich and varied tapestry of so many threads including nature magic and cosmic energies - all culminating in the New Earth and the next step on our evolutionary path. Sarah is the future! She holds the blueprint for humanity's evolution and for Gaia. As we call Sarah in, each time we take on a little more of these blueprints, and then weave them into our own lives and the places and land where we live.

We too are weavers of Sarayei. We will each work with those threads that resonate with our own soul's energy. Sarah is a human face that represents the Archetypal energies that are talked about in the book, but really, these energies belong to all of us. She is here to empower us to skilfully weave the threads into the world's weave, changing the pattern as we go, bringing in the Divine energies! As you read the channelings and words in this book, you will be triggered to have your own revelations & realisations about Sarah. Together we are creating a new mythology. One that rises up from the depths of our collective unconsciousness - a new mythology for the New Earth!! The stories we create will inspire new thoughts, new books, and new ways of being and living together that we couldn't even imagine right now! This vibration is pouring through the Earth into those who are ready to receive it – we are the tribe of the New Earth!

I wish you many Sar'h blessings on your continued journey,

Blessed Be,

Rachel Goodwin,

December 2021, Roskilde, Denmark.

* * *

In the book, the Divine is given different terms; God, Goddess, Sophia, but please use any term instead of these that you like to use.

Some of the information given is in a 'question and answer' format, and has been taken from several live interviews where questions were being asked of Rachel and Sarah.

For the rest of the book, my words will be in italics, and Sarah's channelled words and other quotes will be without.

Introduction

The Silver Thread

Silver is the colour of women's magick, of intuition and the moon, feminine mysteries, dreams and meditation. It is no accident that Sarah has come to us, as a woman, as the daughter, at this time, in a point in our history and evolution where we need to re-remember the Divine Feminine, and heal the rift between the masculine and feminine inside ourselves, embracing, accepting and loving All That We Are.

"My mother the Magdalena, she will come to you and help you heal your wounds. She will hold you when you are in pain and suffering and give you so much love and compassion. And my father Yeshua, he will light up that spark, he will fan the flame, he will make it brighter and help you have clarity to comprehend divine truths. And I Sarah, I will help you bring it all together."

Sarah is a 'new' Ascended Master, meaning that she has only just stepped forward at this point in humanity's evolution… because this is her time--- She's here to mentor us into the 'New Age'; to walk by our sides - not to guide us, but to show us how to find what we already know! Humanity has approached the time where we need to discover our own innate wisdom, and the Divinity inside each of us!

What is an Ascended Master? An Ascended Master is someone who has lived on the earth, and reached a point in their spiritual development where they don't need to reincarnate anymore! This is because they've learnt what they need to learn by being here. Earth is a classroom, one where we can master many things, and raise our vibration to an extremely high level! There are many 'Ascended Masters' that none of us have ever heard of, and there have been many more of them than most of us probably think! An example of a 'famous' Ascended Masters could be Buddha, Jesus, or Quan Yin, as well as Mother Mary and Mary Magdalene. Others who became well known through the theosophical movement are St. Germaine, keeper of the Violet Flame and the Master Morya. The 'known' Ascended Masters are male or female, and have a recognizable face, because they have a specific role to play – a job to perform if you like, and carry out in accordance with the Divine Will. Sarah is here to empower us into creating the New Earth!

We have come into a New Age, and it is a time of great change. Mercedes Kirkel, author and channel to Mary Magdalene describes the process we are going through beautifully here,

'.. the time has changed as we are entering into a new age, the age of Aquarius. It has been said by many that this is the age of equality between the Masculine and the Feminine, and this is true. And for this shift into equality to occur, there is a particular kind of passage required at this time. It is though you are giving birth to the new age...' (Mary Magdalene Beckons.)

As we go through this process, we receive support, wisdom and inspiration from Sarah – she is right there with us, walking by our sides, whispering encouragement into our ears; holding us up when need it, along with the power and strength of her host of Angels!

Sarah holds the Christ consciousness in Unity, she is the expression of *the Sacred Marriage, and holds that expression as a blueprint for humanity. She is the male and the female, the light and the dark, the low and the high. If you were to meet Sarah, she might well be non-binary, transgendered, gay or otherwise. All of us can find something of ourselves in her. She lives on the periphery, not accepted or recognised by the 'norm'. She is the outcast, the rebel, the exiled. She knows our pain and comes to share her gifts. She is human and divine. Sarah is the future!*

"What I wish to offer is support and powerful energies, to energetically support you and spiritually support you as you move through these exciting times of miracles and of change.

I am Sarah and my voice and energy and name will become much more well known in the days and weeks and months and years ahead and you are really the pioneers of this new vibration of energy, that comes in now because it is the time for it to come in, in your evolutionary process.

I am Sarah and my blessings are always upon you.

Blessed be. Blessed be. Blessed be. Amen."

You are here reading this book because on some level you recognise Sarah; something in you has called out, given you a wake-up call, even though maybe you don't know what it is that you're being called to.. Something in you 'sees', consciously or unconsciously the light-image of Sarah! She shows us what it is we can become in ourselves. This quote is from the Sophian Tradition of Gnostic Christianity,

'A matchmaker witnessed the exchange of glance between the Lord and Mary, and she knew in that instant that they were in love and it was destined for them to be together. More than this, to her astonishment, she saw a light-image come out of the Lord and a light-image come out of Mary, and the two merged completely together. She said of this light-image, "I dared not gaze at it, because it was blinding. Flashing fire was coming out of it, and I feared for my life. It was too great a holiness." Because of what she had seen, she did not tell anyone. She only spoke of it to the women disciples of the Lord sometime after Yeshua and Mary were husband and wife.

When it came to pass many years later and the matchmaker died, when her soul passed through the domains of.. the celestial abodes, no guardian would challenge her. Having beheld the image .., the glory of the image was upon her for all to see. As it is known among initiates, one cannot see something that one does not become.'

- St. Mary Magdalene:
The Gnostic Tradition of the Holy Bride, Tau Malachi.

The seeds of our enlightenment and evolutionary process are already within us – Sarah is the catalytic miracle that starts to awaken that process within us; she is the water that starts the seed growing, she is the miracle of life.

CHAPTER 1

About Sarah

The Green Thread

Green is the colour of abundance, manifestation, attraction, growth and plant magic, and Sarah's energy has all of these qualities! I have had some images of Sarah that have stayed with me for years. One of them is that in my mind's eye, Sarah always appears as green (the Magdalene as pink, and Yeshua as yellow). I have a strong predilection for nature magic, and adore this part of her energy - she carries the energy of life itself, the life-force, the bursting forth of spring and new growth. But she can appear in all the different greens of the forest, from the first bright green beech leaves of the year, to the darker greens of the firs and pines in winter, and everything else in between!

What should we call her?

I've always called Sarah, Sarah, just because that's how she introduced herself to me. Some different spellings that come up are Sara, Sahra, Sar'h. For the Sanskrit chants, a 'yei' appears at the end of her, which is the deno-

tation of 'shakti' energy, and she becomes 'Sarayei'. Also the name Tamar is given to the daughter of Yeshua and Mary Magdalene, and some people call her Sarah Tamar. In French, she has been called 'Sara-la-Kali' which means 'Sarah the Black' and which we'll talk more about later. I love all the names and stories, and find they each carry a different strand and energy, and each story shows a different side of her as we interpret the possible meanings and significance behind them!

'Sarah, is it okay to call you Lady Sarah, or do you have another preferred name?'

"I don't have any preference over the actual names that I'm called. Really, it's not very important. What is more important is that people choose the names that they particularly resonate with. Each letter, each sound has its own vibration and so creates its own energy of me. My energy is quite, how can we say… large, and each name will particularly focus on the different aspects of me also, depending on which language it's said in, and how it's said even. So really, it's a personal choice. Yes, I think that's what I want to say on it."

Many years ago, I was looking for a Hebrew interpretation of Sarah's name. It's not unusual to find that modern interpretations of name meanings have missed references from the culture of origin that are really important, and I wanted to get down to the linguistic 'bones' of the name. I was looking for this, because I had the feeling that the standard translation of Sarah's name as 'princess' was really missing something important. It didn't feel right to me at all, and I searched and searched on the internet, and finally came across a wonderful article entitled 'The Engendered Shema: Sarah-Echoes in the Name of Israel' by psychotherapist Elizabeth Wyner Mark. It gave me the information that I was looking for!!

Wyner tells us that the name Sarah originally comes from the story of 'Abram and Sarai' in the Old Testament, when they were renamed Abraham and Sarah. (the suffix 'ai' is the name of God related to the word 'breast', is found in connection to names of deities, mythical beings, and nature goddesses! Sarah is very much connected with nature/ lifeforce energy!)

Hebrew is a sacred language and each letter has a spiritual meaning, and there is deep significance to the addition of an h to both of their names. (I found by searching online that one of the meanings of the letter 'he' in Hebrew is to concentrate on the soul within each person, the godly spark, as that is where we are all one. This was very exciting for me to read, as one of the main teachings that Sarah has given, is to work with our Hrit Padma (see glossary), the Sacred Lotus of the Heart, where our Divine Spark is located, and which we work with in the 'Sarah & the Angels healing system'.)

Wyner says that from 'sar', Sarah, is associated with power and dominion, and 'shadows of goddess worship', as the word 'sar' is derived from the Akkadian 'sarru', meaning king - in its feminine form, it is an epithet for the goddess Ishtar, Queen of Heaven!

In her article, Wyner says that there is a tradition that associates the verb 'sarita' with the noun 'sar' (feminine form: Sarah) and points out a striking semantic gender disparity between the two words. "In modern Hebrew Sar/ (male form)/Sarah(female form) is a title given a man or woman holding the office of cabinet minister…" However, in dictionaries the 'sar' form is endowed with the property of governance 'chief, leader, captain, minister, ruler' in contrast to the 'Sarah' translations, 'princess, noble lady, ambassadress, lady minister.' Sarah can also be taken as a verb. Wyner tells us of another name changing event in the Old Testament, where Jacob receives the name Israel, 'you will be known as Israel because you 'sarita' with God and humans' She explains this text is read out every year in the synagogue, where the verb 'sarita' can take the exact form of Sarah's name, Sarah. One translation interprets this as 'Jacob had power with God'. I find this very interesting. Just as Frejya (the Norse goddess) has been taken by some scholars to be mean 'lady' rather than be a specific name, so we can see that Sarah can also be a title/noun, but also a verb. Then her name becomes *something that we are, and something that we do!*

Sarah's channelings teach us about 'oneness', and working with our divine spark; and not only are we given information, she also gives us teachings so that we can work with these things energetically. In doing so, we are becoming a 'Sarah' to ourselves. By working with our Divine Spark (and thereby everything that is not in rightness with the Divine, i.e., our shadow) we naturally come into oneness; our Higher and Earthly selves come into oneness, and we are able to connect directly to our own Godself, our Divinity. We become a Sarah to ourselves; sovereign, whole and complete in ourself!

Sarayei

Many years ago, at the beginning in my journey with Sarah, I had a Sanskrit chant for her appear in my head one day - it had been going round and round in my head for a while before I noticed it! I've always been a person who likes singing, and it's not unusual for songs to go round in my head, and that particular week I had been learning a lot of new chants. Suddenly 'Om Sri Sarayei Narayani Namostute' was in my head (the meaning of this chant will be discussed in Sarah's little book of Chants, Prayers and Practices.) In Sanskrit chants the female names have yei added to them, this means shakti/power – by calling her Sarayei, her role as a window to an archetypal power of the Divine was made clear to me. It also showed me that Sarah doesn't belong to one culture or religion,

" *...& I say this prayer for healing to encompass all faiths, all religions, all spiritualities, barring no one, no creed; we are all children of the Divine, whatever faith or religion we hold & Sarah also is there for all of us, Blessed Be, Amen.*" *(Blessing service, 2012)*

Sarah belongs to herself!!

Sarayei can also be translated from Sanskrit to mean 'the ocean of the world', or 'the endless ocean'. This could also be taken to allude to 'Sea of Creation'. Sarah has shown many times that she has a strong affinity with bodies of water and the sea.

Sarah Tamar

It is said that this is a name which is used for Sarah, with Sarah as the title, and Tamar as the name.

Tamar (Hebrew: וְרֶמָת) is a female name of Hebrew origin, meaning **"date" (the fruit)**, *"date palm" or just "palm tree". (Wikipedia). Here we see another connection to Ishtar/Inanna,*

'Inanna was also a fertility figure, and, as goddess of the storehouse and the bride of the god Dumusi-Amaushumgalana, who represented the growth and fecundity of the date palm, she was characterised as young, beautiful, and impulsive—never as helpmate or mother. She is sometimes referred to as the Lady of the Date Clusters.' (Britannica.com)

SaRa the Egyptian

In connection to the stories of the three Mary's Mary Magdalene, Maria Jacobe and Maria Salome arriving on the shores of France at Saintes-Maries-de-la-Mer, Sarah is sometimes called Sarah the Egyptian.

Saint Sarah is celebrated annually at the 'Gypsy Festival' in May every year, along with the 'Three Marys'; who were believed to have arrived on the boat together fleeing persecution.

St. Sarah, or Sara-la-Kali (Sara the Black) is the patron saint of gypsies, or the Roma people, and her image is decorated and revered in the crypt of the Church of the Saintes-de-la-Mer, and is the pilgrimage destination of the Roma peoples.

I have a deep sense of Sarah's connection to Egyptian energies, and of

Sarah having had an Egyptian past life as a priestess. There are stories of Mary Magdalene having been a priestess of Isis and also that she fled and took refuge with her daughter and lived among the Egyptians, perhaps as many as eight years - so Sarah may have spent her earlier years in Egypt.

As mentioned, a little later in the book Sarah seems to have a strong solar connection, which ties in with the 'Ra' being highlighted in her name. Someone wrote to me recently, and said that Sa-Ra is a light code, just as is Ma-Ra, which definitely resonates with me...

Stories, myths and legends always have many different versions of their tales, as they are told and retold through the ages. I found this beautiful version on a Roma website, (https://romove.radio.cz/en/clanek/18906)

The historical sources support the existence of two Sarahs: one of the Catholic Church, the second Romani. The first was the servant of the two Marys: Mary Salome and Mary Jacobe, who were expelled from the Holy Land. Sarah accompanied them and they landed together in the village of Les Saintes Maries-de-la-Mer. This account has come down from the time of the reign of King Rene (1448). The Catholic Sarah didn't have a right to canonization and so remains in the crypt, since she was expelled from the church. Romani Sarah is supposed to have lived on the banks of the River Rhone with her tribe and taken on with the three Marys after their landing. Franze de Ville, in the book "Traditions of the Roma in Belgium", describes the event this way:

"One of our people who had the first epiphany was Sara-la-Kali. She came from a noble line and ruled her kin on the bank of the Rhone. Thanks to this mysterious revelation, she knew many secrets. By the River Rhone tribes worked with metals and then traded with them. Roma at that time had polytheistic beliefs (they followed several deities) and once a year they took part in a procession with a statue of Ischtari (Astarte) on their shoulders. They walked into the sea with it hoping for benediction. One dat

Sara-la-Kali had a vision. She saw three holy women calling desperately for help. So Sarah didn't hesitate and went to meet them in a small boat. But the sea was so tempestuous that Sarah almost lost her own life. Finally, in desperation, not knowing which direction was best, she threw her dress into the waves. And lo and behold, by some miracle, it served as a raft and helped her to convey the three Marys to shore. The holy women baptized Sara as a reward and recommended the gospel to her."

There are many variations in the myths from the Carmargue; even one where Sarah comes out of the boat and walks on water as they approach. A clear message perhaps that she is Yeshua's daughter?

But I believe that legends and myths have some deeper knowledge in them. They are not necessarily about literal historic truth, but can also tell a profound spiritual truth. These stories bypass the conscious mind and speak directly to our souls!

The Beginning...

When Sarah first came to me back in 2006, I couldn't find very much said about her, or even a picture of her. This was right at the beginning of my journey. I didn't really understand who she was, I had no idea that it was the beginnings of a relationship that would continue for me and stretch far into the future. I just knew I loved her! For many years, that was enough for me. I honestly didn't care why she was in my life, I felt a deep sense of devotion and loyalty to her. I was born in 1970, the year of the Dog, under the sign of Leo, so I'm about as loyal as they come (which has bitten me in the behind sometimes!) It hasn't been an easy journey with Sarah; I had to go through many dark nights of the soul, to come to a 'good enough' place of integration so that I could offer the classes and initiations that I offer today. Many times I wanted to (and did) tell Sarah, and the whole of heaven/spirit to F**K off. But I always came back to the path. Because it is the only way, there is no going back. The only way is forward! And in the end, well,

I love her, you know?!!

But today, in this day and age, there is much, much more about Sarah. Things are starting to open up with her energy - it's a very different energetic place we find ourselves in than when she first came to me all those years ago, when my hair was still brown and not silver as it is today.

She means different things to different people, and in this book I want to share with you the myriad and wealth of information that we have discovered from the questions that have been asked and the workshops, initiations and classes that have been held.

But of course, first and foremost she is known as the daughter of Mary Magdalene and Yeshua,

'The... legend is that Sarah is the child of Mary Magdalene and Jesus Christ. She's the reason the three Mary's were being persecuted and needed to escape to France. The Marys wanted to protect Sarah from the Romans. Sarah then is understood and considered in this legend as the living holy grail, or as the Sang Royale, the bloodline of the union of Mary and Jesus.' (Mary Magdalene Revealed, Meggan Watterson.)

How Sarah came to me

It was a Friday evening when I first channelled the words, 'Welcome sisters, I am one of the lady ascended masters, and my name is Sarah. I was daughter to Mary Magdalene...' I hadn't been expecting a message from Sarah. I was facilitating a group working with a very special earth energy vortex at the Place of Refuge on the Big Island of Hawaii, and had opened up to channel a message about it. Before this, I hadn't had any contact with Sarah, she wasn't someone I had 'believed in' or even had any particular interest in! ... But when you're channelling, if you don't speak the first words that come through, then you don't get any more information, and I had an expectant group of women sitting around me! So even though I *was a bit self-conscious about channelling someone I knew nothing about, I could feel her energy was pretty amazing, and I decided in that moment to go on..*

Sarah came through and I loved her energy. It swept me up and did things to my heart centre and my consciousness that no other energy had done before - and so I've never looked back.

That first channeling was in 2006, and Sarah has stayed with me ever since, and her presence is never far away. Sarah often teaches me through direct revelation, or sometimes words appear in my head, and sometimes through signs and omens. When my life path has been full of hard bumpy roads, and I've hit rock bottom, Sarah has been the one who comes to the fore, and offers her healing energy and clear vision....

In my experience, Sarah teaches how to get yourSelf out of the mire, by bringing in the light and integrating it with all the muck to hoist yourself up to the next level of vibration! She is an invaluable ally & mentor, and I've been motivated to share this with other people through individual channeled sessions, Sarah initiations, and online courses and classes. All of these things together have given me an insight and perspective into her 'mission' here on the earth, which I want to talk about in this book. Everything that I've included here is based on my personal experience and is my own understanding of Sarah and her work. I'm not presenting it as 'the truth', but rather am sharing with you how I have come to understand her and her work...

The very first Sarah channeling · Love is the Key·

In that very first class in June 2006, it was the last of six weekly classes sharing the sacred places and light beings that I had worked with on the Big Island of Hawaii. We were working with the beautiful energies of Pu'u honua o honau nau, a sacred place of refuge next to the Pacific Ocean, and which holds the perfect emanation of Divine Love. I opened up at the end of the class to channel, expecting it to be one of the divine Hawai'ian goddesses who had come through - but instead Sarah arrived! This is the first channeling I ever did from her.

"Welcome sisters, I am one of the lady Ascended Masters, and my name is Ascended Master Sarah. I was daughter to Mary Magdalene, who also encapsulated the love energy that is present here tonight.

The energy of this Lemurian vortex, ancient and old, has been pouring forth the energy of love since the world began. Yes, this is a gentle energy, a soft energy, but in that softness and in that gentleness is immeasurable power and immeasurable strength.

Everything was created with the energy of love. The energy of love binds all that exists within the physical world. It is the thing that connects you to everything else around you. It is the energy of love therefore, in which we are one with the universe, and can be one with all things.

If you wish to know a thing, or understand a thing, or connect to a thing, then send to it the energy of love from your heart centre, and this will open up many doorways for you.

The energy of love is the energy that when you are feeling tense or cross, & don't understand what is going on around you; this is the energy that you need to call upon. The energy that will flow & soften, and help you see once again the truth of what is around you.

The energy at this sacred site, is like a rose with the petals tightly curled. Its time will come where it will grow and unfurl and show its true beauty to the world.

And there is work to be done to enable this process, and this will be shown to you at the right time and at the right place."

Sarah introduced herself to me as the daughter of the Magdalene, emphasizing the Divine Feminine lineage. This was very important to me at the time, and opened my heart to her straight away! I've always felt that this 'foundational teaching' about Love is the basis for all of Sarah's wisdom, and one that doesn't feel fully embodied and is waiting to come back in....

Sarah's energy is pure, powerful and unique

"My energy can be seen as the bright green of nature, the colour of spring, new leaves growing on the branches, abundant growth... I represent the sacred Divinity which is within each of us" * (the transcendent spark within each of us, that conversely also exists outside of manifest creation.) *Taken from 'Sarah's little book of Healing', page 9.

Sarah represents both of these things, the immanent and the transcendent! She is unique, and I just love her! I have a strong 'soul' pull towards her that I have felt since the first moment that she stepped on the scene. That's the way it is for many people who write to me, saying that they feel such a strong calling, but don't know why.

There has been a lot of interest generated over the years in stories about Jesus's bloodline, starting with books such as 'The Holy Blood and the Holy Grail', and later bestsellers such as Dan Brown's 'The Da Vinci code', which put the idea into the mainstream. BUT...

Sarah is more than just a myth or a nice story

Sarah has a mission and is here to support us in our evolutionary journey of Ascension! The energy that she carries is catalytic – when we connect with her, her energy instantly has an effect on us, and our light bodies start to change. Sarah is a new Ascended Master teacher for the New Age

of Aquarius/the Golden Age and is here to work with us, teaching us new technologies about our energy bodies and how to work with it, as well as how to work with the energy systems of the earth!

'I have come to tell you of my news, that I am returned here once again, not in physical form, but through conduits, sources of energy, through the hearts of mankind, my light, my power is being given birth to on earth. This birth is happening as we speak, as you read these words, my love, my light, the power that I represent is manifesting onto the physical planes. Open your hearts and breathe me in, I am there already, lying dormant, waiting to be awakened.' (Sarah's little book of Healing, page 8.)

Sarah holds the Christlight in Unity Consciousness

Sarah holds the energy of Oneness; she is the Divine Feminine, and the Divine Masculine brought together as one - in her there is no separation. She holds the Christlight in Unity consciousness – but what does this mean?

In her, all things are integrated. The dark and the light, the male and the female, the conscious and the unconscious. Her energy has a magnetic quality (a female quality) returning the lost parts of ourselves* but with conscious awareness; meaning that we know what is being returned to us and why (a male quality).

'No-one can prove of whether or not I ever existed upon the earth, but as a concept of an energy borne from the sacred union of the Divine Masculine and the Divine Feminine, I am most believable! I am the awesome power of my Father, and the awesome love of my Mother combined to make a third most incredible power.' (Sarah's little book of Healing, page 9.)

Where these two things are held together - the divine masculine and feminine (divine opposites), out of this tension is born a 3rd energy, and this is what the New Earth is being created from.

* When we call on her power, everything within us that is split off from us starts to journey back from whence it came! This could include lost soul parts, repressed parts of ourselves, twin souls, our shadow side, etc. A very practical use of this is that Sarah is very good to call on for doing therapeutic healing work- Years ago, when I was a psychiatric nurse, I trained in group analytical psychotherapy and also had several years of my own therapy. Through experiencing these sessions, I learnt the power of 'integrating' difficult experiences and emotions. As a sensitive, I became aware of the energy that a good therapist brings in. The best way I can describe this energy is that a 'groundedness' comes into the room, and that one becomes more aware of one's own emotions, thoughts and feelings - in fact one becomes more present to oneself! When we call in Sarah, and her presence enters the room, this is very much the same as having the presence and support of a very good and experienced therapist in the room, and the likelihood of 'coming into wholeness' is increased!

Sarah is present in the Etheric

Sarah is a presence on the earth right now; she is here on the earth, manifested in/on the etheric plane. This is unusual for an Ascended Master, and reflects her special role in helping us with the evolution of our light bodies and also that of the earth grid* – it also means that she is very accessible!

'Greetings, greetings, arise, arise. I have come, I have come, I am here, I am here. My love, my light, pouring through the earth. Can you hear, can you hear, the sound of my footsteps as I dance my way across the earth? I am jubilant, I am in praise of all that is, I am in love with all, in love with life. I am, I am, I am. Blessed ones, I bring you the news, I am here, I am here, I am here. Jubilations to all, I resound my joy in circles of power across the earth.'

* *By referring to the earth grid, I mean the crystalline/new earth/ golden age grid structure, which is a 5th dimensional ley/energy line system currently being rebuilt on the earth, and which needs to be in place for the 'new golden age'.*

Sarah is an Ascended Master teacher for our time and for the New Age

Sarah is stepping forward as an Ascended Master teacher for many. Her energy acts as an evolutionary catalyst, and some people may just need a 'burst' of her energy at a specific time in their life to shift them where they need to be – but there are others, who have agreed in their soul contract to work specifically on Sarah's agenda and 'life purpose'. For these people, Sarah is available as an Ascended Master teacher/mentor. Sarah is also useful to Starseeds, as her cosmic energy can connect with their cosmic energy, helping to bring them 'down to earth', and grounding their much needed Starseed light.

One of the reasons why Sarah is here right now at this point in our evolution is because humanity needs to integrate the higher and lower self. Sarah's ability to unify and to integrate all that is, lends us the quality of energy we need to help us tease our higher selves down into our physical selves, and our physical bodies up into our 'higher' selves.

But before this can happen, we first need to do the clearing work needed (not just on ourselves, but also our ancestral lines, the cultures we live in, and also of the 'energetic waste' we have left on the earth.

Sarah has her own 5th dimensional vibration of the violet flame

Sarah has some 'power tools' to give us a bit of extra help with this great cleaning up process! She has her own vibration of the violet flame which transforms lower density energies to 5th dimensional and above. This vibration of the violet flame rapidly clears our own personal space (that we live in), and our energy bodes. Sarah has been instructing us in techniques for keeping a 5th dimensional vibration in our homes – and (for those who want to get deep into the process) in the areas of land where we live. She has also taught us how to attune sets of crystals with the violet flame. When my resistance comes up (I'm not good enough, no one is interested, you know how it goes!!) I go and get my crystals, which then shift me through the resistance and I can get on with my work. Of course, sometimes I forget to use them, and get stuck that way, but I always remember in the end. Attuning the crystals allows us to ground these 'higher' energies that Sarah is bringing in, into the material plane. As a tool, they are very easy to use, as you simply need to be in physical contact for them to work.

Sarah has a Host of Angels

Sarah's host of angels are always around her. They are pure whiter than white (it is a whiteness of such purity that we can't imagine it in our limited imagination, but we can feel it in our hearts), and these angels are too numerous to count, but we can imagine them around us in the shape of a horseshoe. They hold the purity of Sarah's archetypal force, and it is through connection to this host of angels that Sarah 'makes it so'- meaning that they carry out the Divine will which she is expressing. Sarah can teach us how to reach a higher level of spiritual evolution so that we can resonate to her host of angels as well!!

"My father *(Yeshua)* performed many miracles.

I am here to light up your hearts so you can perform those miracles yourself.

Remember who you are!" (Sarah's little book of Healing, page 9.)

More and more people are called to work with Sarah!

More people are waking up to and discovering Sarah's energy. Sarah is offering her light and energy to walk with you on your path. For those of you that feel really drawn, she offers a path of self-discovery and transformational evolution!

If you want to call Sarah fully into your life, her energy will lift up that which has remained hidden. She will shine the light into every dark corner so that all is brought into self-awareness, and no stone will be left unturned on the path of self-realisation!

Humanity is on the brink of a New Age, moving into new arenas, new ways of being, new ways of living. This translates into new ways of working, relating, being on the earth, partnerships, managing our resources, and so on, and all of these new ways have to be brought through by each of us.

Many of us who bring in these new ways will in time discover others who are also doing the same work. We can form groups to share our common identity and help each other through the experience that we've gained.

Inviting Sarah in to walk with you on your path is a conscious decision that can only be made by you. Some people may hear it through others (such as clairvoyants and mediums) that Sarah is stretching forth her hand towards you in welcome, but Sarah will only ever be with you on your path when you have taken a decision for her to be there.

This is because this a path of self-responsibility, and conscious co-creation with the Divine, which means that everything that happens needs to be self-generated, ie, generated by you.

Before deciding on calling Sarah into your life in this way, you might like to spend some time, contemplating whether this is a good path for you right now. Evolutionary transformation is not for everyone at every stage in their life, and requires resources, stamina, a strong willingness for self-reflection, and an overwhelming need to live in accordance with the will of the Divine, (which is your Higher Self), so that your final goal is to be yourSelf living here on the earth.

We are pioneers, forging the way ahead, and what we achieve now will require more faith, energy and perseverance than it will in the future. Humanity is entering into a New Age, and we make this effort for future generations to come, leaving them a legacy of our heartfelt love.

Your greatest tool is you!

You are the Divine made manifest and have at the centre of your being your Divine Spark.

If you wish to walk with Sarah upon your path, then simply you need to decide that this is what you want, and then express that to her and let her know!

If you invite her in, she will be there.

There is no-one who she is unwilling to work with, as we are here on earth, we are all in a position to work with the energy of evolutionary transformation, as all life on earth is working with this at present!!

But Who is Sarah?

I love all of the different stories about her - to me they tell of the richness and diversity that lies within her. Each story shows a different side, and through all of them Sarah's wild essence shines out.. she is a free spirit, and defies being pinned down, labelled, defined, or put into a box.

I have experienced many different strands of Sarah, and there are many colours to her cloth! In this book I've shared the ones that have come through thus far..... perhaps you can add some of your own to the weave!

Who is Sarah?! Should we even call her Sarah?! What does it mean that she's an Ascended Master?! What has she come to do? Why is she here? How does it work with Sarah being here? Has she incarnated in a similar way to that which Yeshua did? Why do so many of us feel connected to her?

In the first book 'Sarah's little book of healing' I share the 'I am Sarah' channeling. In this Sarah lays out who she is and why she's come. One of the things she tells us is,

"You are the Divine made manifest, the divine clothed in the wonders of matter. It is time to awaken, time to remember; you are not the consciousness of your body and your mind, they are the physical manifestation of you. Each of you is the Divine, birthed into manifestation, given individual consciousness. I have come to help you remember what you already know…"

Sarah is so many things, and she will mean different things to each of us, but ultimately to me **this** is who she is - she is the Ascended Light Being who has come to teach and mentor us through the process of becoming fully Human and fully Divine. She has also come to show us her full humanity which is being lived through the soul aspects of Sarah. They are expressing her wounds and challenges, so that her Divinity is able to enter in. Then we are through sympathetic resonance**, more able to access our own divinity and apply it to our own human wounds. (you can learn more about this technique in 'Sarah's little book of Healing'.)

** Sympathetic resonance or sympathetic vibration is defined as 'a harmonic phenomenon wherein a passive string or vibratory body responds to external vibrations to which it has a harmonic likeness.' (Wikipedia.) We already have within us the vibrational qualities which Sarah holds, but mostly, at this point in our evolution, they exist only as potential – a seed which is waiting to grow. Connecting with Sarah's energies causes these untapped potentialities within us to awaken and flourish.

Sarah The Ascended Master

We call Sarah an Ascended Master to show that she has reached the point on her spiritual path where she has 'ascended' above the need to live an earthly life – that she has learnt the lessons that 'earthschool' can provide, and that she is in a position to support and guide humanity from a place of wisdom and compassion. Also, because many people are not familiar with Sarah's name & who she is, using the term 'Ascended Master' or 'Ascended Light Being' helps them realize that this is someone who they might want to get to know a bit better!

However, in herself, Sarah is very informal. She walks by our sides as sister, mentor and teacher, and has no need for us to put her 'above' us… She is simply on a different place of the path that we are all walking, and has energies, teachings and experiences to share that can help us and the earth at our present time. I experience 'Sarah' as an energy; this is how I experience all of the light beings that I channel – I read their energy. Often they don't come to me with a name, and I recognize who they are from the qualities of energy that they carry. I think Spirit (see glossary) tend to do this so I can recognize someone over a period of time, and don't get a shock! The first time Yeshua appeared to me in a channeling workshop, I recognized him straight away - as with most children who grew up in the UK in the '70's, bible stories were part of our culture and school life. Honestly though, I was really disappointed; I wanted Quan Yin or someone else Divine Feminine!** (and I also had a big block to Divine Masculine energies) He said to me 'I'm not who you've been taught I am'. In the same workshop, I had a beautiful energy connection to Mary Magdalene, and continued to work with her afterwards. When Sarah first came to me, I recognised energetically both Yeshua's and the Magdalene's qualities being at Oneness in her. That's how I knew it was her.

** I was already trained and initiated as a priestess of the Goddess, and this was where I felt 'at home' and was at my happiest!

Sarah the Human & Healing the #Sarahwound

If you have read Sera Beak's 'Redvelations', you'll have come across the idea that Sarah's incarnation as the daughter of Yeshua and Mary Magdalene was not all love and light!

When I first starting connecting with Sarah's energy, I experienced a lot of fury and rage coming up that was not my own. I worked with it, and discovered it was Sarah's. At the time, she was initially overlighting me and we were going through an intense period of connection. It felt like a teenager's rage, absolute, clear and hot! There were no shades of grey in it. Just fury at Yeshua that he hadn't been there for her, just as 'her Dad', and yet he was being there for others on a planetary level. (Note: I don't have any personal beliefs about their lives or their 'history').

It surprised me, that this rage was still present in her energy matrix. I had connected with her and had had the experience of her being 'ascended'. It seemed that one didn't have to overcome and transform everything in one's emotional and mental body in order to 'ascend'. Perhaps it was another case of 'good enough'? This is a psychoanalytical concept I learnt through my psychosocial nursing work. It refers to Donald Winnicot's concept of the 'good enough' parent. This concept has the idea in it, that being a less than perfect parent prepares your child for managing the harsh realities of later life, as in response to the challenges of your failures, the child develops its own coping skills and discovers that it has resources to be able to cope when things are tough. Although not a direct parallel, the idea come to me, that we have to develop to a 'good enough' level before going on to the next, and that not every thing has to be perfectly transformed and transmuted!

Recently, the 'human Sarah' has been coming up again for me, and my spirit team has helped me understand that Sarah has more healing work to do. She shares with us many of the wounds that humanity currently has. Many of us have been working with healing the #witchwound. The horrors and trauma of the centuries of prosecuting witches has left a deep scar that really is only now coming to the surface to be healed. But also, there is a #sarahwound. It carries much of the same trauma of exile, judgement, not being having one's needs met as a child, and then not being able to meet them as an adult, not being understood or seen, having to hide and remain invisible, not being allowed to be the self that one is, abandonment and physical punishment and suffering. These types of trauma can cause dissociation, a splitting of the self, a rejection of the spiritual, or an over-reliance on it to solve all things. It makes sense to me that Sarah holds the archetypal energy of oneness – how else to become a master of integration and oneness, but by going through the extremity of the polar opposite?

Sarah has been the 'hidden daughter'. Her process has been one of cultural exile, and a coming out of the shadows. It is our process too. As spiritual people, sensitives, healers, witches, shamanic practitioner, (insert yourself here) we too have been reviled, ridiculed, shamed, denied, ignored, hated, abused, and even murdered by the cultures we live in. Sarah's wound is our wound, her process is our process. Although it may sound strange, even though Sarah is already Ascended, she still has this part of her human self that is going through this healing with us, and it is part of our journey into the New Age. Her healing is our healing and so on. She belongs to all of us.

Sarah and Healing the Original Wound

Now we come to the 'master wound', #originalwound!

*Sarah is an Ascended Master who teaches us how to bring our light into the darkness; and it is through working with her that I have been guided with healing the original wound. Healing our original wound is about getting down to our **core issues**. Those wounds are directly around our core being, our essence, who we truly are.*

This wound came into being when we were originally separated from the Divine, and has remained in our subconscious ever since, (waiting for the time when we are ready to heal it!)

Through working with our original wound, we draw forth our greatest compassion, our greatest love, our greatest joy and all of the Divine qualities and all of the parts of our Divine Nature that are needed in this great healing work.

Often it is the situations in our lives that have caused us (or are causing us) the greatest pain and where we have experienced the greatest loss, that are manifesting the theme of our original wound. By working with the wound directly, we can bring about Divine healing to the pain in our pasts and in our present. We are asked in these special times, to dig within us, and heal ALL of the parts of ourselves, leaving no stones unturned.

This can be our service to the Divine, to take our difficulties and alchemise them into spiritual gold.

THIS is Sarah's work here on the earth, to show us how all of those things which we have seen as darkness, pain and suffering in our lives, actually contain the seeds of our enlightenment and ascension. Truly are we blessed!!

The following excerpts are from a shamanic journey which I did in 2010 and gave me some idea of what the original wound is:

'First of all, I was shown the connection to God - there is a golden orb/ light up in the cosmos and I am connected to it and it feels great! *(this is my awareness of being an individuated consciousness but still one with the Divine).*

Then there is a gradual disconnection as I feel myself descending, *(my awareness of oneness with the Divine is growing less and less as I descend into matter).*

Then I am down here at the bottom and all that lovely connexion is gone, *(now I've come onto the earth plane and inside me all is empty and cold and dark, there is nothing, just nothing, it's all gone.)*

Then a gradual re-awakening of love as I find things to love around me, people, things, places, *(and that feels better, what a relief, like coming out of the cold and into the warm)* but then distress coming in at the realisation of always losing these things, never being able to hold onto them *(and all the grief and loss that goes with this, oh God, what pain)* and with this, the total and absolute realisation of being able (in truth & reality) to hold onto nothing, a gradual returning of my face towards Divinity, *(and back to the Light within).*

This time, the return to the Light within, is through my consciousness and using my intent and I am shown that this is the way to re-connect to the Divine.

No mystery, no magick, just so!'

Later on in another healing journey, I received from Mary Magdalene, some 'etheric' healing salve, and applied it to the wound - and as I did so, I discovered that underneath the initial feelings of emptiness that came with the first descent into matter and separation from the Divine, underneath this nothingness, were accompanying rage, grief, howling loss, and extreme shock.

The pain of being separated from the Divine was so great, that it sent the conscious into unconsciousness, (the shock was so shockingly shocking as to be enough to send any form of consciousness into an instant faint back into the comforting, deep sleep of the unconscious).

And so, the pain lumbers on in the depths of the subconscious mind, rearing its head as an occasional illness, or whenever deep loss and grief is felt, it awakens again.

This terrible wound to the newly born ego, in its first descent into matter, is too great to be actually felt on that initial experience, and so it sleeps in the darkest depths of our subconscious minds, only being awoken from time to time, by the (resonating emotions of) grief and loss, and issues around separation & abandonment, until we have sufficiently matured into the light, and brought our healing skills to such a range that we might attempt to heal this greatest wound, our deepest pain.

Sometimes, when we have reached this level of development, then comes into our lives our twin flames, for us to experience this oneness at a soul level even while we are in our physical bodies (we feel at one, not just in our minds and bodies, but in our hearts and most of all, in our souls – because we have found the other half of our soul, and we are complete, what love, what joy) sometimes then only for them to be separated from us again, (what pain, what grief, what loss and abandonment, what rage).

Many people experience that the great light that the soul creates in a twin flame relationship, concurrently brings up all that needs healing (the darkness), and we find ourselves drawn inexorably towards the light (the union of souls), only then to discover it precipitates more 'suffering' (which is really all our unresolved issues coming up for healing.)

All of the loss and abandonment in our lives helps us to experience feeling 'torn apart', and echoes our original loss, which was the loss of our conscious awareness of our connexion to the Divine; because of course, we have never lost God, just that it seems so to our conscious selves. (Our conscious self that is struggling to become consciously God-aware whilst in physical matter). It allows us to come the closest we can at this stage, to experiencing the original trauma of feeling separate from God.

Were we to already experience the actual feelings from the original event, all in one go, we would fall immediately into unconsciousness, the trauma being too great to process. Experiencing separation, loss & perceived abandonment in our lives allows us to start to move towards the original pain, rage, shock that we felt, and allows it to start to be ventilated a little from our system.

The gifts that we develop in response to this pain are gifts of compassion, love and healing. The greatest gift is that we learn that there is no wound so great that it cannot be healed by the love of Divine Mother/ Father God (who is ourSelves).

We are called to bring love into every part of our being.

As the trauma is healed/ uncovered/ brought into the light, so can our God consciousness, which so far has been buried underneath the trauma, once again rise up from its slumbers in the depths and come into the light, evoking the memory and consciousness of who we truly are. And so, slowly by slowly, through our individual healing journeys, can all the material repressed in the subconscious be dealt with and processed.

In healing this wound, our greatest work, we are learning how to become master healers, and to create the Age of Aquarius.

Exploring our Connections to Sarah...

I ran an online course a few years ago to do exactly this – explore our connections to Sarah! I'd never really wanted to find out my own connection, I knew I loved her, couldn't help it!! What else could matter? I didn't want to get into ego problems with being important/not being important enough – our poor egos have a lot to contend with on a day-to-day basis living in this world, and I didn't want to add to it, for myself or anyone else! But I could feel a mounting pressure from my spirit team to offer this, so I braced myself for what might come and got on with it! It was actually a really interesting experience, and a whole picture emerged for me that I have found useful ever since…

…It seems that there are different ways that people are connected to Sarah. The ways that have emerged are: through past lives; through lives on other planets and star systems (for example, the Pleiades have come up in connection with Sarah over and over and over again!); through DNA connection; through being a soul aspect of Sarah; and as a kind of 'sub-division' to the past lives, there are people who have been priests or priestesses of the archetypal energy that Sarah represents, and who may or may not have directly had a past life connection with her, but have woven into their soul energy the energy that Sarah is…. I also know there is one more option, but haven't received the information yet!! Some people have one of these connections, others have more than one – it's a fascinating journey!!

In the channellings below, you can find some of these connections expanded on.

Has Sarah incarnated on the Earth?

"Welcome, I am Sarah.

This question is larger than you think, because it needs me to describe a phenomenon which goes beyond the question which you are asking on a personal level, and goes to a greater level which is connected to humanity and the collective.

There is a strand of energy woven in the web of humanity that comprises of the energy that I represent – the energy that I am an archetypal face for, and this is the energy that humanity are moving into now, and it is the energy that will allow them to step into the 'New Age'/'Golden Age'/'New Earth'/5th Dimension, or whichever way you want to describe it. This energy is the energy of integration and will bring about the shift into 'oneness/unity consciousness' that will allow humanity (in co-creation with the other realms) to create a higher vibration of divinity upon the earth.

At present, polarity is the functioning paradigm upon the earth. When a person descends into the material realm, and her/his spirit creates their spiritual form in a material body, so must they function between the poles of polarity. Polarity is always kept in balance, where there is a wrong there must be a right, where there is male there must be female, where there is dark there must be light. But when a certain level of learning has been achieved, an understanding one might say, that there is no-thing that is not part of the Divine - then it is possible to achieve a higher level of consciousness, that takes into this account of deep unity of 'heaven and earth', and which will allow mankind to live from a greater place of joy, and peace, love and happiness. Mankind is born into the depths of the material world, so that he/she can find their way out, through discovering the light within, and through spinning that web of light and dark – always keeping the balance and learning so many gifts of wisdom as they progress.

Now there are those of you who have walked the path along with me. They too are students of polarity and oneness, and within this soul group, we have studied together in many different times and places and even planets! We can talk about Egypt and Atlantis, and the foundation in the simpler times of Lemuria where oneness was achieved but at a higher level of vibration than we are currently at. Many talk about an experiment having failed, but nothing is wrong here. Things are simply as they are, and each individuated spark of the Divine is always returning to its source, everything around you is masterfully designed to achieve that objective, 'God's plan is built upon a rock', but it can only be seen and understood when one has achieved a certain level of mastery of learning and vibration, and that is why it is important that humanity receive spiritual guidance 'from above'. It is easy to see when one is 'looking down', and not so easy to see when one is on the ground floor as it were!

So, the answers that I am giving you, is not so much about me, but more about you, and who You are! You are one who is here to give the light to others, and who is here to masterfully blend and balance the dark and light, bringing compassion where there is suffering, and peace where there is rage. We have worked together side by side in times gone by, I have had many incarnations upon the earth, of which Sarah was my last, a culmination of all my experience and knowledge, all I had achieved, put to use in being the one to carry the blueprint for the evolution of humanity. I am that that can be in all things, all spheres, all directions, there is no place I cannot be, whether it is the highest of the high, or the lowest of the lows! I am Sarah. I integrate!!

You too carry this light, this strand (if you like, you can see it as a strand of the lifeforce running throughout the quantum DNA of humanity, always bringing the purity of the Divine to everything it meets, causing life to sprout forth, and come into its Divine perfection!) and you can call on me to teach you how to work more with this if you have need. I am here as sister, mentor, teacher, guide, but you must choose to have me step forward onto your path, and call me forth.

I am Sarah and these are the words which I would speak to you this day.

My blessings are upon you, Blessed Be, Blessed Be, Blessed Be, Amen."

** When Sarah showed me this impression of this special energy strand running through the web, I also got the information that it has been deep in the web at many times, in the unconscious of humanity, and then at other times, such as now, it rises to the surface in the weave, and so it runs like a movement or a phenomenon through a culture's spirituality, where it is consciously taken up and worked with. At present there are people incarnated upon the earth who are actual 'soul aspects' of Sarah, and are here to ground these energies into the earth grid, but there are also those 'technicians' or 'engineers' who have worked with this energy of 'Oneness' metaphysically through religion or magic – they are also holding this archetypal force as Sarah did in her lives on earth, and as she does now in the higher dimensions.

We are her workforce if you like, the circle of men and women, together with the angelic, elemental and other plethora of light beings who work with her. She is at the centre of the circle, and we are all surrounding her, as she orchestrates this amazing dance. We move and dance as we will, but always to the music that she sings forth, rejoicing in its beauty.

Sarah the Black

As already mentioned, one of Sarah's names in French is Sara-la-Kali, meaning Sarah the Black. This has a link to the name Sarah the Egyptian, meaning she was dark-skinned, and also the effigy of Sarah in the church of Saintes-de-la-Mer is very dark, like a Black

Madonna. In the channeling 'Sara-la-Kali' in chapter seven, Sarah says, 'I am that which is created here on earth, the darkness; primordial matter. To reach the light of God, transcendent and formless, is to go through me, the darkness and manifest creation of form, matter and all being. But where I am, God is.'

This is Sarah as Sophia/Black Madonna: in chapter three, she describes the healing energy of this aspect of herself in the channeling, 'Waiting in the Darkness'.

But more than this, Sarah the Black means to me an ancient lineology, going back to the beginnings of time. She has shown herself to me as a black woman, and it resonates deeply with me. Inside this energy there is primordial ancient wisdom, wordless and full of power. In this vision where I see the black woman, we have dropped deeper than the mental layer, her eyes shine with knowing, and there is a communication between us without words. It is a paradox that although Sarah is a 'new' Ascended Master, the energy of Oneness that she represents, is older than that of the Divine Feminine and Masculine. It is what we were before the separation. We are coming back into Oneness now, after having gone through the experience of being in separation. The circle is being completed.

Sarah's Twin Flame

A number of people have written to me over the years to ask if I have any information on Sarah's twin flame; one such person wrote to me just last week, and I told them that I've never received any information about who Sarah's twin flame is, which is technically true. My energetic response when I'm asked that question is that Sarah doesn't have one, and I've been thinking this week about why that is. I'm trying to explain concepts here that I can only glimpse, so I am not saying I think this is 'the truth' but that perhaps there is 'a truth' to it in some way. Sarah is on a soul level, whole and complete to herself, she doesn't need another soul part to complete her — because she already is. (Although I sense this energetically, my human side feels a bit sad about it. It sounds a bit lonely…)

Sarah the Forest Witch

Sarah has presented herself to me many times in her aspect of a forest witch! In this manifestation of her energy, she is almost a pure emanation of nature, of life-force (a green woman?!) and aligns to the long tradition of wise men and women, forest and nature witches who worked for their community, healing with plants and herbs and in communication with the natural forces around them. In the same way Sarah also is knowledgeable of herbs and healing, plants, trees, the animal kingdom and nature spirits. She walks in the depths of the forest without fear, with wolves watching over her! As a skilled adept, she is a natural at mastering the many layers, depths and breadths of magical power, and has a close relationship with Saint Germaine (he who was Merlin).

This channeling speaks to the magic of England's ancient woodlands, and it is Lucia, Archangel Melchizedek's feminine counterpart who speaks to us. The energy in this channeling is very aligned to Sarah in her aspect of forest witch!

"Welcome all, I am Lucia the Queen of Light, feel my light in the highest echelons of your being, and know that it is always there, for you.

I wish to hover my wings of light above and around you, as I direct your thoughts towards this most beautiful time of year. As the land awakens and the carpets of bluebells spread across the woodland, so the earth prepares herself and all you people of Britain to be awash with the spirit of hope.

Find some time in your busy day and your busy schedule to go to some woodland near you, and breathe in this most beautiful energy, that the earth has prepared just for you. Feel or see and imagine the beautiful green & violet colour of the bluebells dancing around your aura, laughing and playing, just as the woodland folk, the elves and the sprites dance and play amongst the bluebells. Imagine that you are indeed able to link to the wondrous and ancient energy matrix of the bluebells, and feel the magick & mystery contained therein.

Imagine once the land of Britain, covered in woodland, the forest floor awash with bluebells, for miles upon miles upon miles. Imagine how this would have been in those long-forgotten days, imagine those counties where you live, thickly covered with the scent and colour of the ancient flora, and allow once again the gentle freshness of hope once again discovered to fill the land.

If you can, do this in the woods, but other than this do it anywhere you can. Just by this simple exercise, you can take what already is, and multiply it a thousandfold.

What a joy it is that the land where you live is abundant in the natural beauties of the ancient trees and plants, that it has remained to be protected by those who understand the importance of safekeeping this heritage.

Allow your heart to consider these matters as you felt your spirit swept along in the hope; what do you dare to dream for in your life, what wonderful things would bring magick & mystery into the realms of the everyday? What natural beauty in your life is in need of protection & safekeeping to safeguard its very existence, and must not be allowed to be bulldozed by the quickening pace of life?

Imagine your dreams, your hopes, dancing there amongst the bluebells, taking in that wonderful energy, then breathe them back into yourself, where they can come into being.

Breathe in life, breathe in hope, give thanks for the incredible beauty of the bluebells, of the trees' leaves gently curling into life. All is well, all is well, all is well.

Faeries abound amongst the bluebells, and may your dreams dance and sing there too. Blessings be to all………. Blessed Be."

Sarah as the Holy Grail

'Lady Sarah, would you say that you are the Holy Grail or are you an aspect of the Holy Grail or something other please?' *(Question is from a live interview.)*

"The Holy Grail is an image of something that exists as an etheric creation. So, if I were to give an example of the sun. The sun has been understood in different times, in different ways, and has had different names, different genders and has been understood very, very differently.

With the Holy Grail, this is something that exists in other cultures, but will have a different name, which will give it a slightly different energy.

So, the Holy Grail is an image of cup or a bowl which is a receptacle. And often we see the cup or the bowl as being a divine feminine image and yet, there's something about the Holy Grail, that is holding energy of the divine masculine as well. (*In the Grail legends there is sometimes a Holy Lance or a Sword.*) And that possibly is because of the active dynamic, the active component. The Holy Grail is not something that just sits there, holding a divine energy or a divine liquid, but it also has an active effect. It's doing things, it has a power and presence.

So, this is the story that came into creation with the Jesus stories or myths as I would like to say. Because of course, even if we take the view that Jesus was an actual physical person having an actual real life, still much of the stuff around him are stories and myths.

However, stories and myths have their own value. They reflect what is in the collective unconsciousness and yes, the collective unconsciousness can hold a shadow. But it also holds the divine knowing, that people have because of course each person has a piece of the divine in them, they are created from the divine. They have a divine spark within them, even if it's unconscious, that is still there and so that part of each person gives out stories, gives out impressions - it does things.

The Holy Grail came along with the stories of Jesus throughout time and has also been connected to King Arthur and the Knights of the Round Table. And there is a mystery and a presence to these stories, that the divine spark in each of us responds to because it recognizes that there is a divine truth there and there is a longing to go towards that Holy Grail.

So, I have a symbol which was channelled for me some years ago and this symbol when it's worked with, very much becomes the Holy Grail. And one of the ways to presence that symbol, is to imagine that you are being brought down into the centre of that Holy Grail, and this has been called "Coming into Sarah's Embrace." Once you're in that cup of the bowl energetically, an alchemical process occurs, & things are worked within you. Things are brought together that have been separated, which causes things that are not of reality that are illusionary, to suddenly disappear.

This is one of my archetypal forces that I hold, this energy of integration. And this is directly linked to this energy of the Cosmic Christ which can also be linked to the divine spark that exists within each thing that is alive in which you see around you on the earth.

And this can also be linked to the ancient Vedic system where everything in creation is brought into being by Narayana and Narayani - the divine spark and the Holy Grail itself. I would say that the divine spark is the Narayana, and the Holy Grail is the Narayani and this is a longer mystery than I can explain here. But to make a shorter synopsis of it, The Holy Grail is these energies that are present in manifest creation and what this represents is that divine spark - but which actually exists (in divine oneness) outside of manifest creation, it 'exists' in transcendent reality.** I think I'll leave that there."

** *the divine spark is both transcendent and immanent, existing in manifest and unmanifest reality.*

One of the Sarah healers, Besymih, received these beautiful words when she had her initiation into Sarah's healing energy,

> 'Sarah brought her known and activated Chalice
> to remind and activate mine!
> All my cells drink the Divine Nectar of Sarah's Chalice!
> Sarah is the Chalice.
> I am the Chalice.
> We are the Chalice.
> We are all one!'

In 'Mary Magdalene, Bride in Exile'. Margaret Starbird says of Sarah, 'But is that drinking cup really ethe Holy Grail of myth and legend? ..there is the suggestion that the Sangraal/ 'blood royal' was not really an artifact at all, but a symbolic reference to the bloodline itself.. The vessel of the royal bloodline, the sacred contained, would have been Mary Magdalene herself, extended to any child born of her union with Jesus, but especially to a daughter, because a cup or chalice bears distinctly feminine symbolism.'

But what about the Merovingian Kings?!

I remember seeing 'The Da Vinci Code' at the cinema in 2006, and thinking that Sarah, Mary Magdalene and the Divine Feminine were really moving into the collective consciousness! Dan Brown and the stories about the bloodline and the holy grail sparked a lot of interest in the Merovingian kings. But I found as time went on that I had this reaction to it: I don't remember from reading the bible in my religious studies class that Jesus was that interested in the whole idea of kingship (In fact, I remember that he was really against the idea!), and why would it matter if his descendants were royalty or not? I'm not sure Sarah would be interested in being royal, as royalty spend most of their time tied up with the most mundane matters, (well, I'm thinking of the British royals here, as I'm British!) and having to pay a lot of attention to things that would be meaningless to many 'spiritual' people.

And as to the idea of Sarah herself actually being incarnated physically here - what if Sarah were walking around on the face of the earth?* Would she rescue everyone, save the whole world? No, of course not. I think if Sarah were alive today, she would want to be the sort of person who could empower other people. Because we are ALL a spark of God, just as she was, and is. We are ALL here learning on our spiritual path, at different places on that path admittedly, but we all have the same destination goal. WE are the change we wish to make, and when we get all excited about Sarah and Jesus and Mary Magdalene, we can remember that WE are the ones who can save the world! With some help from Ascended teacher guides such as Sarah! This is our job now, and is what Sarah has come to remind us. Meanwhile she has some really class A 'power tools' to help us along the way!!

*more said about this later!!

Sarah shows us that 'she is us' and we are the Grail!

Here Sarah describes our soul/higher self as being our inner grail, that part of us which inspires taking a path of healing and spiritual development...

"Welcome, welcome, I am Sarah. Today, I would speak to you of the grail. The Holy Grail. There are many ways for this wonderful symbol and image to be interpreted, but today, I would speak to you of the interpretation of the grail as representing your soul and divine self. It truly is a symbol that is common to each individual person in mankind, as each of you has the divine spark as the centre of your being, and it is the place from which you are each individually created.

It is the part of your being that knows how to apply balm to your wounds, that can bring love where there is hate, and patience where there is only haste. When remembered, (because it is simply 'forgetting' that causes the loss of the divine self) each person comes into their full maturity as a soul - birth into the material plane causes a temporary loss, a 'forgetting'. But because you are Divine Light, you are always returning to that which you are, Divine Light, which is the source of yourSelf.

Everything happens within divine timing, spring comes after the winter, and in the same way, the soul blossoms and becomes embodied fully, when it is the right season for it to happen. Each season has its purpose and function, and so each phase in your development as a soul has its purpose and function. The blossoming of the soul cannot occur until you are in the right stage of your development. When your energy is moving in the correct way, so will the blossoming (enlightenment) occur.

This enlightenment comes as a oneness, so that everything in your being has access to the oneness at the centre. Imagine that you are a circle, and your divine spark is at the centre. At the moment, there are other circles (blocks) between your everyday mind, and that divine spark. As these circles between you and your divine spark are dissolved, so do you naturally come into alignment/ oneness. The circles are created by anything that is not in alignment with the divine. I am Sarah, and these are the words which I wish to share with you today, blessed be, blessed be, blessed be, Amen."

Sarah/ Solaris

I've drawn the sun card for Sarah before, and felt a great significance. But I don't have a channeling to give you, only a sense of it. I had a vision of Sarah once as a female Druid on the Isle of Iona, standing a top of Dun-I (which means 'The hill of Iona' and at 333 feet above sea level is the highest point on the isle). It felt incredibly right to see her as a female druid, and in tune with the Sun aspect of her - Druidry being a spirituality where the sun was and is of special significance.

A couple of years ago I received a message from a Facebook friend, sharing that she had the name 'Solaris' come to her for Sarah. So interesting! Solaris is a name which literally translates as 'sun' but is gender neutral! I love that! Very Sarah!

Sarah Primal Earth Goddess!

This is very interesting! I feel Sarah is referring back to ancient days, which we would consider perhaps to be uncivilized, or barbaric, and where life was very basic and simply lived. She gives us another perspective on that – and possibly is referring to the Neanderthal people?

Channeling is from a live interview.

"So, there is a pattern here in the ancient days, of a primal and I've got the word 'rude', meaning a very basic connection to the earth.

The age that you are living in today, is very mentally orientated and there is a strong emphasis on the mental layer, and has been being developed very strongly in this part of humanity's evolution.

However, many of my past lives were more connected to the physical and connected to the spiritual, without this strong mental layer of energy. There was a much more direct experience of the earth, a much more profound and direct way of living and experiencing the earth without the problem of 'thinking' constantly coming into the equation.

So, it was possible to live a life much more directly in contact with the earth herself, with the tree spirits, with elemental beings, and of having been able to draw out much more power from nature. There were fewer blocks and obstacles in the way with less man-made creations causing disruptions in the flow of energy.

So, when I connect to the question that you asked about - my past lives, there's a huge power that comes through from the earth, from the power of nature, from this direct creation force if you like, that's very embodied. A very divine energy being embodied through nature and through the lives of the people as well.

So, although you might think of past peoples as having been more primitive, there has been much more purity of divine consciousness than there is now, because this strong emphasis on the mental layer causes a lot of blocks. This is one of the reasons why working with my energy can actually help overcome these things. I have a strong imprint in my energy from these past lives which help each of you also to connect directly back up to these beautiful forces in in nature."

How to build a practice with Sarah

'I wanted to ask if you could enlighten us on whether there are special herbs or crystals, trees, chants, or oils that people who want to increase their connection with you, that might be beneficial for them to use.' (Question is from a live interview.)

'So, for each person, there will be a different thing that will hold this energy for them. It's quite important to have a practice in order to connect to my energy. So, if you want to build up a stronger or deeper relationship, you can connect to my energy each day by doing something very simple like lighting a candle or just asking for my presence to come in and then meditating with that presence. Also, I would say, anything from the forest! You can ask that my presence enters in for that and then keep it in a special place or on an altar if you have one.

Really my ways are one of self-mastery and so I would encourage each person to develop their own special relationship with me and of course, it will be found that there are correlations between what people discover. But I would encourage each of you to discover your own special relationship with me and to sit in those moments of connection with me and ask for a sign or for a colour or for an essential oil or for something which will be special for **you** and then be open to the inspiration that you receive. Be open to the signs and omens that come your way.

Now there are some natural correlations between me and the colour green and again at the forest in spring and the forest in winter and the forest in autumn, but especially the colour green in all its different aspects. And so, the crystals could be peridot, they could be bloodstone, they could be moldavite, they could be serpentine. There could be many, many possibilities. But really, it's the ones that jump out for you because as you connect to my energy as a practice, then you will start to recognize my energy and then you'll see something in the world around you and it will be jumping up and down in front of you saying "I am holding the energy of Sarah" because as you connect to my presence you become attuned to my presence and then you become attuned to the things in the world around you that also have a similar vibration.

With the essential oils, lemongrass, quite a challenging scent for some people, but then my energy is quite challenging. Rose also which is softer side - the energy of love, but that's also very nice. And lavender, which is holding the energies of the violet flame in the inner, in a certain aspect. I think that's enough for now.'

Sarah doesn't belong to any religious hierarchy

'Thank you that was very interesting. Following on, may we know more about your angels who are part of your spiritual team, Lady Sarah?' *(Question is from a live interview.)*

'So, I tend to work with other masters and beings of light that are working with the same outline that I am. I do have a strong connection to work within the earth, but I also have a connection to the Star Councils. The energy that I hold, is a cosmic energy and it's not related to any religion or belief system and there are other names for it in other systems. Paramatman *(see glossary)*, is one that is jumping out.

But I suppose that this is the point where I want to speak about that I don't particularly feel that I belong in any religious hierarchy, whether it's Christian or otherwise. In my past lives, I have been present in many different cultures and of course in my life as Sarah, I was part of a Jewish system and so I have actually never had any lives as a Christian on the earth which is not to say that I have anything against it. In my way of seeing things, all religions have their own special quality, and they are all equal. They're all equally important to the people who are in those religions and I don't affiliate myself to one or the other in any particular way.

If I were to affiliate myself to something, it would be to the powers of nature, these raw, primal forces, but in truth I am connected to all of the spheres because I hold the energy of integration. I am able to connect to anything, on any level, at any time, from whatever point I'm in, which is unusual for an ascended master, as most ascended masters are in their particular sphere of specialisation, which has a specific vibration. But with me, I can connect to anything which means that I can also work with anybody in the higher dimension. (in this, Sarah means she can work harmoniously alongside, for example, all other light beings, masters & deities)

So, I do have a team that I work with on the earth and I'll be talking more about this in the time to come and I am also part of a Council of Star Elders. I'm working more cosmically, but again and this is this is quite unusual because I have this fluidity, an ability to integrate. I'm not limited to who I can work with and I can be pulled into any other system of energy and will be able to integrate well with it. There are no clashes, it will always work.'

Sarah the Star Elder

'Thank you. May I just ask, what is the Council of Star Elders? What's the purpose of the council and what kind of work does it entail?' (Question is from a live interview.)

'We're looking at the level of energy for this solar system - The Council of Star Elders. One of the things that they are working with, is the energy flow in the whole of this solar system. All of the planets or the manifested creations in this solar system are interconnected and they all hold different aspects of each other in the way that the energies are flowing through and around. They all give something to each other.

If you think of it as like the Solar System being a family. A family is made up of different personalities and each one contributes something to the whole and so there's a necessity of looking at how these immense beings are working together, the problems that have been having, what challenges they have been having, if they need a bit more help, if something needs working with…

So, for example, the earth herself is sending out earth energies out into the solar system. She is contributing sacred energies to other planets; she's also receiving. Each planet has its own specialisation and vibration, so there's a much bigger kind of picture out there than the one that we see if we're having a physical incarnation on earth.

But earth herself is an ascended being. She's taken on the job of humanity and is a little bit held back because her physical body –

humanity, is made up of the Earth's physical body. So energetically, she's like, you know, like a pregnant mother. When you're pregnant, you have to take things a bit easier, you have to slow down, you can't suddenly go to work, go dancing. You know, you can't light the candle at both ends. And it's the same with the earth. She's had to slow down her evolutionary progress a little bit.

However, just the same as having a child is incredibly rewarding and powerful process where you develop incredibly, so the earth is also getting a lot out of having humanity. It might not look like it, if you're a person with all the difficulties in this day and age but you know, taking over eons of time, it is an incredibly powerful and rewarding process to the earth!"

'What are your thoughts on the Galactic Beings coming in at this time? I paint with spirit and angels come through and many others. The Galactics and cosmic beings are coming in more recently and have been bringing in the violet flame.' (Question is from a live interview.)

Rachel: 'So, Sarah has a really cosmic aspect and that's been showing itself more recently. Let me just ask her about that and then at the end I'll quickly channel anything she wanted to say that we didn't get to….

So, I think that this is something that is going to come out more. With the work I've been doing with her, it's very much about the earth, healing the earth, taking us to our next evolutionary level.

Now I have done some live channelings from her where she's part of a Star Elder Council *(see glossary)*, so for people who work with star seeds and galactic energies - really try calling on Sarah and see how you get on! Recently, there's been quite a few little clues and they've all been pointing towards the Pleiades, she has a strong connection to the Pleiades. I don't think that's the only one. There's a lot of connections with Venus as well and that's kind of the Christ family, and also Sirius but more is going to be coming in the years ahead as more star seeds work with her and bring through the information.

I'm doing channelings for people and they are getting messages about working with her galactically and it's quite a different energy and yet, she holds all of this together.

I think she's an amazing, ascended master to work with for the New Age, for all of us because her energy is coming up from the collective unconscious and it's coming into us. We already have this energy inside of us. It's just about us birthing it basically, that's what we're doing.'

Sarah & the Lineage of the Blue Rose

Sarah is part of the Blue Rose Lineage, which is connected to Venus. I connected consciously to the energy of Blue Rose before I knew it existed. There is a point in the Ascension Grid energy system, in Roskilde where I live – one evening I went out for a walk, Venus was shining brightly, and I was mesmerised by her all the time I was walking, I couldn't take my eyes off her! I came to a place, near some ponds that are filled with spring water (from the Magdalene spring and others), and as I stood on some old paved stone, I felt this most incredible and beautiful energy run through me into the ground. The next year, I read Mary Farell Tobin's channeling about the Blue Rose lineage, and recognised the energy in it as being the same I had also felt standing by the pond!!

This is part of Mary's channeling, "The lineage of the Blue Rose was embedded in the hearts of many in the times of Avalon and entered the land of France through the teachings of the companion to Yeshua, The Magdalene or as she is known to some, Mary Magdalene..... It is a strong lineage, heart centered, bearing the gifts of healing, prophesy, song, and dance. They have knowledge in the use of crystals and stones, I have imparted much knowledge through the lineage of the Magdalenes." *(see Links for the whole channeling)*

Sarah and the Akashic Records

'Sarah, what is your link to the Akashic Records?' *(Question is from a live interview.)*

"Welcome, I am Sarah.

The Akashic records are held within the fabric of the earth. Gaia has taken on as a sacred charge to assist in the development of the human race. She has given you part of physical body so that you can take on part of her physical form, and use those physical vessels to fill with your spirit. But also, there are the Oversouls of all of the life on earth for all of the different species and lifeforms, whether stone, plant, animal, fae and so on and so on. These Oversouls, which are a kind of blueprint (except they are also filled with all of the information since the beginning of time until now, as well as the perfection of the original blueprint) and these 'blueprints' are also held in the energetic body of the earth. Earth doesn't just lend her physical material to you, she also lends her energetic matter, so that all the necessary 'equipment', can be engineered. Humanity's evolutionary process for example, is entirely stored within the earth's energetic matrix, everything that has ever happened, and all that that entailed on the mental planes, emotional planes, etheric planes, causal planes and so on, is stored within the earth, and this is what you call the Akashic Records. Some people are very good at retrieving information (so using the energy from the mental plane) from the Akashic records, and some people are very good at reading the energy of certain times and certain places so that they know what energy healing needs to be performed, in order to re-create Divine Balance. You could say that Gaia is the oversoul & indwelling spirit of the earth, and I have close connections to her; we work in partnership together, and I assist her in her duties.

I can be a doorway to these records, whether you need them for information purposes, or for energetic purposes – whatever your needs may be, if you have work to do with humanity, either collectively or individually, call on me as an Overseer of the Akashic Records, and I will assist you.

These are the words which I wish to speak this day, my blessings are upon you, Blessed Be, Blessed Be, Blessed Be, Amen."

How we are connected to Sarah

A few years ago, I ran an online course, 'Exploring your connexion to Sarah', where we discovered many things, and sometimes I still do 1:1 sessions with people helping them find their way with this if they need the support. It seemed that the connexions that people were discovered were either through a DNA connection; a soul connection – either through being a soul aspect of Sarah, or through having known Sarah in past lives; from being part of the lineage of working with the archetypal force that Sarah represents; from being 'held within' and part of the energy matrix that Sarah weaves for the New Earth, and that has its ancient origins in the beginnings of the Earth and is that of being a powerful creative being - which could be healing work, magickal work, or being an 'earth engineer', (and many others which I haven't mentioned), from being connected through other planets and even star systems as a Starseed. Discovering these origins can be helpful in informing about who you truly are and adding to the rich tapestry of 'what you have come here to do'!

Soul Fragments

This is the information that Sarah has gave me in response to a question being asked about a person's soul connection to Sarah, and I've shared that information here, because it also applies to so many of you too!

"The past informs the present. We are the sum of our memories, and yet we are more than that. Memories can be shaped and changed.

Traumas can become healing memories. Some things can be laid to rest. Yet there is another memory within the body. This is the memory of the soul. The body is imprinted with all that the soul wishes us to know, understand and follow in THIS lifetime. It is your body that is your guide. When you have a thought about something, feel into your body and ask – is this true?! If your body lights up in response, then you have your answer. When you read these words even, your body recognises what is true for you, or what isn't. When you see, hear or read the truth, your body has a resonating chime, and this is how you can accept those things you know as truth.

You have a clear vision. You know you are on the right path. There are other things which are yet to be revealed, but which are already held within the matrix of your physical self (the body), which is in truth, an extension of your soul. So you will be led towards all things that you need to know, at the right place, at the right time, and in the right way.

There is a trinity here between the Divine Feminine (Mary Magdalene), the Divine Masculine (the Master Jesus), and the Divine in Oneness (the daughter Sarah) and yet in physical manifestation, Sarah is bringing the teachings and the guidance of how to be in oneness in a physical life, even whilst (we live) within the physical laws of polarity. She does this as Ascended Master, guiding from 'above' from her Ashram (see glossary), and from the etheric, where she is in (etheric) physical existence. She also does this by taking form simultaneously, by incarnating many, many pieces of her soul. So there are numerous aspects of Sarah's soul which are incarnated here at this present time, although most of her soul (which is vast) is not incarnated on the earth, but only enough to help birth and anchor this archetypal force that comes to help humanity usher in the 'golden age', and to take up their new responsibilities as co-creators with the divine."

The picture that I get, is that very very small fragments of Sarah's soul are each able to take up physical existence as an incarnation, and that this is done in this way, so as not to overwhelm the ancestral line of those families, or cause complicated difficulties to that individual person living that life, but allows for this soul to be integrated into the community and allow a life to be lived, whilst at the same time, grounding this archetypal force, and allowing it to manifest in whichever way that (incarnated) life/ person chooses. It also creates a web/net of light across the globe that means that change is inevitable, because a new 'colour' (energy) is now present amongst the weave, and things cannot stay the same, because they are not! (the same)

And then Sarah is impressing these words upon me:

"I am Sarah, and I tell you, all is well, all is well, all is well. Nothing is awry and all is well. Each moment is created in response to the will of the Divine, each moment perfect and preparing for the moment ahead. Blessings are upon you, each and every moment of your life, blessed be, blessed be, blessed be, Amen."

Again, this channeled information came through in response to a question asked about what the connection to Sarah was, and I have shared this information here because it too, applies to many people who will be reading this book!

Sarah, teacher, healer, sister, mentor. An Ascended Master for our Time.

Sarah is an Ascended Master for the Age of Aquarius. She's always been around, but in a less obvious way. It's like she has been in the subconscious depth of humanity but is coming up now into the consciousness because she needs to. She has much to teach us; to help us connect with our higher self and our divine spark and make it more a part of ourSelf – so it becomes *integrated. Then we can live from that place, creating the New Earth and the Golden Age and move into the 5th Dimension.*

Sarah's a great and incredibly useful ally. She's not here to tell us what to do, she's here to act as a catalyst for us becoming our own sovereign power. She empowers and tells us what we need to hear rather than what we want to hear. It is very unusual if she makes a decision for us, but instead, she gives us the keys that empower us in making our own decisions.

Regarding the healing work we do with Sarah - healing isn't the best word, but is the closest word that we can use. We work a lot with Ascension codes and downloads. We go through a lot of transformational shifts in our energy bodies. And that is one of her main roles, to keep us going through that shift. She's teaching us directly; metaphysical techniques which help us deal with this time of transition. Her healing system is very much involved in that. (see Links for 'Healing with Sarah & the Angels')

Chapter 2

Gaia

The Blue Thread

Blue is primarily associated with the earth's seas and oceans – and therefore with water! Sarah and the New Earth are intertwined for me, and the NASA images of earth from space, with the blue and the green, represent both Sarah and Gaia in my heart. But about 71% of Earth is water covered; Gaia is much more than just a grounding force, she also represents the blue of healing. Water holds peaceful and calm energies, but can also be deep, dark and dangerous! Our lives on the earth plane throws many challenges at us, and Gaia gives us the opportunity to live those lives in physical manifestation, and to learn and to grow...

Since the very beginning of when I started working with Sarah, the earth has been a recurring theme. For many years this confused me; I wasn't sure how it all fit together, but that was before I had a clear understanding that this is an evolutionary journey we are on – us AND the earth. 'We are the Earth' was a teaching that Sarah gave to me early on. We are made out of the earth, everything within us comes from Gaia. We are walking around in her body. No wonder we are so intimately connected! Of course, we forget this, with our mentally sophisticated and constructed lives. We wonder why we feel better when we go 'out in nature'. It's because WE ARE NATURE! We have removed ourselves from our natural habitat, into buildings vibrating with all sorts of artificial frequencies that don't particularly suit our physical bodies and energy system! We are here to be guardians of the Earth, to watch over the ley lines, to keep the energy clean, to make sure there is not a buildup of psychic residue on the planet.

We are re-remembering many of these things right now, whilst being in the middle of a massive changeover! We are really learning on the job as the energy grid system on the earth is being re-built from scratch, and it needs a lot of hours of manpower from us to get it up and running! Sarah could be described as a project manager for the work that is going on currently on this construction site called earth, and we are her employees! For years, many of us have worked with 'our stuff', which is, as we know, is a never-ending journey (it's the journey that is the thing, not the end goal, lol).

Now it's the time to step up a level, and be working in groups together on the 'clean up Mother Earth' project. The construction site is full of psychic debris from the last aeons, and although Gaia can manage some of this herself, we also need to take responsibility for what we have created, and clean up the energy that we/humanity have put upon the earth.

It's time for us to remember that we are ALL native to the earth, it is the place where we live, where we come from, where we are all born. It is our home. Yet in the western world, we have much to learn from cultures who remember how to live on the Earth,

This beautiful excerpt is from 'Braiding Sweetgrass', where she tells of the Thanksgiving address from the Onondaga Nation given to start and end the school week,

'… in a language older than English, they begin the recitation. It is said that the people were instructed to stand and offer these words whenever they gathered, no matter how many or how few, before anything else was done. In this ritual, their teachers remind them that every day, "beginning with where our feet first touch the earth, we send greetings and thanks to all members of the natural world." Today it is the third grade's turn. There are only eleven of them and they do their best to start together, giggling a little, and nudging the ones who just stare at the floor. Their little faces are screwed up with concentration and they glance at their teacher for prompts when they stumble on the words. In their own language they say the words they've heard nearly every day of their lives.

Today we have gathered and when we look upon the faces around us we see that the cycles of life continue. We have been given the duty to live in balance and harmony with each other and all living things. So now let us bring our minds together as one as we give greetings and thanks to each other as People. Now our minds are one.

There is a pause and the kids murmur their assent.

We are thankful to our Mother the Earth, for she gives us everything that we need for life. She supports our feet as we walk about upon her. It gives us joy that she still continues to care for us, just as she has from the beginning of time. To our Mother, we send thanksgiving, love, and respect. Now our minds are one.'

— **ROBIN WALL KIMMERER**

Your body is the Earth

"Welcome I am Sarah. The message I have for you is to become more closely aligned to the earth. The earth contains many things that are of mother/father God, and are a direct way to experience the opportunities for a Sacred Life. Humanity holds much wisdom as a group soul, but often the earth is overlooked in her own wisdom as a very high source of teachings and information. Because you are made of the earth, you can receive these teachings physically into your body. Gaia can give them directly to you, the same as if you were a pupil of a great spiritual guru! See the earth as your teacher, directly giving you the healing, cleansing, purification and transformation that is needed for you to advance spiritually. The earth needs people like you, because as you grow and become more and more spiritually pure, so you can be of greater service to everything here on the earth plane, including Gaia herself. The earth needs your help and she has much to offer you.

Feel into the earth when you go outside. Listen to where you are led to go, by listening to your desires and wishes. Where will it bring you joy to go? Where do you need to be? In the same way that you listen to your body, and sense what food you need to eat & what will be best for you… learn to understand your body as a compass, directing you in whatever direction you need to travel.

This is Sacred work and there is much to learn. I am Sar'h, and you can call on me for help as often and whenever you wish. My Blessings are upon you, Blessed Be, Blessed Be, Blessed Be, Amen."

Living on the earth is a blessing

"Welcome, I am Sarah. What I would like to share today, is the thought or feeling or energy of that living on the earth is a blessing because it might not feel this way right now to many of you. I'm sending this energy through, so that you can remember to concentrate in your day-to-day lives, on seeing the small moments of delight and of magic especially when you are able to go outside and to connect with the elements of the earth and the air, the sun, the sky, the trees, the plants, the animals.

This is one reason why so many people love their pets… it's because it connects them to the realms of nature and to the earth. All of the animal kingdoms have a stronger connection through their senses to the physical realms of the earth - one that is much more easy for people to disconnect from with all of their mental distractions. The mental realm very much can take people away from the body, from the earth because your body is the earth, and you need the earth. So, remember that in each day, to do simple earth-based things – feel your feet on the earth, take a breath of fresh air and notice it and be aware of it when you are outside.

Also, when you are out in nature, there are nature elementals who tend to all of the flowers and the trees looking after them and caring for them, adjusting things when needed and it is the same for the animal kingdoms of which you are a part of. So when you are outside, you can be attended to in this way as well by the nature elementals! They don't really like to come into houses so much, but they are happy to work with you when you are outside, so remember this when you are out on your walk and invite them to come and be with you and do their job - because it actually makes them happy to do their job of being around all these different things… these creations of the divine. It's their job to take care of them and you are included in this as well.

These types of elementals are very much in my realms, they recognise my energy, they know who I am, we are in a state of oneness together one might say. So, when you work with my energies call me in, they will also see that in your energetic aura and be happy to come close to you and give you assistance.

I am Sarah and these are the words which I wish to speak to you this day.

Blessed be, blessed, blessed be, Amen."

I am Sarah and I give you my blessings, blessed be, blessed be, blessed be, Amen."

Healing of the Earth

'Can we use Sarah and her angels, to send healing to the elementals, tree spirits and so forth?' *(Question is from a live interview.)*

Rachel: 'I've found the elementals, the fairies and nature spirits and the like, they very much have a mind of their own and know what they want themselves. But if you call on Sarah and her angels, or just call on Sarah because her angels will come with her. They're very good to have with you when you want to work collaboratively, with the elemental kingdoms, because she's very connected to their energies and so they'll like you.

What stands behind Sarah is Sophia. Sophia is Queen of the Elementals and Mary Magdalene, as Sarah's Mother is obviously part of this lineage. If you want to do any healing work with the fairies and elementals, I would tune into them (Sarah and Mary Magdalene), and ask them (the nature spirits) what they want, because they always have something to say about that!'

'How are the elementals and Mother Gaia doing at the moment? Is there anything in particular you feel we should be doing to assist them and also to support the bees, animal kingdom and pets? Some pet owners have noticed a change in their pets' behaviour and would welcome guidance on how they can best support them.' *(Question is from a live interview.)*

"So, I would ask each of you now to sink down a little bit into your earthly bodies, to come down into connection with Gaia. Now Gaia is already an ascended being, not in her physical body perhaps but in herself, in her consciousness and the reason I say 'not ascended in her physical body', is because she has made the sacrifice of having humanity be alive upon her using part of her body. And so, she waits patiently and assists humanity where she can. But there has been a way of thinking, of regarding the heavier earthier realms as 'less than', & not as 'spiritual' - although this is definitely changing in the spheres of those who work with the Divine Feminine in the body and dance and sensuality very much blessed by Mary Magdalene's presence for example. But you too are all of the earth, you too are all of the animal kingdom and you contain everything within you that they do. You are much more aligned to them than perhaps you realise. However, you have this strong mental layer to your energy field as well, so you have something extra.

So, a good way to make contact with the elementals, with your pets, with the animal kingdom is to quiet down your mental activity and come into your heart. Perhaps you could try doing that now. Take your awareness down right into your heart centre. If it feels right, invite in the presence of the Magdalene, my mother. Feel the physical space that you occupy. Place your hands on the earth if you can or even just on the chair that you are sitting or the floor but connect down to the earth. How does it feel to you? You are connected through all of these layers, through all of these energy lines. You are the earth; you are the earth. You are the earth in all of her beauty and her wondrousness.

Everything is made from the earth, from her body – your beloved pets, the whole of humanity, and your houses - all of you are made from her body. Even the elementals are made from the vibrational fabric of the earth. It is simply of a different vibrational level. They too are physical, just a higher physical vibration. This is how you can help all of these different kingdoms whether it is stone or animal, elemental or plant. Take a moment to connect to the earth and through all things that live on her in that way. Invite me in when you do this exercise because I can act as a bridge. I bring everything into integration and oneness and love is the key. Love is the key. Love is the key to everything. But just place your hands on your heart again now. Breathe into that place knowing all is well, all is well, all is well.

This is a divine truth that all is well and everything that is happening around you in the world today, is happening because you are all on a journey back to the divine. This is the journey back to the divine. It is inevitable, unstoppable. Feel that truth in your heart. All is well, all is well, all is well. And then place your hands back down again on the chair or the floor or the earth and connect once again to the different kingdoms.

If you wish to help them, do this exercise, and then ask them: how can I help? How can I be of service and see what comes to you? Each of you has your own task, each of you has your own purpose in the world which is linked to your soul essence, your past lives, the experiences and skills you have accumulated over the eons. Each of you has come to help in your own way. All is well, all is well, all is well. You can also just simply spread this divine truth throughout the kingdoms, working throughout the layers & bringing a centeredness and a calmness. This doesn't mean that there is not action to be taken, responsibilities to be owned up to.

However, even while you take that action, even while you own up to those quite large responsibilities, it is good to do it from the heart place as you place your hand back on your heart again saying all is well, all is well, all is well. If you can do this and act from the place that all is well rather than from the trauma, from the fear, from the pain, then your actions will be the most aligned to the divine will, to the will of the divine spark that each of you has within you.

This is a practice - not something that you should expect yourself to fall into. This is humanity's next step, to come back into alignment with the divine spark within - which is held just underneath the heart centre at the position of the Hrit Padma *(see glossary)* – two or three finger widths underneath the heart centre. To start the practice now is to support the evolution of humanity.

Humanity is starting to bloom now, it might not be apparent, it might not even be visible and yet in truth it is happening. Perhaps you can see it in some of the people that you know. Perhaps you can even see it in yourself. It may feel like a slow process to you but once again with that perspective of looking above with the ascended eye, these little lights on the earth are coming brighter and brighter joining together and becoming fields of flowers.

I am Sarah and this is what I wish to speak. Blessed be."

A channeling from the time of Corona

"Welcome, I am Sar'h. As you have been feeling, this is a time of great light coming in, and as you have also felt the light and the darkness is, as a polarity, in balance. The vibrations of the planet are rising, and humanity is going through a great time of change. Notice the word 'great' keeps occurring here, because this is something that occurs only once in many millennia. More and more people are waking up to my energies, some who are more sensitive are aware that it is me, others just notice a presence of fresh life force and hope in their lives, even in this time of difficulty.

I am able now to step more into the world as it is, I am more able to be present in your day-to-day consciousness and in the world paradigm. There is more space for me to come in and to be in.

I, as I have discussed with you many times, represent an archetypal force of the Divine. It is not 'my' energy, but one that I am an archetypal window for. When people 'look' at me, or focus on me in some way, they are able to access this archetypal force. This force can be described as oneness consciousness, or cosmic consciousness – 'in me, there is no separation'.

When you connect to my energy, all things within you start to come into oneness, in sympathetic vibration. This includes your lower and higher self. Right now you are experiencing the speeding up of this process. I am a catalyst, where I am present, these processes happen with more speed. When you are ready for the process of becoming one with your higher and lower self, I will be there. When you need to take a break, I will step back, but will remain at your side. This is why so many of you are feeling me so intensely right now, I am facilitating this process.

Right now the earth is surrounded by a corona of violet flame which is burning off that which is no longer necessary. This is for the earth, and for humanity, and for all that is in physical existence on the earth (this includes all of the plant, animal, crystal/stone and elemental kingdoms).

As light codes come into you from the sun, and the stars and galaxy around you, the whole earth is going through a process of enlightenment, or of being 'lifted up'. Many of those passing are taking ancestral heavy energies with them as they pass, as all people do when they die – but right now, because many more are passing, this effect is more pronounced, and so each day the earth is carrying a less heavy burdensome energy. I do not say these things to lack compassion, or to say that it is a good thing that so many are passing in this way, but I say it because it is so, these are the metaphysics of the situation, if you will.

In the midst of darkness, many have found peace, many souls have been lifted up to a vibration of the light that has never before been achieved, and this includes those who are passing, as well of those living right now; it also includes 'awakened' and 'unawakened' souls. Those who are passing, are not remaining earthbound, they are moving swiftly to the next place on their journey. They are supported by the outpouring of love and compassion that there is for them from the Collective. They are able to draw sustenance from this, to know that they are cared for, and there are many, many angels supporting each person that passes over. The light vibration that your galaxy is currently passing through, is of such a refined and high vibration just now, that it supports many processed that only a short while ago would have been impossible. Many of you have been brought on line by this 'cloud of enlightenment' that you are passing through in space, and many Ascended master guides, angels and light beings are taking this opportunity to do work that supports the growth of the planet and of all life upon the planet.

Remember that you are blessed, even though from the outward appearance it may not appear this way for all of you. No matter what the situation is in your life right now, just being present upon the planet as a lifeform at this moment in the history of the earth, gives you a light quota that is available to your soul and your soul's development. Your soul will remember this matrix of light that is on the earth right now, and will be able to use it in future incarnations, even those who pass will be able to do this. It is an ability to access the light, no matter what the outer conditions are, no matter how dark and how heavy. This light matrix is Divine Grace in energy form that is flowing through all of your energy bodies, and as I said, once experienced by the soul, then that soul will always be able to access this 'light grid of grace', even in future incarnations. It is one of the Divine's tools to start to balance up the light and dark on the earth right now. Organically, there is a lot of heavy energy on the earth that needs to be cleaned up right now. You are all becoming master workers, and this is your task now, to always access the light, and bring it into the darkness. Not to raise one above the other, but to join them together. All is one, all is the divine, all is well.

I am Sarah and these are the words I would wish to speak to you this day, blessed be, blessed be, blessed be, Amen."

Sarah's Violet Flame and how to live 5th dimensionally in a 3D world

Right now, many of us are struggling with how to live in a 3D world whilst bringing through and holding the energy of 5D (and higher) inside ourselves. *The family systems we live within, the society, towns, workplaces, and schools we are living in, all have challenging energies, and can make us feel like we are being pulled apart. The more time goes on, the more the gap seems to widen, and our 'inner' and 'outer' life becomes further apart. It also becomes harder and harder to tolerate the incompatibilities between 3D & 5D earthly life as it creates an inner tension inside ourselves - we are working and living within systems where it is difficult or impossible to live out our inner truth and values and be 'ourselves'... and this can manifest as stress and depression – as well as worsening 'ascension symptoms' (if you're not sure what these are, just google them, there's lots of info around.)*

My work with Sarah in recent years has been about how we can shift more easily from 3D to 5D. Sarah holds the energy of 'oneness' so she can be in any dimension she pleases! This also means she can teach us how 'to dance' in between the vibrational spheres.

A couple of years ago, Sarah gave me a 'net of light' meditation, (see appendix for link) which creates energy integrity around <u>all</u> of our energy bodies (aura), because for many of us, the energy downloads and rapid transformational growth that we are going through can cause some problems with 'holding it all together' energetically! In the ‹net of light› meditation, Sarah lends us her support in keeping our energy integrity, so we can 'hold it all together', even through times that would otherwise put a lot of strain on us.

Sarah has also given us a meditation to create a 'net of light' around the homes that we are living in - this is to create a 5D web of light, that maintains the frequency for us (so at least we get one place where there's some respite from 3D energy!) I'm really amazed that this is possible, but I've experienced it personally that this is really happening!! This meditation has the image of a seed (matrix of energy) being planted down through our own individual energy system which then 'grows' very organically out into the personal space that we live in (see Online Classes for this class 'Growing your own Ascension Grid').

Finally, I've been working with Sarah's violet flame more than anything else! I have been a 'violet flame junkie' since the very start of my spiritual journey - before I ever did anything 'spiritual', I sat every day FOR 2 YEARS and did a violet flame meditation through all of my energy bodies and physical self, without actually knowing why - I was just compelled to do it. I very first came across this practice from the Aetherius society in London, but the violet flame crops up over and over again in different esoteric teachings, and I've even had a spontaneous past life memory of being a priest of the Violet Robe in Atlantis, when the fields were failing and everything was collapsing!

The violet flame is known as a tool to transform and transmute 'negative and inappropriate' energies. I actually have my own take on what this is really about, but I'll be talking more about this and what it all means in my upcoming workshop here (see Online Classes for the Sarah's Violet Flame Attunement.) And I've been using this particular violet flame for quite a few years now, as Sarah has her own vibration of the violet flame that she works with. But the last 6 months has led me to work with Sarah's energies using crystal matrices, and OMG has this led to a stepping up of the energies!!

From working with Sarah's violet flame, I have discovered that it transforms the heavy energy patterns of 3D to 5D. Or rather, it creates an energy matrix around us that allows us to shift away from the well-trodden path of 3D and operate instead from the lighter and much happier tracks in the 5D groove!! The crystals that 'came forward' to hold the vibration of Sarah's violet flame were lilac amethyst, and when I'm holding them (I have them in a little bag that fits in my pocket), I've experienced that many 'core' issues which I haven't been able to shift before, (even though I've used my ‹tool box›, such as EFT, shamanic journeys, vibrational healing, dreamwork and so on) are now just not having the same hold over me anymore! It's as if when the crystals are physically on me, the energy matrix of the lilac amethyst creates a space where I'm 'lifted away' from these old energy patterns – and that the space between me and the old energy pattern has given me the objectivity I need, and so the chance to act and behave differently. I have been able to shift relationship patterns that have haunted me for years, (even though I have had different therapies and healing modalities until I was blue in the face)!! Often these 'core' patterns of behaviour are the result of past life patterns plus ancestral patterns (i.e., your family dynamics that have been passed down), and they are also given strength and power through energetic resonance. By this I mean that because a lot of other people have done the same thing as you, and have behaved in the same way many, many times before you, then this vibration of energy has a power and has created a well-worn track for you to slip easily into. The power of that vibration pulls you into vibrating at the same energy level! Behaviour patterns exist as a thought form, or energy matrix. This is the well-trodden path, or groove that I was referring to before. For example, if a family member has been hurt by a sibling, and lashes out in return by saying something hurtful – this is a behaviour pattern that has been repeated many times before. If you have your own personal habit of lashing out when you feel hurt, unfortunately this isn't the only 'energy pattern' that you will have to overcome. The strong and powerful energy matrix of that behaviour pattern has been reinforced over and over again by many other people and means that if you are going to do something different - which could be taking a breath, and saying that you feel hurt rather than retaliating, then you first have to resist the 'path of least resistance'. Which is being drawn into the same old energy matrix and behaving how all those other people have behaved before you!

Sarah's violet flame shifts you up to the 5th dimension. From this higher vibration, honesty, integrity, thoughtfulness, compassion, wisdom (and more) are easier to access. You are able to access the thoughtforms which exist at this level of vibration, and although the thoughtforms haven't reached the same level of 'reinforcement power', than the ones in 3D, because you too are lifted up to this 5D level, you are 'physically' closer to them, and so they have a greater power over you!! It takes work and consciousness to access the 5D matrix, but attuning crystals to Sarah's violet flame really helps! When we access this 5D network, we are also able to access the sympathetic resonance of the thoughtforms/energy patterns of all the people who have previously created positive patterns of behaviour, whilst operating at a 5th dimensional frequency. It's been some time in the history of humanity since 'we' as a majority have operated at that 5D frequency, but it has happened. When we **can** shift to get there vibrationally, those eons matter less than you would think; the shared vibrational frequency brings you into the same shared energetic space with the behaviour and energy patterns of those who have gone before! Sarah's energy integrates.... 'In her there is no separation'. This means that even if you are needing to work within a 3D workplace or function within a 3D family system, then you can still access your 5D resources and respond in a way that is good for you! With Sarah's support you can 'straddle' (not the most elegant image I know!) both worlds - which is where many of us are right now.

I have the blessing of living in a town in Denmark, where there are numerous natural springs running through. These are no ordinary springs, but create (along with the earth energy lines that are also running through the town, as well as energy portals and chakra points) an Ascension grid. From connecting to these energies of the grid, I'm able to 'see' how we can move forward on our path into the New Age/New Earth/5th Dimension/Golden Age - however you want to call it. It's coming, it's on its way. (Or rather, we are on our way to it!) But we, in co-creation with the angelic, elemental, the stone and plant people, and the animal kingdoms, still have some way to go! In the meantime, 'Spirit' are giving us some extra help in the form of these tools - which are providing a 'fix' or 'patch' for us to get us through until a time when the new system is ready to come 'on-line'! Several years ago, I bought an (Amazon) kindle fire tablet for my youngest son, to play some games on when we were flying frequently, as the old android one got smashed. But I was really annoyed to find out that all of my son's favourite games that I'd bought on Google Play were now inaccessible. Amazon had designed their own tablet which blocked out any attempts to use Google's platforms. This bugged me for several weeks, until after some searching, I found that it was possible to rewrite some of the code on the Kindle, and create a 'go-around'. Now I'm no coder, but I found the information that I needed, and after some fiddling about, I got it to work. Now I didn't change the original programming of that Kindle, but I got it to do what I needed it to do by using a 'fix'. And that's what we need to do with our 3D problems in our daily life. We can't change that old programming of everything - that old system is too gargantuan to be dismantled, and actually we don't need to, because there is a new 5D system on the way!

But many of us are suffering right now - our nervous systems are overstretched and overburdened and we need some help right here, right now, because we are having to live in the world as it is!! Spirit doesn't want us to collapse under the weight of the effort that many of us are needing to make, and they know what huge efforts we are making. Sarah is really stepping forward now to lend us her more than phenomenal energies! HELP IS AT HAND!

The time of Corona

I channeled this during the first year of the time of Corona, and the channeling specifically refers to that time.

During Corona, we have been able to see how polarising challenges and emotional stress can be. The truth is no one thing can be ALL right, and the other ALL wrong. Each of us are imperfect, and that's OK. We can BE with that. No ONE has ALL of the right answers, no SIDE has all of the solutions. Each SIDE holds a perfect piece of the whole. Together we are ONE. Blessed Be, Amen!

"Welcome I am Sarah.

As you have been feeling this is a time of great light coming in, and as you have also felt the light and the darkness is, as a polarity, in balance. The vibrations of the planet are rising, and humanity is going through a great time of change. Notice the word 'great' keeps occurring here, because this is something that occurs only once in a millennia. More and more people are waking up to my energies, some who are more sensitive are aware that it is me, others just notice a presence of fresh life force and hope in their lives, even in this time of difficulty. I am able now to step more in to the world as it is. I am more able to be present in your day-to-day consciousness and in the world paradigm. There is more space for me to come in and to be in. I, as I have discussed with you many times, represent an archetypal force of the Divine. It is not 'my' energy, but one that I am an archetypal window for. When people 'look' at me, or focus on me in some way, they are able to access this archetypal force. This force can be described as oneness consciousness, or cosmic consciousness – 'in me, there is no separation'. When you connect to my energy, 'all things within you start to come into oneness, in sympathetic vibration. This includes your lower and higher self. You are experiencing the speeding up of this process. I am a catalyst, & where I am present, these processes happen with more speed. When you are ready for the process of becoming one with your higher and lower self, I will be there. When you need to take a break, I will step back, but will remain at your side. This is why so many of you are feeling me so intensely right now; I am facilitating this process.

Right now, the earth is surrounded by a corona of violet flame which is burning off that which is no longer necessary. This is for the earth, and for humanity, & for all that is in physical existence on the earth (this includes all of the plant, animal, crystal/stone and elemental kingdoms.) As light codes come into you from the sun, and the stars and galaxy around you, the whole earth is going through a process of enlightenment, or of being 'lifted up'. Many of those passing are taking ancestral heavy energies with them as they pass, as all people do when they die – but right now, this effect is more pronounced, and so each day the earth is carrying a less heavy burdensome energy. I do not say these things to lack compassion, or to say that it is a good thing that so many are passing in this way, but I say it because it is so, these are the metaphysics of the situation, if you will. In the midst of darkness, many have found peace, many souls have been lifted up to a vibration of the light that has never before been achieved, and this includes those who are passing, as well of those living right now; it also includes 'awakened' and 'unawakened' souls. Those who are passing, are not remaining earthbound, they are moving swiftly to the next place on their journey. They are supported by the outpouring of love and compassion that is there for them from the collective, they are able to draw sustenance from this, to know that they are cared for, and there are many, many angels supporting each person that passes over.

The light vibration that your galaxy is currently passing through, is of such a refined and high vibration just now, that it supports many processes that only a short while ago would have been impossible. Many of you have been brought on line by this 'cloud of enlightenment' that you are passing through in space, and many Ascended master guides, angels and light beings are taking this opportunity to do work that supports the growth of the planet and of all life upon the planet. Such an outpouring of light happens only once in a millennia, as I mentioned before and it is happening now.

Remember that you are blessed, even though from the outward appearance it may not appear this way for all of you. No matter what the situation is in your life right now, just being present upon the planet as a lifeform at this moment in the history of the earth, gives you a light quota that is available to your soul and your soul's development. Your soul will remember this matrix of light that is on the earth right now, and will be able to use it in future incarnations, even those who pass will be able to do this. It is an ability to access the light, no matter what the outer conditions are, no matter how dark and how heavy. This light matrix is Divine Grace in energy form that is flowing through all of your energy bodies, and as I said, once experienced by the soul, then that soul will always be able to access this 'light grid of grace', even in future incarnations. It is one of the Divine's tools to keep the balance of the light and dark on the earth right now. Organically, there is a lot of heavy energy on the earth that needs to be cleaned up right now. You are all becoming master workers, and this is your task now, to always access the light, and bring it into the darkness. Not to raise one above the other, but to join them together. All is one, all is the divine, all is well.

I am Sarah and these are the words I would wish to speak to you this day, blessed be, blessed be, blessed be, Amen."

Chapter Three

Healing & Sarah's Angels

The White Thread

White is the colour of Sarah's Angels and the high vibration of spirituality that they hold and project. In truth, where-ever Sarah is, so are her host of Angels – they are One. But to separate them out, helps us to see and connect with the beauty, the 'higher than high-ness' that they are, and also that is the same energy as the Divine Spark within each one of us... There is so much healing, truth, cleansing, peace, unity, purity in this white of Sarah's Angels. White contains all of the other colours – in Oneness!

"The healing of yourself is the greatest task you can undertake in this lifetime. Until the healing is occurring within, mankind cannot heal itself on the outer layers of itself i.e., the society, culture and world that you live in. "

Taken from "Sarah's little book of Healing".
'God enters through the wound' Carl Jung

Sarah is at the core of her being, first and foremost a healer. It is what we have all come here to do; to heal, to become One. 'Sarah's little book of Healing' outlines Sarah's philosophy towards 'becoming whole'; the essence of her healing work and how to use specific healing techniques for working with your daily life as a way of integrating all that you are!! It's also a foundational book for those who want to become a healer with the 'Sarah & the Angels' training course. The channelings here give more information on Sarah's Angels, and expand on that which was given in the first book. Since the first book, published in 2014, Sarah's Angels have really stepped up our light quotient, and revealed themselves in greater and greater ways!

And as was said, Sarah is at her foundation a healer. When her presence is present, things start to heal themselves! In truth her Angels are there to assist us with our evolutionary process, and with the vibrational 'lifting up' of our energy bodies. Whilst this is technically a healing process, it is bringing us into greater wholeness; it is a 'higher healing'. We can differentiate between the healing that one can find in Sarah's little book of Healing, and the healing that then occurs when her Angels are invited in; the first, we could call Soul Healing and heals the emotional, mental and spiritual, and the second, we could call Higher Self or Divinity Healing and brings in energies of 'the highest on high', and then informs all the other layers of healing. Both are needed, and both are beautiful ways of healing!

Calling Sarah in

For people who are new to Sarah and would like to ask for her help with healing, what are the first few steps they should take? Where should they start? *(Question is from a live interview.)*

"Welcome, I am Sarah. Getting to know me and getting to know my energy of course, is really simple. What do you do when you meet a new person? You get a sense of them. How you feel when you're with them and you feel; do I like this person? Do I want to stay friends with them? How will my relationship work with them?

And so, it is with me. A very simple thing you can do is to call my presence in, and there are different ways that you could do that. You could get some special water from the sea, or from a spring or stream and place it in front of you, or you could find a leaf or flower, or you could light a candle.

Ask yourself, 'what do I signify for you when you feel into my energy; what do I mean to you?' And then pick that thing that means something to you, whether it is something from nature, or a colour or something from the elements or perhaps some beautiful piece of material. Choose something that represents that meaning for you. The possibilities are really endless. And then each time you want to call in my presence, have that thing there with you and start to get to know me.

You could do this for a few minutes each day and you could ask for healing. You could ask for some help with some matter that has been troubling you. The important thing is that you do it little and often and then our relationship will grow and deepen, and other inspirations will be put your way.

My blessings are upon you. Blessed Be. Blessed Be. Blessed Be. Amen."

Rachel: 'So, I was seeing quite a gentle little drop, drop, drop, drop and she does have quite a few different faces. One of them is helping us connect with the divine love inside us. It can also be connecting with the wild person inside us.

Sarah has a very strong magickal nature energy so it could be connecting to that wild wisewoman (or wild wiseman) inside of ourselves.

It can also be about really getting to grips with our own light and making these things conscious. She does have quite a few different roles and really you can only find out by just saying hello each day!

Lighting a candle is a really powerful way of bringing her in, but I'm also aware these days we're more conscious about particles in the air and breathing difficulties so a candle isn't necessarily always the way to go. But anything elemental: water, fire, air, earth - those things. Colours too. It's also great to go out into nature and connect with her.'

Sarah's energy can help repair your DNA

"I AM Sarah and I am here as an Ascended Master for the Age of Aquarius for the new earth. I hold the patterns, the energy matrices, the blueprints. Just connecting to my energy helps your DNA start to re-sequence itself because of Sympathetic Resonance. I hold the energies for the new earth and the new humanity and I come here as sister, teacher, mentor, to walk by your side, to lend you my energy and its catalytic presence, to help you become the more of what you are."

(Sarah's book of Healing.)

Calling on Sarah's Angels for healing help

How can we approach Sarah for assistance with distant healing, sending healing to others or maybe even to pets? *(Question is from a live interview.)*

Rachel: 'I think that's where Sarah's angels are really useful. So, Sarah's angels are very much kind of her technicians if you like. They're the ones that make things. So, she has her job to do. She's aligned with the divine will; this needs to happen, and the angels are the ones that carry it out.

When it comes to healing or times of crisis or distress, they are very good to call on. So, if it's you or your family, we have to really think about asking people's permission. So, you can only really do this if you know people are happy for you to send them healing. But if they are, you can simply ask Sarah's angels. I would just light a little candle and put it in my amethyst cave that I love, and I like to put a little candle in there and ask Sarah's angels to watch over somebody having an operation or someone I know that's having a hard time or whatever. But I wouldn't go beyond my sphere unless I've been specifically asked by Spirit *(see glossary)* and what I mean by that is if I was watching the television and I saw there was terrible trouble somewhere in another country, I wouldn't ask Sarah's angels to go along and start doing healing with that and the reason for that is this.

Sarah has come here to offer very specific energies at this time. She has a very specific job role and a lot of this is about our evolutionary process. So, the people who are ready to work with Sarah, are attracted to Sarah. That doesn't mean everybody in the whole human race is ready. And to be exposed to her energy too soon and when I say her energy, I am including the angels in with her because like I said, they come as one package.'

Is there anything we can do with Sarah's angels, that is simple, to help with healing trauma held in the land due to natural disasters, war, pain, arguments, torture, and ancestral karma? *(Question is from a live interview.)*

Rachel: 'Any place that we go to physically, we can apply healing *(it's always good to tune into your guides first, or take an oracle card and get some guidance)* and what Sarah is saying is simply take some water. It can be water that you've collected from a natural water source, or it can just be tap water, it doesn't matter. Simply hold a bottle or a bowl and ask Sarah's angels, to put healing into that water and then take it around and sprinkle it on to that place.

I would also, while I was doing that, visualise that I have Sarah's violet flame around me, like a cloak because it's a wonderful protection when you're doing earth healing. Sarah is involved in a lot of earth healing. I have classes on my online school for working with Sarah's violet flame and also Sarah's Violet Flame Temple in Glastonbury. Sarah's violet flame attunement gives a lot of techniques. *(See Online Classes.)*

Yes, the healing is needed definitely, but 99% of it right now is the violet flame because we have to - it would be like if you wanted a wound to heal, you'd need to clean it first. You wouldn't leave it dirty. That's what we're doing with the violet flame, we're going around cleaning.

There are a lot of vibrations of the violet flame. Of course, you can just ask for the violet flame, but Sarah's violet flame is specific to working with us going to our next level of evolution and that goes for the earth as well, because the earth and the wounds on the earth, are generally caused by us and that's why we have to clean them up.

And that's part of our 'coming into our mastery'; that's part of our learning of how we can learn how to clean these up. And at the same time, Spirit teaches us stuff. The elementals work with us, the angels, it's all part of this cooperation thing but it is important that we know we have that ability to shift things on the planet. It's not true that we can't do anything. We can actually do a lot especially when we work in groups.

We're only just learning how to do this en masse and powerfully, and Sarah is one of the new Ascended Masters that are coming in to teach us about all of this stuff.'

Sarah's energies blends well with others

So, for people who are already working with different healing systems, I just want to reassure them that they can also work with Sarah's healing system as well. There's not going to be any possible issues with using two different energies and any potential conflicts? *(Question is from a live interview.)*

Rachel: 'So, years ago, I used to offer a chant service because I like doing chanting and I like using Sanskrit chants. I also use Hawaiian chants quite a lot too. With the chants, I found that if I called in Sarah and then did the chant, which could be calling in Ganesh or Lakshmi or the Durga, Pele or Laka or whoever, her energy just blended with it beautifully and actually amplified it.

So, it's that thing again, that Sarah is in all of the Spheres. She compliments things beautifully. I've never found anything that she 'bangs up' against. She's useful in every situation. So, the energies from any spirituality, you can put Sarah in it, and it works. It's really amazing.'

Sarah's Angels connect into Highness

Could you say anything about, how working with Sarah's angels differs in terms of the healing that people are perhaps more familiar with, in systems such as Angel Reiki? *(Question is from a live interview.)*

Here, Sarah is specifically talking about the techniques we use when working with Sarah & the Angels Healing System (see Links)

Rachel: 'The first thing that I'm getting is that it's that kind of circle that's coming together and I see their wings *(the angels)* coming up and making a connection and again, although they need her to make things manifest on earth, it is a lot about integration. So, Sarah's Angels have this ability to connect into highness, for us or through us you could even say, and then we like bring down what we've learnt with the healing system.

(In the healing session) We bring down these higher fine particles of light and then Sarah helps us manifest that onto the earth plane with her energies and with her violet flame because things need clearing out of the way. And it applies to anything 'new earth' really. So, anybody who is involved in bringing through new energies or new systems for work, the way we live, the way we eat, the way we farm – they are going

to be part of it and the more conscious we are of them, the more we can bring them in, the more they can get involved.

So, they have this magic of being able to take these things that aren't in our vibrational sphere yet on the material plane, and help us bring them down *(and ground/manifest them)* and actually, they do make it very easy energetically wise, for this to happen.

Of course, the real hard work is then at the physical end because things take time. You can't grow an oak tree in a second. Well, perhaps you can if you're Saint Germain! It's going to take us time to bring in all of these systems, but Sarah's angels are very much the ones to call on.'

You are Blooming into a New Era of Growth!

Sarah has said before that her energy can be likened to that of spring, which means that she holds the power of initiating something new. A huge burst of power is needed (often after a period of gestation where it seemed nothing was happening, but it was just unseen) to bring in a new life, or a new project. This channelling has a beautiful energy in it, and as Sarah has done many times before, she uses the metaphor of a garden – which helps me remember we are all organic beings growing naturally, following our pattern of growth, just like the flowers and the trees and all living creatures...

"Welcome, I am Sarah. My blessings are upon each and every one of you. As I speak from this side of the earth, spring is truly upon us and all of the blessings that come with it, the chance of something new – new life, new growth. I am a good person to call upon when you have new projects in your life that you perhaps feel need a little bit more power and umph. I will gladly come along and give that energy.

I have the power of bringing spirit through to the manifest world and this is not my power in truth but rather an aspect of the Divine that I am an archetype for, I am a face for, or an 'energy colour' – whichever way you want to describe it.

You can call on me even to help your garden grow out in nature. You can ask me to bless the water that you pour on your house plants. You can bless the water you drink to help *you* grow or your children grow, or your pets grow in those times where change is needed and perhaps you wish for the fresh verdant energies of spring!

I am Sarah and I am here specifically as mankind blooms into a new era of growth. It is time to cast off those old chattels, those old beliefs especially the guilt and the blame and the resentment and anger and bitterness. It's fine that it's been there. It's ok it was right for that time but now, now something beautiful and wonderful is coming for humanity. All things come in right timing, right time, right place, right being, and you are in this cusp now – this turning point. Can you feel it as I speak? Can you feel those blossoming's starting to occur in each and every one of you? Those of you who have ears to hear the light within you, has already sparked, has already grown so much.

My mother the Magdalena, she will come to you and help you heal your wounds. She will hold you when you are in pain and suffering and give you so much love and compassion. And my father Yeshua, he will light up that spark, he will fan the flame, he will make it brighter and help you have clarity to comprehend divine truths. And I Sarah, I will help you bring it all together. I will help you fully, fully embrace your humanity and fully, fully embrace your divinity. You have come to be all that you are and so it shall be.

Blessed be, blessed be, blessed be. I am Sarah.

Those of you who have come here to work with me, you are ready to hear my call and so it shall be. I am Sarah and these are the words which I wish to speak this day.

Blessed be, blessed be, blessed be. Amen

My blessings are upon you."

Description of Sarah's Angels

Lady Sarah, you have your own angels from what I understand, who work alongside you and you give them jobs to do. I don't know very much about them. How many are there? Are you able to enlighten us about your angels? Can you tell us what qualities they have and if people want to work with them, which I'm hoping that they will, can you give us some guidance on how people can get to know your angels like we're getting to know you as well please? (Question is from a live interview.)

"So, the first thing I want to say is they come in the shape of a horseshoe and they are a beautiful, beautiful shining light in an incredible purity of whiteness that is beyond white as we know it and this energy is the pure force if you like, of the Cosmic Christ energy.

So, I hold an archetypal energy of the divine masculine and divine feminine, brought together in the sacred marriage which then creates a third entirely other and different energy from the first and the second. And this is, at the same time, newer in the human evolutionary system, but it's all actually a more ancient energy because it was what comes from before. It was present in Lemuria and lived in this consciousness of this light that the angels hold. So, although I can say that my consciousness in the lifetimes that I had on earth was able to sit in this this energy of Cosmic Christ light, but it is actually the angels that hold that pure force and not me.

So, they are, they are the team around me but because of my spiritual development, I am able to resonate with this energy and I have worked with it and made it part of my own soul energy, but it is the angels that hold that force. And so, when things need to be done, I call upon the angelic realms to make it so.

They are a collective force, although the idea about a horseshoe shape is one where one can imagine six or seven angels around oneself and then perhaps sitting in the centre of that horseshoe. In actuality, this host of angels is an uncountable number. They are an awesome and powerful force, but when I need to work with it or when other people want to call on these angels, you're just calling on the part of that force that you need. You don't have to worry about being crushed by the presence of thousands of angels suddenly turning up. Just to say, that is how they are. Yeah, considered all or made up, it is of a huge Legion of angelic beings together.

What can we learn about Sarah's angels generally and how many angels does Sarah have assisting her? *(Question is from a live interview.)*

"Welcome, I am Sarah! My blessings are upon you and as each of you listen to me on this day, or in the days or weeks or months and years ahead, perhaps you can start to sense or become aware that around my energy is another energy, of the angelic realm. If you like, you can see this as a beautiful divine white light, whiter than white.

It is through these angels that I can carry out my divine will. My divine will of course, is in alignment with the divine because I am at a level of advancement that means from the place that I speak today, I am speaking with clarity and perspective.

It is much more difficult when one is living in a human body on the human earth, to have such a clarity of perspective all of the time and yet it can be achieved in moments throughout the day as I'm sure many of you have experienced many times.

The moment of clarity when looking at a pool of water, or hearing a breath of wind, or seeing a bird fly up in the sky and with that moment comes a drop of information, a clarity, or an insight in the same way when you work with oracle cards or runes or whatever healing tools you have, the same thing happens.

It can also be that if you call upon my angels, which of course do not belong exclusively to me. I am but a representation of a divine archetypal force, one which seems complex at first, but is in essence what happens when you bring together the divine feminine and the divine masculine in oneness. Yet I have at this time on earth a more particular job, role, position as it were, with very specific things to do and the reason why I am mentioning this ability to see things clearly when one is not in a physical body upon the earth, is because those angels that work with me can assist in bringing about that clarity.

You have the understanding very close to you, of your soul. You can tune into that soul and your soul has many, many life experiences, and wisdoms that you can tap into, just like that if you have the right catalyst around you. Calling upon my angels and imagining them in a horseshoe around you, can give that perspective. Know that angels that I work with exist as a collective, so trying to place a number on them doesn't really work. They are large. They are Legion. They are many, but they are in oneness. However, you can each of you, call for one particular angel to work with should you wish. SO, there are as many angels as is needed at any one time. The number is infinite.

I am Sarah and these are the words that I wish to speak just now. Blessed be."

Rachel: 'The number seven comes up with these angels very often, but not so much as a literal thing, more of a vibrational quality of seven. This can be a problem as our minds want linear facts and yet actually, Spirit don't really provide them. It's us that can interpret what they give us into linear facts as much as we can, but it is more that our human brains do that but it's always worth asking the question because you'll always get something that you need to know.

It was interesting that Sarah used the term Legion to describe her angels because that's often associated with more evil demons!! However, Sarah is about integrating the light and the dark, with both aspects being seen as part of the Divine.'

How Sarah's Angels work with healing

What kind of healing can Sarah's angels assist us with? Can we literally ask for healing with anything, for example healing finances, relationships, illnesses, even like personal issues such as life changes? I'm trying to get a sense of the vastness. *(Question is from a live interview.)*

Rachel: 'I have written a small book called Sarah's Little Book of Healing and I wrote that a number of years ago before I got really specialised into the healing system that we've got now, where we're working with Sarah's flame in the 3 different aspects of white, green and violet. Initially we only worked with her flame, as it exists in oneness, & that is actually very useful for physical healing. Now I used to be a nurse, I was trained as a psychiatric nurse in the UK, that I'm only qualified to deal with mental health but, I was trained in the legal/medical system and we've been taught to be very careful about ever making claims about anything medical. And I'm, not making any claims here but… this is what Sarah has taught me over the years.

There's a picture on my website: rachelgoodwin.dk. and there's a Sarah page. If you look on there, there's a painting of the flame that Cheryl Yambrach Rose did. Now that flame is very good for physical healing and Sarah wanted me to mention that because she knows I wouldn't actually say that myself because I'm too legally trained not to make claims. I'm not a believer in any particular system of healing. I believe in listening to your own intuition and doing what you're called to and what feels right for you whether it's allopathic or alternative or whatever 'ive' it is, and that we should have the freedom to use everything at our disposal, but Sarah particularly wanted me to mention that. Let me see what else she wants me to mention as it's a big subject or else this will be a three-hour lecture.

She's saying that working with her and the angels and I suppose she's talking about the healing system that we've put together. It's particularly a healing system for the New Age because it kind of is an antidote to all of our ills if you like. When I say that, I don't mean disease, I mean energetically wise; all the things that we need to heal to become whole and move onto our next phase of evolution.

So, one of the things she's talked to me about or given me information about, is that all the seeds for the new earth, everything, it's all here on the earth already. It was already there right from the beginning but what we don't have for the right conditions, is for everything to grow and it's us bringing through our Divinity from ourSelves, bringing in the right conditions that makes those things grow.

These energies, if working with Sarah and her angels and also, we haven't even touched on Sarah's violet flame yet. She has her own violet flame vibration which is phenomenal and is a whole day's workshop all by itself. These things and the things she's teaching us how to use, they hold the antidotes to the modern age basically, which is a bit vast so let me ask her to be a little more specific.

So, in the healing system that Sarah has given us, we call on Sarah and her angels together because they are kind of a package… Of course, we can work with the angels alone, but Sarah is the one that actually grounds and manifests that energy and that's her being this lovely bridge between different spheres/realms.

So, if we ask for Sarah to help us with prosperity for example, there is something such as divine abundance. However, there are a lot of things in our society that twist the money system and twist how we feel about abundance and of course it's difficult for us to see - because we live in this culture. So, when The Secret came out, and yes, you can visualise getting a new car. But, if we ask Sarah to heal our prosperity, she will also heal anything from within us that we have brought through from our family system or our cultural system so that healing will go much more deeply, so that we can manifest true prosperity consciousness for ourselves.'

Do you think Sarah would give any names of these healing angels, because sometimes, people find it useful to have a name and they just call in the angel's name. Would that be possible? *(Question is from a live interview.)*

Rachel: 'They exist as a collective so if you call on an aspect of that, it's like you having your own angel. You could ask for signs and omens for what that name might be. So, I would think it's very individual to each person. The only name I've been given is for Saraniel, who is like Sarah's 'great angel'. He is the Keeper of the Flame of Divinity, which is our divine spark but is also kin to the vibration of her angels. So, there's not like a row of them with names. I think we really have to think of them as oneness and then when we need one of them, something comes, that's just the right thing that we need. It's almost like you get something unique each time.'

The Great Angel Saraniel

"Welcome I am Saraniel, keeper of the Flame of Divinity.

This spiritual flame is the spark of divinity which is at the centre of your being, and is held within existence, yet is outside of existence.

I am all things, yet I am no-thing, I am zero, I am in the void and yet in the whole of manifest creation. I am all these things, and yet I am calm. I am peace.

I hold the depth of being that knows that he/she is part of the Divinity, a being inside of that being. This peace can unfold for you over time, in stages, at first it can unfold when you read my words, and you can experience the truth of the peace of being which I bring.

Then as you continue to call on me, and experience my presence and the peace of being, you can discover for yourself, that the peace of being is inside of you. That you can feel it, because it already exists inside your heart, held in the chamber of the sacred heart, the Hrit Padma**, where your Divine Spark sits, resting there.

Feel the peace that I bring. Sit and breathe it in for a while. Notice how restful it is to be in this place. Here the peace of being. Here you are at zero. Here your divinity is. Here in this place, you can receive all of the inspirations and wisdom that your GodSelf wishes you to have. Here in this calm, you can listen and receive.

All comes from Divinity in this place. It is well.

Then having received, you can use that wonderful tool that is yours! Your personality, your ego, to go out there into the world and make it all so! This is why you have a personality, an ego. Each of you, uniquely so, uniquely special; none the same as before. None can do the same job as the other, each of you with your own special task to bring to the world.

I am calm, I am peace, I am that depth of being that resides inside of yourself, your divine Self, the flame within the flame.

You can imagine my light as a flame around you, a flame of pure brilliant white, and feel yourself resting in the heart of the flame, resting in its embrace. You can feel the depth of my being, and yet all is light. In this place, you can meditate and allow for those inspirations to arise from purity, from the Divine Spark, your Divinity. Just simply allow whatever arises.

If you wish, before you enter into the sacred flame, you can ask for specific guidance. But once you have entered into the depth of being, the flame of brilliant white, let go of all your thoughts and intents, dreams and wishes.

Let go of your directed consciousness, so you can - in purity, be purity and allow the Divine, your spark of pure inspiration, to share in your consciousness. And honour these inspirations, they have come from Divinity. Of course, you can choose whether to manifest them or not, but always honour, love and revere their sacred essence, their Divinity.

It is well, to live in this way and Sarah has come to show you how to live in these sacred ways, each of you finding your own special path to live your Divinity.

It is good. It is well. All is well. Blessings be upon you, each and every moment of your lives.

Namaste. Saraniel."

** *See glossary.*

The Work we have come to do!

There is so much contained within this channelling, and enough to keep us busy for a lifetime! In many ways it contains the essence of Sarah's healing, and gives equal purpose to the dark and the light. This channeling was brought through in winter, those months where the land is resting, the life-force drawn back and slumbering until spring, and the energy encourages us to be more introspective, going within to find the treasure inside.

"Welcome brothers, welcome sisters, welcome all. I am Sarah. Many of you are pondering the seriousness of your paths! At this cold and dark time of year, where introspection comes more naturally and especially during the quieter months of the new year, you may find your thoughts turn to the responsibilities which lie upon you, to become your new true selves and manifest your very being into your lives!

'What if I can't be what I am?', you wonder, 'I don't even know what *I am!*', you worry, 'and even if I did, I don't know how!' These are all natural fears, doubts and worries arising from your ego selves, there is nothing wrong with you that they are there! It is a natural and normal part of the process to have these and other thoughts of worry, doubt and fear.

You are expanding yourSelves into new states of being; humanity is growing, changing, evolving, and you are at the very forefront of this expansion! This change has never been undergone before. You are pioneers; courageous and brave!

Courageous and brave, because your courage and bravery will see you through your doubts, worries and fears. I will help you to discover your own individual ways of working with them, recognising that they are an integral part of the process, and that by working with them, there is much to be learnt from them, many gifts of wisdom they have to impart!

Courageous and brave, because you are stepping into the unknown, 'going where no-one has gone before', and taking humanity into previously uncharted spiritual territory. Your light bodies, your auras are resembling more and more the auras of the masters; you are holding more and more light, and as you do, you need to work more and more with the darkness that is within you.

As you integrate this, (the darkness and the light) it will take you onto the next level of your 'being'.

Your 'darkness' could be seen as the raw, unformed energy of the universe, waiting to be given form and direction. Those issues subsiding in the unconscious part of your mind could be seen like potter's clay, waiting for you to wake up to their reality and eagerly seize the opportunity to make something beautiful. Left unformed, this clay does unto itself, and sits around making mischief, 'I'm not worthy', 'you're not loved', 'I wish I could be ascended, if only I had that kind of potential', 'I can't get what I really want', 'it's not safe here on the physical'.

This unformed clay takes on the form and substance of your ego's past experiences, the thoughts and beliefs that you surrounded yourself with from that experience, and then sits around playing them out, eon after eon, until the day, you notice it's there, and start to consciously create divinity! Within the seed of darkness, is the light, and within the seed of light, is the darkness! This is a mystery and one which cannot be explained by the logic of words alone!

Held together, the dark and the light, they create beauty, synchronicitous creation, each moving in perfect flow with each other until that moment they become one, unity consciousness, a new creation. The dark does not overcome the light, nor the light overcome the dark. They are perfect, whole and complete in their oneness.

So, take care, not to stamp the darkness out of your life. Treat it gently, and with love, for it holds the seeds of your enlightenment! It is your path into the light!

Ask the darkness in your life, the darkness in yourself and your fears and doubts, why are they there? Talk to these things as if they are people, for to be sure they have their own personalities. Treat them with the respect and honour that you would like, don't damn them for their existence, and criticise them into submission. They are here to teach you The Way!

Don't ignore them, and hope that by sending them into the light, you will be able to see the way forward. If your only solution to your difficulties is to throw more light, you will become blinded by the light! Sit with the darkness of your more difficult feelings, your more difficult situations, the ones you wish were not there. Allow them to be there so that you can notice them in the first place. They have come to teach you the way!

Treat them with the love, respect and honour you would give your greatest spiritual teacher, and ask them why they are there. Listen to them with patience as they tell you their stories. Maybe they want to tell you about long ago, this life, or others. But accept what they say, as they tell you their long-held secrets. Honour the truth of their emotions.

Let them cry out their pain, stamp out their anger, or whimper their fear. Let them be what they are, be how they need to be, without interference or judgement. Just let yourself be with them. And when they have told you all they need to say, and been all they need to be, then you can ask the whole of your being, 'how can I help myself with this?' Allow a moment of quietness inside yourself for impressions to come through.

You can also ask, 'what do I need to know?', or any other questions that seem relevant, and the spiritual teachings of love, power and strength, in fact all the wisdom that you need to heal this part of yourself will come through.

Called into being by your intent, the perfect salve to heal your wound can flow naturally from the inner part of your being.

In this way, love (light) can heal pain (dark) creating a new sense of well-being and safety that no matter what happens to you, the solutions are always there (the light and the dark coming together to create a third, but totally new creation). Comfort (light) can heal anxiety (dark) creating a feeling of trust in being in right relationship with the world, (the light and the dark coming together to teach you a divine truth which either the dark or the light could not have achieved on its own!)

All is well, all is well, all is well!

You are the very object of your own creation; all answers lie within you! I say these things to you so you can see, that the very things you seek to escape, can be seen as the objects of your salvation, holding all those precious gifts that are here just for you, right now!

Take each moment of 'darkness' that comes to you, whether as feelings within yourself, or as in those situations in your life that seem imbued with the quality of darkness. Thank them for being there, for they are your teachers.

Do what you need to do, sit down or write, or speak quietly in your own mind, draw or paint your answers, and allow yourself to go into the inner landscape of your mind, of your very being, to draw forth the healing that is there for you.

Many of you have learnt these ways of being quiet inside yourself, and allowing inspiration to come forth. Allow yourself now, to take each moment that is not filled with light and love, and ask it what it wants to tell you, so you can bring forth the divine in service to the integration of your higher being with your lower self! Each one complementing the other perfectly, and grounding deeply your Divinity here on the earth.

If you wish, you can call on me, Sarah, to hold the space for you as you do this work, and cast my light and love around you. I hold the energy of integration and attraction as all things are magnetised through me (love) into the whole (divinity).

May all things be well with you and blessings shine down upon you in each and every moment of your lives,

Blessed Be, Blessed Be, Blessed Be, Amen! Sarah."

Waiting in the Darkness

The female and the male, the dark and the light, the low and the high. We live in a world of polarity.

Sarah represents the dark and the light. Both of them held together. Not one at the expense of the other, but both of them held within ourselves.

For our lives here on earth, the goal is not to eliminate the darkness using the light, but to learn how to contain both within ourselves. This is quite a trick, and requires a different mindset than the one we have been using (most of us) up until now.

Many have been focusing on the light, learning how to bring attention to qualities of peace and joy, love and light; some have learnt to go into the darkness, to express pain, acknowledge wounds, feel rage and be with what is there.

The way of Sarah is to go into the darkness, this is her Dark Madonna/ Sophia aspect. When we go into darkness we take with us the love we have for ourSelves, for Divinity, for each other. Thus prepared, we take with us our ability to bring the grace of the Divine into the darkness, (being God/ ess as we are).

In the darkness lies the most incredible gifts of learning that we could ever find, the treasures are beyond compare.

When we do this, we can see what it is that has caused the pain. We can see what it is that we have made that pain mean. From this we can find a new way of being, a practice that leads us towards a life of spirituality, peace and enlightenment!

These two quotes put some more words on the Dark Madonna's/Sophia energy, and are from Caitlín Matthews, 'Sophia: Goddess of Wisdom, Bride of God':

'The Fall, so often considered a terrible thing, is a fall into experience; like falling of the epileptic to earth, it may also have its other face, for then we fall into the embrace of our dreams and fears and know them for what they are, face to face.

'[...]the fearful face of the Black Goddess is really the veiled Sophia. The rebirth of the mystery initiation brings us into contact with our own power, which we have failed to take in our own time. Part of the reason for this is that we live in the shadow of the Judeo-Christian Fall for which Woman bears the blame. The experience of Psyche and Kore shows the vulnerable face of Sophia, who is not afraid to fall, to learn by seeming mistakes. They show that the descent into death is the only possible pathway to ascent or spiritual rebirth.'

    Sarah is an Ascended Master for the Age of Aquarius and She awakens everything She touches. Her energy alone has an effect even for those who aren't conscious of her.

    But used in conscious co-creation, Sarah's energy has the power to bring about evolutionary change, enabling us to be the hands and feet of Sophia here on the Earth.

    Sarah's energy is beautiful, it has a light, transcendent quality that people seem to just love and find very easy to be with, but don't let it fool you!!

    The more time you spend with Sarah's energy, the more you find that it draws out the darkness in you; all that lovely light finds its way into all the hidden parts of yourself that you were subconsciously hoping would never see the light of day!!

    This is the inevitable part of the spiritual path; lighting up the very darkest corners of the psyche and possibly one which we leave until last - it's a hard path to tread, (…and there were good reasons why we left all that stuff in the furthest corners of our subconscious).

We have to be ready to deal with it when the time comes for us to lift the lid off our own shadow... But - when we finally get to grips with the darkness within us, the rewards can be greater than we ever dreamed.

In many of the sessions where I work with clients, their greatest light, talents and abilities are hidden in the shadow.

Doubts, fears, wounds and traumas are traced back to the past, often in our childhood, but showing a greater pattern.

All of our biggest traumas that we have incarnated tend to show up in our childhood. They are the energy patterns that we have brought with us into this particular lifetime so that we can heal them, and working with them as they have presented in this lifetime gives us the greatest opportunity for connection and integration.

The opportunity to work with the issues which have wounded our younger selves can give us access to much more compassion than we would otherwise have; as we imagine ourselves as the vulnerable, helpless and innocent children that live inside of us.

But whether we work with these issues through the inner child or through past lives or in whatever way does not matter, it simply matters that we do the work in the way that is best for us.

Once that pain has been fully accepted, we can access the resources we need to heal it. Then is our light released to where we can experience it fully and it can shine out from us for all to see. Our light in joined together with our darkness, becoming one. Becoming something other. And as this happens, our light grounds itself through our minds, our bodies, our hearts and manifests through the physical universe into our lives.

This is Sarah's mystery.

"Blessings be upon you.

I am Sarah.

Darkness is a time for you to develop your strength, overcome your fears and light up your life.

Until the darkness comes, what little will you know of these fears?

When it comes, batten down your hatches, go into the quiet spaces, fill up your reserves with food and water, as you may not be going out for some time.

Be with what you need to be with. Say hello to what is there. Try not to judge, to dismiss, to cast away. It has come to tell you its story. And it deserves to be heard.

We are drawn ever towards the light, back home to ourselves, but we do this by going through into the darkness, those darkest places in ourselves, where we have hidden our most shameful secrets, our deepest pains, those things in ourselves which we wish never to see again, never to feel or hear or even know about.

And yet they are there, waiting in the darkness, waiting to be owned, and honoured and acknowledged as part of ourselves.

We could see these parts of ourselves as our children. Those children born out of wedlock, and born of rape and brutality and war. Do we leave them as orphans? Neglected, unfed, uncared for? Kept back in the shadows so that the decent people might live a life uncast by their reflection.

Or do we say, come, come, come out into the light!

Come bring, your pain and your suffering, bring all that you are. We are ready to hear you!

This is my gift to you, of love and light, beauty and darkness, all together, all whole, all as one. To love what is there, what is. To love it as it is, in all its putridness, and deformity and decay; in its ugliness, and terror and intolerable pain. To love whatever is there, as yourself, as God, in all its entirety.

All is God.

And from the rich, damp and dark, fertile places can a new life arise. Born from the darkness, released from the very fetidness that was so foul in shadows; the vileness taking on new life, new love as it becomes the very medium for growth into the light that was always longed for, the journey into enlightenment that you craved.

Look, look into the darkness.

For I tell you this is the primal matter of creation that will give you the spiritual growth you long for. It is your fuel, your unformed clay waiting to be given shape. It is your mud from which the lotus will reach up and be given unto perfection.

See what it is there, let yourself be with it. Let your hearts be full of joy even as you undergo the sacredness of the journey into the shadows.

All is well, all is well, all is well.

You are God ever expanding, ever being, ever growing; light and life, death and darkness, all are one, all are part of the same journey of creation.

All is well, all is well, all is well.

May blessings be upon you, each and every moment. Dedicate all that you are, all that is in your life, to God, to your inner divinity.

All is well, all is well, all is well. Sarah."

Sarah tells us how to experience a healing...

Dear Sarah, why does God allow our hearts to be broken?

"I sense the sadness in you, and the confusion as you ask this question, as part of you knows well, that this is the wrong question. It is not a question of 'God allowing' or 'not allowing'. All things are within you; the pain, and the healing which will heal that pain. Just as the body knows how to heal a cut, so does your soul know how to heal the emotional and psychic wounds within you.

You live in a universe of polarities, so wherever there is the wound, there is the healing available. Your souls know the path to the healing that you need, they are the key. So the question is not 'why does God allow our hearts to be broken?', but 'why are you not seeing the healing that is being offered to you.' This is the meaning of the 4 cups. The hand holding the cup belongs to the Divine, which is all (which is why it is invisible, it is connected to nothing and everything) and the person, the sad looking person, is looking away, and focusing on their sadness.

What if you knew that to every wound you experienced, there was a healing? What if you knew, it was just a matter of patience, and persistence, faith and trust? For you to keep strong with the idea, belief and expectation that a healing can occur (by using visualisation or positive affirmation or prayer and so on. Dear All that Is, please guide me to my healing, please may all the help I need to get better come towards me, I am always healed, I am always bringing towards me the sacred healing I need, so mote it be, Amen.)

And then to not allow that hope to be crushed by despair but to always know that you are being led back to wholeness on the path that brings you the greatest grace, learning and soul growth, so that the beautiful light that you are grows ever brighter.

What if all these things were true - and even in the moments of doubt and despair, which of course, will come, must come, because this is a world of polarity, and we must allow all things to be, without allowing ourselves to be powerless in the face of them, what if you could allow yourself the possibility that these things are true, and act 'as if' they were true anyway, even though in that moment you don't give a damn for God, or healing, or whatever, because you've totally had enough!!! Then these moments of darkness can be negotiated through with little damage, out into the calmer waters on the other side.

I am Sarah, and I tell you that when you have experienced the polarities on both sides of the waters, then you will not ask these questions anymore; because you will have experienced loss, and then in equal measure, something beautiful and divine. You will have experienced pain, and then in equal measure the love and healing you needed to recover from that pain. You will be whole, and healed and will not fear being broken anymore, knowing that God/Goddess always supplies you with what you need, if only you allow yourself to look.

I am Sarah, and I tell you this. EXPECT your healing to be there, to come from God. KNOW that everything is happening in Divine Timing. BELIEVE that everything is happening for your highest good. PRAY OR AFFIRM for the things that you need. ASK for your heart to be healed. KNOW that mother/father God loves you, and WANTS you to be happy.

I am Sarah, and I tell you, all is well, all is well, all is well, Blessed Be, Amen."

Sarah is here to help us bring our Divine Spark into consciousness

- The Hrit Padma**/Divine Spark – Sacred Lotus of the Heart

This is a huge part of 'what Sarah has come to do', and it will come to the fore much more in the years to come. This is the 'real' healing, what will bring us into wholeness.

This is the story of how we came to discover this part of Sarah's work…

In 2006, a year after I had some deeply spiritual experiences working with earth vortexes in Hawai'i, I was guided to start an 'earth healing' group. The images I was given were to continue with the work being done by lightworkers of 'cleansing' the planet, and clearing the pollution of earths' subtle bodies. This was to prepare the matrix for carrying higher energies, to assist the process of ascension of the earth and humanity. As the group started, each month we would work with clearing specific energies within ourselves, often related to abundance and then to assisting with clearing specific places and towns. Initially we were working with elemental energies, and called on Pele, the fiery Hawai'ian goddess of the Volcano, who I had powerfully connected to during my sacred journey to the Big Island, Pele's current home. After a few months, another presence began making herself felt, and this presence came forward as the ascended lady master Sarah. This involved much soul searching for me, as I had not been previously aware of Sarah's life, and felt concerned that I was my imagination was holding reign. As time went on, Sarah began to reveal the teachings she had come to give, I was supported by my spiritual circle, and I began to realise that the teachings that were being given were giving us profound experiences and providing us with a new way of living. One of the most profound was our discovery of the Hrit Padma chakra. That particular month I was guided to write a meditation for the group where the focus of conscious awareness was placed in the different spheres, for example, focusing on the physical body, then the mental body, then the emotional body, then the higher self and so on. This was so that we could become more aware, as a daily practice of where our consciousness was residing. As part of the journey we would take our awareness up to the highest heavens, to the highest possible vibrations of our higher, our original selves, and then bring that focus of attention down into the centre of ourselves, into our physical bodies; coming right now into the moment, into the now. When I had been working with these practices during the week as I prepared for the group, I had noticed a physical sensation like an energy, just underneath my heart chakra but above the solar plexus. Although I had been aware of it, I had no idea what it was, and so gave it no significance, and thought maybe a possible clearing going on. So in the group that month, we did a journey with 'being at the centre of ourselves'. The feedback after the group was very interesting! Several people noticed what I had also experienced, which was that the focus of attention, being 'out there' at the highest heavens, felt the same as being 'at the centre'. This we thought sounded all very quantum physics, because we had an inner knowing that 'out there' and 'in *here' was although placed at two different locations, one and the same. The next revelation from the feedback was that two other members of the group said they experienced a sensation when they came into the centre of themselves, just underneath the heart chakra but above the solar plexus. I was really excited at this point as I hadn't mentioned my own experience to the group, thinking it was not anything of importance. So, at the end of the group, when I did the channelling that month, the group asked this question, 'We sensed within ourselves this core place of 'now', of our being, just below the heart, do you have any more information, is it a new energy centre?'*

Sarah spoke:

"At the centre of your being, is the place where all things are, and also is the place where nothing is. It is the place where your very being is, and also is the place where your unbeing is; and is yet the space where you are connected to everything, in this one central spark of your being. It is like the centre of the universe, constantly creating and recreating, destroying and ending and beginning all over again in each moment. When you bring yourself into the now, into the moment, this is where you are, each time, coming into that …single particle where the universe is destroyed and then born again, and in that moment is all of the potential for all things. This is a great mystery, and one that connects you up with your divinity, and also to your physical manifestation here on earth. It is the place where your very spark of being exists, in between heaven and earth, because where heaven and earth join, there is a fusion. But that spark, that divinity is the fusion, and energetically it exists within your bodies in the place the heaven and the earth energies are in fusion. From this place, you can energetically create all things, all potential is there, in this place. You have access to all that you need here, from heaven and from earth, fused together, as one."

That night after the group, I had a nagging thought which wouldn't leave me alone, and I started to reference this new information by looking through my books to see if I could find anything out. Up until the early hours of the morning, I discovered references to the Hrit Padma, a chakra point between the solar plexus and the heart centre, described as being two fingers' breadths beneath the heart centre. I didn't get too much sleep that night as I was too excited by what I found. I investigated it further online to find further references, and found this chakra point described as the seat of the soul, and references to Narayana, who is described in the Upanishads as the Divine being as it was before it separated into Brahma, Vishnu & Shiva. I also found references stating that in the majority of humanity, this chakra point is blocked, which helps to explain why our societies are living very much from their 'egos', and we have the problems current in the world today. After months of working with the energy at this point through chanting and energy exercises, I have come to realise that clearing the energy to the Hrit Padma is a path to enlightenment. If the energy pathway to our Divine Spark is a clear channel, then we are 'in oneness' with our Higher, our Original Selves. The New Age of Aquarius would be greatly assisted in coming closer to us as we would wish it to, if we worked more with this energy centre as a collective. The teachings for the Hrit Padma, which have been around for a long time, are now becoming more and more significant, and are available to all. Ascension for not just the masters, but for all of us, is our birthright, for we are the Divine made manifest.........

** *See glossary.*

Chapter 4

The Flames

The Violet Thread

Violet is the energy of transformation and transmutation. It is preparing the way for humanity to come into vibration with the New Earth in oneness consciousness, and Sarah's Violet Flame is a most powerful tool for us to use. In truth, the violet flame is only one aspect of three, of her flame, but it is the most relevant to humanity right now. We still have a big work to do of letting go of the old, and allowing the blessings of the Divine to transform it into the new...

The flames are the purest essence of the Divine archetypal force that each of the Ascended Light Beings hold; Mary Magdalene (Divine Feminine), Master Jesus (Divine Masculine), Sarah (Divine Oneness).

The Magdalene flame has given the love we need to heal our wounded self, release the anguish of the past, and joyfully embrace our inner child. The Christ flame has provided us with the strength and wisdom to face our shadow and light up the darkness!

Now the daughter, Sarah is bringing forth her flame that holds the energies of divine abundance and dynamic manifestation for us to bring forth our whole and healed selves and create on Earth with our divine potential bringing about the dawning of the New Age:

"Each of us holds the key to manifesting God's plan here on earth.

Each of us holds deep in our heart, the seeds to our own joy & happiness.

Each of us needs to dig deep now, & prepare the ground for the planting of the New Age. What colour shall your garden be, what size, what shape? You get to choose; it is your desire that will show you the way forward, what plants you need to pick.

Each of you holds your own individual piece of the puzzle, without which the picture will be incomplete.

You see how important you are, how special, how divine?

What will you choose?" *Lady Sarah.*

What's the point Sarah of these flames'?!'

"Welcome all, I am Sarah!

It is good to ask these things, and not just accept 'this is so', it is good to know WHY you should do a thing, instead of accepting blindly that this is the way forward, because it has been said that it is!

When God created the world, the Elohim imagined what was, and so it was!

Humanity was their finest creation, and their greatest joy!

We were made to reflect the Elohim, and each of us in humanity playing an individual role, no two the same, and yet when we are all added up as a whole, we are the perfect whole; each one of us needed to make that whole.

And so it was with the Elohim, when creation was in the process of being formed, each one of them, in the circle of perfect love and light, did their own particular role, played their own particular part, no-one could do as the other did, only that one could do its own unique and needed part. And so, they loved and appreciated each other, as together they formed the miracle of creation! Humankind having been made in their likeness, each one of us perfect in our individuality, each one of us perfect within us, has only those God qualities and functions that the Divine Presence within us has manifested, and each of us has our particular parts to play, that no other can do!

But because we are living within linear time and space, (and I say we, because even though I am not here in an individual physical form, I am with you still in physicality), then the Divine creation of humanity that the Elohim formed is still unfolding.

It is not that the Elohim made creation and humanity to be an ever-fixed form, and although at the moment of creation, all the elements of what it was, and will be in creation were ever present in the original blueprint of perfection.

But creation is an ever-unfolding thing. You could see creation as aligned to the growing of a flower.

First, the seed starts to sprout because the right conditions for growth have been achieved, then the shoot starts to grow upwards in the darkness, emerging into the light. As the stem grows, the bud of the flower grows larger and larger until the day where it starts to open and reveal the beauty hidden inside.

You could say (although this is not an exact analogy) that the Divine Masculine (the Christ Flame) is what is needed for the stem to grow tall and strong, straight and true, and then the Divine Feminine (the Magdalene Flame) is what is needed to form the perfect bud with all the beauty therein, and then you could say that the joining of these two perfect energies, into the union of the 3rd energy, the threefold flame**, is what causes the bud to reveal itself in all its true beauty.

And you could say that the saturation of the plant in each stage of its growth by exactly the right energy at exactly the right time, is what causes everything to grow in the right way. That if the second energy came too soon, the bud would grow too big for the stem to support, and if the third energy came too late, then the stem would wither and die, before the flower had a chance to unfurl.

So, although, as the Elohim had created, all of the elements were present in the original creation, the plan needed time to grow and unfurl with each element being present in right time, right place, and this is how the flames have assisted humanity in growing perfectly!

Right time, right place, right being! All is well!! So, it is not that the flames exist because you have something missing, or that you are deficient in some way, but that this is God's perfect plan for you built upon a rock, each element coming through of the plan in the perfect way to achieve the most beautiful and divine manifestation of heaven here on earth!

And so it is, that my father and mother in heaven have prepared the way for me, and I am here now to facilitate the unfurling of the bud that holds all the beauty therein! This is my work and my power and is my perfect part to play in creation!

All is love, all is joy, all is perfect in wondrous creation…

You can see as God sees!

Blessings, Sarah."

** See glossary.

Sarah's Violet Flame

Sarah, has her own vibration of the Violet Flame! This violet energy transforms and transmutes negative and old energy. It's what we need more than any other to lift up our vibration and the earth's if we want to shift into the New Earth energies and the New Age of Aquarius! Sarah's vibration is specifically for this job - as she's come at this time to help mentor us into successfully doing this work!

'I'd like you to talk a little bit about your violet flame. You have your own aspects of violet flame, Lady Sarah. Can you tell us about how it differs from say for example, the violet flame we'd associate with Saint Germain and Lady Portia and so forth please?'

"St. Germain is the overall guardian of the violet flame in its entirety. My violet flame that I work with, is specifically for preparing the earth and humanity for the shift that they are going through, right at this moment. So, it has very specific functions and works in very specific ways and it is able to shift and transform very quickly, lower and heavier energies, to higher and lighter energies.

The world as it currently is now, is not in a state where it can shift and transform in an instant to the fifth dimension and higher dimensions. There is a process of change that it is going through. The lilac violet flame is directly connected to facilitating that process and change. It is not that the whole of the world needs to be transformed. It just needs to be transformed to a certain level of vibration and then all the new things that have been made - because at the moment there are many new grids and new ley lines and new things, so many things then can be woven together into the fabric of reality.

All of these new things can suddenly come online at a certain point, but there has to be a little bit of 'lightening up' before that happens. This is very much in between an 'in-between time' at the moment. We're in between the old and we're in between the new, and for many people who are sensitive, it's a difficult time, because you are not in one or the other, but are being pulled between the two.

So, the lilac violet flame creates a bridge. It's very challenging to stay/live a life that's entirely in the fifth dimension in the world as it is right now (because of the energy fluctuations). However, you can call on tools like my violet flame and learn how to surround yourself with it. And also as you do this, you're also part of this clearing process because it is an incredibly effective tool to using and clearing land, clearing here all of these things, all of these places where humanity has left a layer of waste and debris.

And when I talk about this, I'm talking about all of the thoughts and all of the feelings and all of the actions that people have taken in the past that have not been in right relationship with the world and then having created a backlog of energy waste and all of these things that is humanity's job to clean these things up. Of course, the earth, Gaia could do it. The earth could do it overnight, but it wouldn't be good for humanity if she did, that so she's not going to do that.

However, it's part of humanity's learning how to be masters themselves, as part of that job, of coming into self-mastery, is learning how to clean all this stuff up and there's many systems out there, many parts to follow and mine is just one of them where you can learn how to do this do this clearing."

'I'd like you to talk a little bit about your violet flame. You have your own aspects of violet flame, Lady Sarah. Can you tell us about how it differs from say for example, the violet flame we'd associate with Saint Germain and Lady Portia and so forth please?' (Question is from a live interview.)

Many Ascended Masters have their own vibration of the violet flame that they work with, as does Sarah and as do many lightworkers! We have often developed these in past lives such as Atlantis, and they suit our particular soul purpose.

"St. Germain is the overall guardian of the violet flame in its entirety. My violet flame that I work with, is specifically for preparing the earth and humanity for the shift that they are going through, right at this moment. So, it has very specific functions and works in very specific ways and it is able to shift and transform very quickly, lower, and heavier energies, to higher and lighter energies.

The world as it currently is now, is not in a state where it can shift and transform in an instant to the fifth dimension and higher dimensions. There is a process of change that it is going through. The lilac violet flame is directly connected to facilitating that process and change. It is not that the whole of the world needs to be transformed. It just needs to be transformed to a certain level of vibration and then all the new things that have been made - because at the moment there are many new grids and new ley lines and new things, so many things then can be woven together into the fabric of reality.

All of these new things can suddenly come online at a certain point, but there has to be a little bit of 'lightening up' before that happens. This is very much in between an 'in-between time' at the moment. We're in between the old and we're in between the new, and for many people who are sensitive, it's a difficult time, because you are not in one or the other, but are being pulled between the two.

So, the lilac violet flame creates a bridge. It's very challenging to stay/live a life that's entirely in the fifth dimension in the world as it is right now (because of the energy fluctuations). However, you can call on tools like my violet flame and learn how to surround yourself with it. And also as you do this, you're also part of this clearing process because it is an incredibly effective tool to using and clearing land, clearing here all of these things, all of these places where humanity has left a layer of waste and debris.

And when I talk about this, I'm talking about all of the thoughts and all of the feelings and all of the actions that people have taken in the past that have not been in right relationship with the world, and then having created a backlog of energy waste. All of these things - it is humanity's job to clean up! Of course, the earth, Gaia could do it. The earth could do it overnight, but it wouldn't be good for humanity if she did, that so she's not going to do that.

However, it's part of humanity's learning how to be masters themselves, and part of that job, of coming into self-mastery, is learning how to clean all this stuff up and there are many systems out there, many parts to follow, and mine is just one of them where you can learn how to do this clearing."

Sarah has a Violet Flame Temple at Glastonbury, UK!

Sarah's Violet Flame Temple in Glastonbury was one of the seeds that were planted in the earth in times gone by - by Sarah herself. Working with Sarah, Gaia and the elemental and angelic kingdoms, we activated this Temple in 2020! (You can still experience this – see Online Classes!) Since then other temples have been created in the UK, US and Denmark. Also called the Violet Flame Spiral Temples, they gently and slowly clear the landscapes where they are placed - the spirals are there to clear the earth of the collected thought forms and energetic waste of humanity. The temple in Glastonbury is the Mother Temple, and is helping the earth prepare for the next stages.

"Welcome! I am Sarah. So, this Violet Flame energy matrix, Temple Spiral at Glastonbury! These are interesting times, and this is just one of the energies of my threefold flame**. The violet flame is preparing the way for the rest of the energies and you are warmly invited to join in on this journey or not as you wish.

But this is a time of transmutation and transformation on the earth and these times are never easy, so try and walk your path with ease as much as you can. Take away the stresses that you know don't need to be there. Perhaps you just put up with them out of habit. Just blow them away gently off your path now. Give up the responsibilities that you don't need to take on as yours, because a time is coming when your biggest responsibility will be to ground down into your own essence and truly manifest what is there. I AM Sarah and I tell you that you are walking into important times, that you will remember for the rest of your life. Important times where you see the light of the Divine truly manifesting in your life and it becomes more than how it is now. It becomes bigger and brighter and larger because it comes from within. It comes from inside you and you can illuminate it all around. I AM Sarah and I am here as an Ascended Master for the Age of Aquarius for the new earth. I hold the patterns, the energy matrices, the blueprints. Just connecting to my energy helps your DNA start to re-sequence itself because of Sympathetic Resonance. I hold the energies for the new earth and the new humanity and I come here as sister, teacher, mentor, to walk by your side, to lend you my energy and its catalytic presence, to help you become the more of what you are.

I AM Sarah and my blessings are upon you.

Blessed Be. Blessed Be. Blessed Be. Amen."

** See glossary.

'Dear Sarah, can you give some advice on how we can work with the energies of the terrorism present on earth and also the response to it - is there a way we can assist with these issues energetically?' *(Question is from a live interview.)*

"Welcome, I am Sarah, I have a violet flame which can be used for this purpose. It is important that you first use it on yourself and then again when you finish. Everything that happens within the world, is a reflection of what exists within the collective unconscious of humanity. You have to understand that these energies have been built up over thousands and millions of years. When you transform these energies, you do it in truth from the inside, but looking outside of yourself to the outer event is also useful, because it connects you up in a very powerful way. All of you have access to the negative energies that need transforming because you are in physical manifestation as human beings and therefore have direct contact with the oversoul of humanity which contains these energies. Right now there is a need to transmute the pain, fear, and anger into an ability to heal. This is the next step.

First, call on me, Sarah, and ask for my aspect of the violet flame.

Think of the issue that you want to send the violet flame to.

Draw the violet flame into your body, up through your feet from the earth. You are drawing the violet flame up through the New Earth grid*, which exists underneath your feet as lines of energy on the etheric planes and supports the energetic creation of the new earth. In this grid lies everything that is needed for humanity to find the solutions for a peaceful, harmonious and loving existence. So when you draw up the violet flame from the New Earth grid in this way, you are also drawing up the solutions, possibilities and potentialities to the difficulties. My violet flame will take the old energy and transform it into that which is in accordance with the vibration of the New Earth; this is the particular quality of the aspect of the violet flame which I command.

First, fill your physical body with this violet flame. Breathe it in slowly, breath by breath until your whole body is filled with the violet flame. Then start to send it out. See, feel or have the issue you want to send the violet flame to in front of you (for example, you could have something that symbolizes the issue, such as a globe, a map, or the issue written down on a piece of paper, or something printed out and you can then hold these things in your hand) Send out my violet flame, you can say, 'Sarah's violet flame, Sarah's violet flame' over and over if you wish. You can also chant 'Om benzo satto hung' if you like to use Sanskrit chants, and imagine that as you sound the words, it is sending out the energy of my violet flame. Then when you have finished, firmly let go of the issue which you have been sending energy to. Give it into the safekeeping of the Divine, or the angels, or of me - whatever feels the best way for you and know that everything is happening in Divine Timing, and that 'All is Well, All is Well, All is Well'.

Once again, imagine the violet flame is coming into you, this is the violet flame in all its aspects, and this time it is coming from the higher dimensions above and is coming into your body from the top of your head, all the way down into the earth. Fill yourself with it one more time and then send it down into the New Earth grid which exists as lines of light beneath your feet.

Say to yourself 'it is done' and feel a sense of completion.

I am Sarah, and I give you this practice so that you can assist in transforming the energies that are held within humanity at this time, and are coming up now so that they can be focused on. Have hope, keep a brave heart, and know that nothing you do is wasted. Every thought, every thing you do to help the situation is heard by heaven and then your efforts are multiplied by the angels and archangels, the elementals and the devas, and the earth herself. It is a great work you are achieving, and all is well, all is well, all is well. Blessed Be, Amen."

*See glossary.

Sarah's Flame of Unity

'Sarah, can you share insights about your flame?' *(Question is from a live interview.)*

"Welcome, I am Sarah. So, the best way for each of you to understand my flame is for each of you to experience it! It's a little like talking about healing or reiki and telling somebody about it cognitively and really the only way that they can understand it, is by having it, by living that experience.

So, let's do that now wherever you are as long as you're not in a situation where you can't close your eyes. Just close your eyes and feel my flame rooting itself just underneath your feet and growing up around you and coming to the top just above your head. Now this is the flame of Unity Consciousness. It's a flame that unites all the pieces of your soul. It's a flame that unites all the parts of your being and it makes it possible for you to experience the divine truths while you are in physical incarnation. Some people perhaps would call it an enlightenment flame or an embodied ascension flame because while you sit within my flame even though perhaps you haven't already achieved a state of enlightenment you are closer and more able to experience that state of enlightenment so sitting within this flame and just allow yourself to let go of your worries and your fears, your cares, and your burdens just for a moment, just for a minute or two.

Allow your body, your mind, your heart, your soul to experience a state of being in oneness with all that you are coming into peace, coming into centeredness. Just rest, rest now, coming into balance nothing to do but just sit here for a moment breathing quietly, being quietly and you can allow my flame to infuse every part of your being every cell in your body resting, letting go of any stress, letting go of anything - you just don't need it anymore!

Take a deep breath now, breathing in this beautiful energy of my flame. Breathe in healing to all parts of your body where healing is needed. Breathe out all of that, all of that, that needs to be let go. Feel the lightness from the flame, feel the lightness that is in truth your being, the lightness that is in truth yourself at the centre of yourself. This is who you are, this is who you are, and you can experience this state, this lightness even while you are living on the earth and this is where we are guiding you to be.

This is where humanity is stepping towards now as you become more and more integrated. See the path ahead, the path of humanity lined with this beautiful energy of this flame, my flame, this aspect of the divine that I am a portal for, that I am a face for, that I am a doorway for. A beautiful circle of you and the ancestors going back to the beginning of time, going all the way around. See this whole circle lit by this flame of oneness, this flame of unity. All is well, all is well, all is well.

I am Sarah and I tell you all is well, blessed be, blessed be, blessed be, Amen.

Inspiration through Sarah's Flame

The year after we activated Sarah's Violet Flame Temple in Glastonbury, Sarah asked us to activate the White Flame of Divinity in a similar way (see Classes); this occurred in 2021 coming in through the New Earth Ascension Grids in the Pacific Ocean near to the island of Kauai, and being grounded in Saintes-Maries-de-la-Mer in the Camargue in France, and the sacred town of Roskilde in Denmark, which is blessed by more than two dozen springs!

"Welcome, I am Sarah.

There are still more things for you to understand about the power of this flame that I represent—this aspect of the Divine that I represent because you are still growing in your consciousness and although you are starting to see the light at the end of the tunnel, and when I say that I mean you are coming out of a long, long, long process of transforming and transmuting all that needed to go before you could start to take on the energy of this unified flame.

That light at the end of the tunnel—in this case, is the energy of the Unity flame of the Christ Consciousness, but it is still a way off yet and so your understanding and comprehension of how these things will work, will continue to grow and expand in the days, months and years ahead.

And so, it is that in the year of 2021, the white flame of Divinity - this aspect of my flame will be grounded here on the earth during the month which is dedicated to my Feast Day in May. Even just talking about this aspect of the white flame of Divinity brings it in and it is attuned to the same vibration of my angels—my host of angels and to the Divine spark that sits within each of you.

It is that amazing purity whiteness of Divinity that is, of coursea in truth in all things and yet can be felt more clearly when we focus upon this flame—this part of the Divine and perhaps do that now. Imagine my flame in whatever way you want to see it and see part of it as this pure divine white light and feel it sitting around your head and shoulders lifting you, expanding you, allowing you to encompass and embrace all that you are. My blessings are upon you. Feel this energy streaming into you now. Take deep breaths, deep lungfuls of it into your body. You are breathing in etheric particles of the divine as you do this.

All is well, all is well, all is well.

I am Sarah and my blessings are upon you.

Blessed be, blessed be, blessed be, Amen."

Sarah's flame is coming upon the Earth

In 2022, the 3rd and last aspect of Sarah's flame, the green energy of manifestation, of life itself, will be activated and anchored, and then in 2023, the flame will be activated and anchored in its 'oneness' state as the Unity Flame.

"Welcome I am Sarah. My flame is soon to be birthed upon the earth, but until that time you can start to 'pull it in' through me, through my presence; I am a portal. Once the flame is present upon the earth, it will be grounded here, just as the Magdalene flame and the Christ flame are. 2023 has been hailed as an important date in terms of the 'Ascension calendar' and indeed, my flame will be present on the earth by then. But it is going to take some work! Always, your presence must be involved (by this I mean the physical presence of humanity). You have underestimated your capabilities. In the times ahead, you'll receive a much clearer vision of who you are, and what you are capable of. Currently, you see yourself as being the centre of many divine forces, as orchestrating this in part, in alignment with the divine will, and this is true, and yet you are more than that. These things are not available to your understanding until you have passed a certain level of ego structure. When you come into a place of being able to be of service, (and by this I do not mean, coming from a place of sacrificing yourself to others, I mean being able to stand from a place of strength, balance and self-love and then sharing what you have with others), then you are able to see your true ability to shape and create the world around you.

For now, let me share some information about my flame. I am the 'result' of the sacred marriage – when the Divine masculine and the Divine feminine come together, I am born, and yet I am greater than the sum of my parts. I am oneness, I am unity, I am something that existed before polarity, I am something that is older, and came before the masculine and the feminine. I am the Divine remembering itself, I am ancient.

All this is a paradox, because in 'human terms' I came after the divine masculine and the divine feminine on the storyline of the 'holy family', and yet this energy has been present on the earth plane before, this energy of oneness that I embody. This energy was present in the times of Lemuria, but at a time when matter was not so dense but was much more loose and pliable, and less solid.

Now this level of energy is returning to earth, returning to humanity as a level of consciousness. You cannot embody this oneness vibration in your physical bodies just yet (because it is too far down into density) – yet it can affect it, bring about healing, & cause a raising of vibration nonetheless. But your consciousness, which resides in planes above that of the physical, (yet whilst retaining its connection to it) is able to rest at this level of vibration, and it is to your consciousness now that I speak, it is to your consciousness now that I send my message of connection to this energy of mine, to my flame. Concentrate on the flame, rest your mind upon it in meditation. Immerse yourself in it, and ask me to plunge your whole being into it, and sit and imagine you are breathing it in and out.

I am Sarah and this simple practice will do more than you know. I am Sarah and my blessing is upon you this day, Blessed be, Blessed be, Blessed be, Amen.'

CHAPTER 5

The New Age: New Earth, New Humanity

The Platinum Thread

The frequency of Platinum vibrates to the New Earth, and is held as an energy Matrix by the whale and dolphin collectives. Platinum helps us connect to our joy, to our Ascension blueprint, and to keep our energy high, as we learn to become our Higher Selves here on the Earth.

'Now the time has changed as we are entering into a new age, the age of Aquarius. It has been said by many that this is the age of equality between the Masculine and the Feminine, and this is true. And for this shift into equality to occur, there is a particular kind of passage required at this time. It is as though you are giving birth to the new age....' Mercedes Kirkel, 'Mary Magdalene Beckons, Join the River of Love'.

This is why Sarah is here, to guide us, to be sister, teacher - to walk by our sides, as we co-create the New Earth! She holds the blueprint for the New Humanity; just calling in her presence has the effect of that blueprint starting to work on our energy fields! Something in us knows that which we will become, and calls us towards it, and Sarah is a great mentor in this process! This is why she has stepped forward at this time, to fulfil her role as a New Earth Teacher/Mentor/Guide. She is an Empowerer, always she is showing us what is already within us, coaxing out that knowledge, wisdom, power, compassion – whatever it is within us that needs to come out fully into the light! She also holds many New Earth codes. She has taught me how to create sacred power places, in co-creation with her, her team of angels, Gaia and the elementals. I sometimes think that the two colours that speak the most to me of Sarah, are the blue and green of the earth that is seen from outer space. That comes to me over and over again.

This message came in 2008, in a group I used to run, called 'Raising the New Earth'.

Sarah and Humanity's Evolutionary Journey

"Welcome all, I am Sarah. I have been watching over, and attending to this group, this evening, and directing the course of the thought processes, and helping that direction to take the best course, so that understanding may occur. I have the benefit of having been incarnated here on earth, and so I am a fit subject, in that I understand the ways that humanity can achieve their next evolutionary phase, through their own intent, and by their own means.

Evolution is often thought of as something which is done *to* you, this phase of humanity's evolution is one that must be done *by* them, and this is why the direction of consciousness, to facilitate the greatest understanding, is so important at this time. Because for your evolution to occur, there are truths which must be understood. And of course, not everyone will sit down and read Steiner, or even think about the Christ Light; but when these truths and understandings are brought in by groups of people, so they connect to the greater consciousness, and so other ways can be found, through myths and stories, television plays, books & films, these things can begin to infiltrate the greater consciousness of humanity.

Humanity is at a stage now, where its evolution must be controlled by their own selves. The Divine cannot do this work for humanity, but can only encourage and facilitate. And this is part of my work here, to encourage and facilitate and make signposts and directions as to which way humanity can look and be aware. And so it is that this evening, although I have not directly spoken or been brought through in any of the exercises, I have facilitated the whole process and it has been directed by me, in the best possible way, so that hopefully as much can be understood as needs to be, at this time.

There is much that can be achieved by energy work, by mantras, by geometric symbols, by colours, by all of these things. And yet still, the light of your consciousness, and the understanding that comes with it, is a vital part of this process. And so, the teachings and understandings that are provided, are as much a valued part of all of those practices which you build into your daily lives. Mankind stands at the brink of directing its own evolution. Truly these are exciting times!

These things though need to be expanded and directed further out; the understandings and truths that I can provide - should you wish to connect to my energy, are ones which will greatly benefit humanity, should they be shared and taught onwards. So, I would urge you always to think about how you can share these thoughts and understandings with each other, whether this be through writing or speaking, or even telling stories. I would urge you to think about how this can be taken further out, into the reaches of humanity. Because anchoring the light will do great wonders, and yet without the light of conscious understanding, the effect will be limited.

As always, I thank you for being here and taking part and doing this work, and giving up your time, and this is a shared wonder that we work together. Lastly, if it feels right for you, remember to connect to the Elohim, they will assist you, on your path of light, and can do this in a very tangible way. They hold the particles of light, that will help you take on your Ascension body, and connecting with them, will lead you each time, a step closer to that goal.

As always, I shower down blessings of love and light upon you, and share my joy that we do this work together. Blessings be upon you each and every moment and every day of your lives, Blessed Be. Sarah."

Hi'iaka & the Light

This channeling comes from Hi'iaka who is Pele's sister in the Hawaiian pantheon of Divine Beings. Sarah's Temple of the Sacred Flame is really the Earth herself, and she has her Ashram (see glossary) on the Big Island of Hawaii! In my experience Sarah blends seamlessly with other spiritual cultures, but the Hawaiian pantheon also seem to blend seamlessly with her in return, perhaps because they both have the same Lemurian energy. Hi'iaka is referring to Imbolc, which marks the beginning of Spring. An energy very aligned with the Sarah archetypal energy. Spring also can be seen in the evolutionary phase we are in right now, that time where much work has been done, and we are ready and waiting to see the new shoots appear.

In my eye, Hi'iaka has some similarities to Sarah; she was the patron goddess of hula dancers, chant, magic and medicine – all things which Sarah is also connected to. Hi'iaka also lived in a grove of Lehua trees (which are sacred to her), and where she spent her days dancing with the forest spirits.

Hi'iaka was conceived in Tahiti, but carried in the form of an egg to Hawai'i by Pele, who kept the egg with her at all times to incubate it. From this, she earned her full name, Hi'iaka-i-ka-poli-o-Pele: "Hi'iaka in the bosom of Pele". Hi'iaka was the first deity of this pantheon (the Pele family) born in Hawaii. (Source: Wikipedia.)

"Welcome all, I am Hi'iaka. Born from darkness, I carry the light for mankind to raise their consciousness up into the heavens whilst still remaining firmly here on earth. Born and formed from my elder sister Pele, she who holds the fire to burn and create anew all that is dark within a man or woman. From my sister's power am I created, an image of what mankind too can be. I am love and laughter, dance and play. I hold the power to overcome evil and am skilled and adept in using my magickal abilities. Child I am not, woman I am.

A useful ally I am for the coming of the New Age, whilst Pele can assist you in breaking from the old and walking on a New Path, I can take you along that path, and walk with you. I can be there to guide and empower and teach you the skills and abilities I have learnt along the way. I can teach you how to be a New Human Being, living from love and light in the New Age of Aquarius, these are my realms, the realms of light, where from time to time darkness may enter in, but these things hold no terror for me, I have much assistance around me and I have great powers available to me, and all is well!

Of the light, I would say 'start to appreciate what is there'. Humanity searches for the light in all things, hungers for it subconsciously without ever realising that it is the spiritual light that they long for.

Imbolc* then is a time when the light can be seen to be visibly appreciated, as the light is returning to make the day longer than the night, after the long, dark, cold winter and holds the promise of spring and summer days. As you feel the magic of hope and light and rejoice in the snowdrops, let your minds turn to the spiritual light that you have created in your life. Perhaps you can remember a time in your life when there was no spirituality in your life to comfort you, no goddess mother known to you to light up your darkest hours, to offer comfort and solace, guidance and wisdom when you were lost and afraid. If you can remember these times, and then coming back to the present, think of all the little differences that have come into your life now. All the ways you have learnt to connect to your inner selves, your true selves, and the light within. All the experiences you have had connecting to the Divine and the Divine Mother, sometimes alone, sometimes in groups, sometimes your own personal experience, sometimes being shown the light through the energy of another.

Think then of how much light you have welcomed into your life. How through your own dedication and soul wisdom you have reconnected yourself and your daily life back to the ancient Mother. Celebrate your own courage and wisdom in taking these spiritual paths.

And thinking this, you can if you wish, re-dedicate yourself to the Divine, and spend a few moments contemplating your spiritual practices.

Are they as you would wish, have you dropped practices by the wayside that you wish to re-embrace, are there new practices that you wish to add to your life that you know will bring you even more sustenance and light than you have currently. Allow your minds now to suggest any practices that will bring as much light as you wish into your daily lives.

I am Hi'iaka, light of the New Dawn, of the New Day, if you wish I can show you how to dance through your lives here on Earth, in love and joy and light.

I am Hi'iaka, carrier of Consciousness/Light. All is well. Aloha and farewell."

*Imbolc is a Celtic festival which marks the beginning of spring, and is generally celebrated on the 1st February.

Priest/esses! The future is already there...

This channeling came through from the 'goddess of creation'. When I see Sarah's ancestral line, Sophia and the goddesses are standing behind her, each one stretching further and further back in line as Ancestral mothers. The further back it goes, the larger the Ancestors become. I get an impression of Russian dolls, because they all fit inside each other. All of our genealogies are like this. WE are the divine spirits we call on.

"Welcome priest/esses. I am the goddess of all creation, and my force is your force. You have within you, the ability to dream and manifest new worlds, new consciousness. It is important now, that you remember or concentrate more strongly upon reaching up into the highest heavens and connecting to the Divine Blueprint, to the plan which the Divine has not just for humanity and the earth, but for the whole of creation. For what is happening here on the earth plane, in physical manifestation, has a roll-on effect throughout all of the dimensions.

This is how the Lemurians created the world. It was in a way much easier for them, because before they descended into matter, they had a permanent and perfect connexion to the divine source; they lived in a blissful state of ecstasy. But they spent their lives dreaming and they wanted to face the challenges of physical life; they wanted to see what they could do. And so, they reached up and connected with the potential of all creation, and then they brought it through and dreamed it into being. This is the task now of humanity and all lightworkers must lead the way. But you as priestesses are particularly important, and the work that you do, creates foundations for others to build upon. Connect up then to the highest source that you can. Make yourself a perfect vessel as you can. Clear away blockages that impede your chakras that impede your energetic flow, and when this is done, you will be able to connect to the whole of the cosmos.

The future is already there, all possibilities already exist. The time is coming now to focus upon the highest possible potential, and draw it through into being, draw it through into manifestation. This you can do; this is your power. *This is your power.*

Call then upon the elemental forces in your life, call upon the guardians of the elements, the angels of the elements, the goddesses of the elements. Ask them to teach you what it is that you need to know, because each of you has a unique understanding of the universe, and a unique task to perform.

This then is my message to you. A reminder of your own power, and the work that you are to do. May blessings be upon you. Blessed be."

Connecting to the Elohim

Sarah works closely with the Elohim. Rudolph Steiner describes the Elohim as Creator Angels, and says that we too are created from the Elohim, 'The .. Elohim could form the earthly nature of man by breathing into him. What streamed into man with the air was the essence of the Elohim themselves..'

"Brothers/sisters, we are one, we are the Elohim. Welcome to you this day that we spread our message, our love, our light across the earth. Welcome, welcome, welcome.

Each time you think of us, and focus your energies on us, our energy of the Elohim is a little more present on the earth, a little closer to the physical realm. We would entreat you now, to open your hearts & minds a little wider, to come a little closer, to welcome us in, for we are here.

We are here to assist you on your journey of evolution, for humanity now has physically reached its end-point in the current evolutionary cycle, and in the days and years to come, you will make an evolutionary leap of breath-taking proportions, where a new vessel for your physical incarnations is grown and manifested here on the earth plane.

This may seem a little bizarre, a little 'E.T' for some, but in truth, for each of you to reach the climaxes and heights of the New Earth, the New Age, you will need some new equipment to achieve this. The old ways and bodies are too limiting and would not allow you to reach the glories and heights to which you will achieve in your new physical forms. Mother/Father God's perfect plan for humanity is indeed built upon a rock, and we are assisting now in carrying out the Divine plan, in co-operation with the lightworkers who are currently incarnating on the earth.

So, we would ask you to lift your minds and hearts to ours, as there is much we would do to assist you in your process of ascension, much of which is involved with this process of upgrading humanity's earthly vehicles. Even connecting to us for as little as a minute each day, will allow us to achieve great things, as directly then, we can set about setting in particles of light into your energy fields, particles of light which carry the momentum and force to carry you to the new millennium of the Golden Age.

The Divine wishes now, to assist you in this way, and for us to give you this energy directly. We are spirits of form, beings of light who are involved directly in bringing about the evolution of humankind, and we would work with you now.

When you wish to connect with us, light a candle with the intent that this connects you to us. White would work well for this purpose, but really any colour that calls you is sufficient. Light this candle and picture us encircled around you in perfect balance, continuity and form. As you feel the perfect grace contained within, allow us to lift you, heart, mind, body and soul as you say quietly to yourself, or inside your mind, 'Elohim, Elohim, Elohim'

We will lift all that you are, here with us, raising your physical vibrations with particles of etheric light which will remain present with you after you have 'returned to Earth' and are going about your earthly lives. To do this exercise, even for one minute each week will be of benefit, not only to yourselves, but the whole of humanity, as it is allowing us to bring you a little closer to us, where you already are outside of manifest creation, but closer to us too on the physical plane, manifesting a little more each time of heaven on earth.

These things contain great mysteries that reveal themselves to you, at the right time, and at the right place, and in the right way. We are the Elohim, your beloved brethren, and we bless you now, with beautiful particles of light that rain down gently upon you now…………

All is well, all is well, all is well.

Namaste."

Sarah's support with the evolution of our Lightbody

Sarah, many people are currently experiencing Ascension symptoms such as anxiety and anger which are proving a challenge to manage. Could you share some insights on how to deal with them in order to help ourselves and also for us to assist others? (Question is from a live interview.)

Sarah has so much to offer to us during our time of evolutionary change. Indeed this is why she is here! She is sister, guide, teacher and mentor! She has stepped forward to walk with us, while we, in co-creation with the Divine and all of the realms and kingdoms, usher in a new era!

"Blessings, I am Sarah. This is such a huge evolutionary change that you are going through at this time. It is really phenomenal. Of course,

you are in the midst of it living right in the middle of it and you can't see with that perspective from above just how massive this process is that you are going through - although of course many of you sense this and know this deep in your hearts and know that you need support. You know that you need assistance, and we are here, you are not alone.

The Ascension symptoms that are commonly experienced are often about needing to come into alignment and in truth this is it at its most simple… that evolutionary change that you are going through. You are coming into alignment with all aspects of your being from the highest to the lowest.

Now when I use that terminology, I am not casting any shadows of judgement that the highest is the best and the lowest is the worst. It is simply a way of describing these different levels of your being, all of which are equally valued, equally necessary, and equally loved by the divine and so you must love all of these aspects of your being. You are here to become fully human - to invite the wholeness of your divinity into your humanity; integration is the key.

Now if you are able to call on my energy this is what I suggest:

You can imagine my light, my ray, my spirit coming and standing with you. Now I am able to be present upon the etheric layer of the earth. This is quite unusual for an Ascended Master and is related to my capacity to be integrated with all things. This means that I can affect your etheric body in a way that many higher beings cannot. I can come closer to the physical layer because I am in all of the spheres. There is no vibrational dimension I cannot connect to because I hold this energy of integration and oneness. In me all things are in oneness.

So, as I was saying, invite my spirit in, my light, my presence and imagine my light shining down from above your head and bringing you in a state of alignment starting from your higher chakra going down to your lowest chakra.

Ascension symptoms are caused by a dissonance* between the different chakras in your body, all of which exist in different vibrations and different dimensions which is a little mind boggling if one thinks about it too much and is not really important. What is important is that you consider your intent to come into alignment from the top to the bottom and so I would simply ask you to do as I suggested. Call in my spirit, call in my light above you and my light beneath you and ask that I help you to come into alignment and see yourself between these two points of light, straightening up as it were parts that are a little too far to the left or to the right or to the front or to the back. See them coming into oneness throughout your energy body.

Now of course there will be reasons why those things are out of alignment - but doing this meditation will help those things come up into your greater consciousness, and it may be a good idea to pull an oracle card or a rune or whichever tools you like to use when you do this meditation. This will give you a clue as to what it is that you need to focus on, and what you need to bring your awareness to, that will help you come into greater alignment.

There is also my *net of light (meditation, see appendix)* which you can pull around you to keep your energy body in greater integrity. As I said, the Ascension Symptoms are caused by different vibrations of your energy being pulled too much this way or that way and not being in harmony and balance. And it is very difficult when you are living in the world as you are being so bombarded by many different frequencies, downloads coming in, lower vibrations coming from this way and that. It is a huge challenge that you are passing through and you should not blame yourself in any way for struggling with these things.

However, you can call upon me and ask me to place my net of light around you. *This is a little like the starry sky at night and it comes and sits around your energy body* so you can just simply imagine it with little points of light in the night sky – a comforting cloak that helps give you some protection from the bombardment of the outside world and helps you maintain the energy integrity within your own light body.

You are going through huge changes in your light body at this time and this is something that I will talk more about in the months and years ahead but for now this is enough to know that you can call on me and that I will give you assistance. It doesn't matter if you call on me and you feel no different because you wonder if I am really there at all. If you call on me, I am there. Sometimes for various reasons it could be difficult for you to sense things in a very sensitive way but have faith, have belief, have the knowing that you are a powerful being and if you call for help to me, I will be there whether you feel it or not.

So, know that I am always there to help you. I have come forward now for this time particularly. I have been waiting in the wings. I am an Ascended Master for this time, this now, this age, this eon. I am here. I am here. I am here. Take a deep breath and feel this reality within yourself that all is well, all is well, all is well. The Divine's perfect plan is built upon a rock and everything is happening within divine timing and divine grace. You hold your own perfect piece of the plan, each of you perfectly unique, a perfect piece of the puzzle that together makes up the whole. Comfort your fears - assuage your fears. You cannot know the whole, you cannot see the perspective and that's ok - but know that the Divine can and you are each a spark of the Divine and my blessings are upon you.

I am Sarah and these are the words that I wish to speak for now. Blessed be, blessed be, blessed be, Amen."

the dissonance that Sarah is referring to, is when some of our chakras are out of alignment, which stops the flow of energy in the energy field

An Evening with Sarah:

The next set of channelings came from an evening event in the town of Roskilde in Denmark, where I live. We can use this first paragraph as a way of connecting more deeply with ourselves and with Sarah before we ask for guidance from her.

"Blessings I am Sarah. I would first of all invite you to focus upon your heart centre. And that space just above your heart centre, the higher heart. As you focus your awareness there, my presence is all around. And I invite you to bring my presence closer into your energy field. Closer in, deeper, to that heart, and higher heart centre. In this way can you breathe me in. Breathe in that life force, that life force energy. And in response through your heart centre, your higher heart centre opening and blossoming. Feel your energy system relaxing and sinking down a little deeper as it fills with the support and the strength that I hold and represent. And as you rest down into this energy, I invite you to ask me the first question."

How can you help us Sarah?'

"In the way I started this conversation by offering, giving an invitation, which ended in the statement I made that that offer and invitation of breathing in, of accepting my energy, is a support, a strengthening around you. In this way have I come to the earth at this moment, in this present time. The energy body which you are in is becoming something other than what it is. This is a difficult process. At times a painful process. At times a joyful and wonderful process. But a process that requires a huge 'using up' of energy. If, for example, I can use the metaphor of an electrical appliance such as a kettle, that is plugged in and then uses a lot of electricity to boil the water - at the moment your energy bodies are using up a huge amount of power. If you were that kettle, you would be sucking up huge amounts of electricity because of the changes that your energy body is required to make in this process of it becoming something other than it is right now. It is not quite correct to say that it is transforming. Because when your energy body becomes 'this other', it will not be what it was before. It will become something other than itself. I realise these words are inadequate, but I hope that they can create an impression that makes or gives a little sense of understanding. To support this process, I create an energy grid, a net of safety, of stabilization. Something that can be described as a net of safety and support and strength that is around you. When I say strength, I don't mean in the sense of brute force but a strength that means you can hold yourself together more easily, or more correctly, or more efficiently. It is difficult for each person to hold on to the integrity of themselves when they are going through changes such as each of you are going through at the moment. I can't say 'humanity' because it is not the whole of humanity that is going through these energy body changes at the moment. It is a certain number of individuals that are going through this energy body change at the moment. This is one aspect of my work. This is one aspect of the things that I and other beings of light have come to do. But it is the one that is the most relevant to speak about at this moment and for your understanding."

Rachel: 'So that was interesting. That was sort of a new concept to me that she was talking about there. I was sort of getting this image, people talk about all these ascension symptoms, and that we are getting downloads, and this and that and the other. And I was sort of seeing all this incredible change going on within someone's energy field and Sarah being this holding force around it. Because the pressure of all that change is so intense. It's like getting to the point where it's actually too much for some people. It's too intense. It's too much. So, we can call on her to sort of be this holding force around us.'

Sarah what is your mission here?'

"At this moment in time it is a question of alignment. Bringing help, supporting those who are ready to hear, those are ready to come into alignment to do so. And by that it is a process of the line of energy from above and below, and below and above. And the place of connection there is here in the heart. There is a question that you have been discussing about how to come into clear contact with the I AM presence, with the Higher Self. And very simply speaking, if one is just talking about each person's energy, it is simply a question of that person's energy system coming into alignment and being in a straight line, as above, so below. Of course, the process itself is less simple and requires more work than the simple way there is in explaining it. But this is the process now that I am approaching and that you are approaching and it starts with the centre of yourself, the centre of your being, which is here, around the heart. When that place is stable and strong and balanced then it is possible to come into alignment above and below. When this process happens, you have the connection from your Higher Self, you have the connection from your Earthly Self, you have the connection with your Soul. There is a clear flow between all the different parts of your being. Each one of them knows what the other needs. Where it needs to go. Each one knows how to help the other. They all work together in a beautiful and fluid cooperation, aligned with one another. The communication is clear. This is the mission that I am approaching and that you are approaching right now, to work in co-creation with each other."

Why is this development, this work, important to humanity?

"The first level of the answer is to say that I speak from the level of vibration of the Ascended Masters who are as you know, people who have carried on further down the road spiritually and have evolved into a higher, finer spiritual matter. We are in alignment with all the different levels of our being. We have integrated in that way. If you could look at the energy body of human beings, you could see this bit is over here, and this bit is over here, and that bit has gone over there. And they all need to be gently brought back together so that the flow can happen once again. So, from our perspective of where we are at the moment, we are focusing on helping humanity develop into what we are already, but we are doing this with the motivation or end concept, or the hope that, humanity can do this while they are still on the Earth. This is the Divine's plan now, that humanity become Ascended while still being incarnated upon the Earth. In addressing the question of why this should be important to humanity, for a number of you this is your life purpose. Your Soul has agreed to come here at this time to help push humanity to its next evolutionary phase, its next step in the development. I use the word push because this is a huge step that is being taken. And as I said before with the energy body, it requires a huge amount of energy and of power. So, for some Souls the question about which we speak consumes their lives because they feel very driven to want to help in this process, although they may not be sure exactly what that is.

So why is it important to the whole of humanity? I would say that from my understanding, this coming into alignment is a raising of consciousness. That is the only thing that will overcome and transform the problems and negativity that exist within the realm of humanity at this present time. Of course, these things have a huge amount of learning in them, of poverty and of disease and of mental cruelty, and all of these things which we can see on the Earth, the many problems we can list and discuss at great length. But in this mission that I have, in this next step of Evolution for humanity, there is this possibility then of integration with all that One is. So not ascending away from, not leaving behind the personality, but instead bringing to it one's own innate and natural Divinity."

What do we need to know about our evolution and the earth's right now?

"I suppose the most important thing for you to know is that this is happening because you are ready for it to happen. The Earth has her own complex cycle of evolution and she has at some point in that history of evolution agreed to take on the extra work, if you like, of the human race. And in this way her evolution has become tied to that of humanity. So, when I speak about readiness and being ready I don't speak about the Earth. She has agreed to carry that extra work of humanity, and her readiness is not in question.

But humanity has come to a point now where it is ready to take the next step. And a big step it is. But also, it is a question of having to, and this is partly the question that is being asked of humanity now. And that is being tested. And that is, "Are you ready?" because you can't carry on the way you have been. That road is not open to humanity any more. Staying the same is not an option. The only option now is to go on the road ahead. And so many changes are being brought about that are difficult to keep up with because these changes are necessary.

I suppose if I were to give you a metaphor that could be likened to it, it would be of a child that is growing and has reached so high now and so tall that they cannot fit anymore in the house that they are living in. So, they have to go and move out and climb out through that little door and go and find a bigger house to live in. So, I'm not saying that humanity cannot stay the way it is because of something terrible or bad that they've done and now they're being punished. That's not it. That's not what I'm saying. I'm saying, as far as I can, because it's very difficult to describe these concepts in a linear language, that humanity has reached a point in its growth now where it cannot stay at the same level of consciousness for the metaphysical power that it holds. And that is what this energy body change is. You have grown out of the energy body that you have been living in. You have become too big for it. You need a new house in which to live. A new energy body that will befit you and befit your ability to create."

How are you connected to the Earth grid here in Roskilde?

"The archetypal force that I represent is one of Integration, (which of course is an energy that belongs to the Divine, but which is something that I hold something of, in myself and therefore I can become a face, if you like, for that energy of Integration.) But one of the qualities that this (*archetypal force*) has, is that one can be in contact with many different levels of vibration at once. So, for example if one has Integrated the whole, then from that Integrated energy you can connect to very high vibrations or very low vibrations and everything in between. And that's ok. It doesn't cause a problem for me to be connected to any of the energies in any of the spheres in manifest creation. herefore, in this work of supporting humanity and the earth in going through this process of change, this Integrative quality that I can use and teach to other people so that they can then become that themselves means, that the problems, the difficulties, with working with energy, with these very low vibrations and these very high vibrations - these things can all be brought together and mixed together, and made whole and made into divine fullness. And in that energy miracles can happen and wonderful things can occur and the divine's work can be undertaken. So, a person who has gone through this process of Integration in themselves is a very powerful person, in the sense that they can't be knocked off balance because all those energies in themselves, all those energies that have existed within them, the high and the low, the divine and the diabolical, the good and the terrible - they have all been accepted. They have all been allowed. They have all come into Integration.

Now, there are places on the earth that have special energies and all of these different energies can be utilized for different purposes. So, for example if one wanted to connect to very high energies, one might visit a place on the earth that is naturally aligned to the crown chakra because it would assist you through sympathetic resonance. It would assist you simply by being there physically to also open up very easily to that high crown energy. There are also places on the earth where the energy systems have been rewired into working on very specific things in the human energy field. And these have been done deliberately, sometimes by ancient cultures who worked with ascended masters, beings of light, angels, beings from other planets, even. There are places on the earth where this has been done and people visit these power places now and enjoy the benefits of how those places can interact upon their own energy field. This is the process now that is being undertaken in this part of the world where you are living here, in Scandinavia, in Denmark. There is an energy system here that is becoming. It hasn't become it yet. It is awakening. But this process needs people. It needs a co-operative process of co-creation between you, beings that exist in physical manifestation, and the earth, and the angels, and the elementals, and all these other beings of light, such as myself. And my role in this is my mission is one of supporting humanity in evolution. And here in this place where you are living there is a great work that is being undertaken to create an energy system that impacts upon the human body and the human energy field to assist it in this process of becoming the 'other'. Of course, I don't mean that you have to come here 'as the only place on the earth where this can happen and your energy field will change.' But the fact of it existing as it is **its own piece**, and it is one part of the whole. Just the fact of it existing will affect the whole of the earth grid. It will affect the whole of the earth grid in the way that because it exists here it means that it is much easier for humanity to connect to this ability to become 'the other' in that sympathetic resonance. Because it exists here it will make it much more possible."

Rachel: 'That was interesting. So, what I was getting there I was imagining like Machu Picchu and these old civilizations, those ancient power places. They all had their purpose. Those places got created and are doing a specific job and then this is getting created here because this is what we need right now. And then I was sort of imagining the different energy places, the power places around here and each of them have their own purpose for coming into that alignment. So, if you went to this place, it would make you more grounded and if you went to this place, it would bring you into vibrational resonance with your higher self. They each have a specific purpose of helping the energy body shift. So, it's like a computer program or something that's getting wired up to do this one specific job. But the fact that it exists here means that everywhere else all over the earth, that vibration suddenly becomes much more accessible. If you come here, it is really powerful but just the fact that it exists…'

To find the Source of all life

I have a crystal skull called Maya, and she is made from selenite (which is associated with the moon). This teaching very much aligns with 'life as daily therapy' which is the Sarah teaching from the first book (page 17), but I also love the simplicity of this message and yet it's incredible magick!

'Welcome, I am Maya and I am of the moon!

The light you see on the moon, is the reflected light of the sun, and so is creation the reflected light of the Divine. The moon looks as if it is shining out its own light, as if it is its own light source, but this is an illusion, as the true source of light is coming from elsewhere, from the sun.

So it is with reality, if you would wish to see the true source of life, then you will not find it by looking at reality, you will discover it by looking elsewhere, for reality is the reflected brilliance of the Divine.

When you are looking at the beauty of the moon, on a dark night, the sun is not visible, and so you would not perhaps make the connexion that the light is coming from the sun, as no clue is apparent that this is so.

So it is with the Divine Source, there is no outwardly apparent clue that is obvious to the eye as to where the source is coming from, the source of all life.

To find the source of all life, you must not look upwards, but inwards, inwardly at the centre of yourself, at the heart of all things is the Divine. There in the centre of yourself is the Divine, sitting waiting for the day that you come to discover this truth for yourselves.'

Sarah through the Ages

'Has Sarah been working with us through the ages, and has her interaction with us changed (i.e. In the way she communicates with us?)' *(Question is from a live interview.)*

"In all honesty, the energy that I carry has been slumbering in regards to humanity in the collective unconscious. The divine masculine and the divine feminine as understood as coming together with the sacred marriage, was created as a powerful energy matrix, that was also anchored here on the earth.* The oneness that I represent (as an archetypal force), was planted here within that energy matrix as a seed. It was not the time for it to flourish then. When a thing happens in the space time continuum, there are always echoes backwards and forwards, because time actually exists in physical manifestation, and it exists as one whole piece of 'material time', all woven together as one fabric, one tapestry. Powerful events, which have happened during the course of earth's and humanity's evolution, are always sending off the powerful vibrations, into that tapestry where humanity is living and existing. My time, which is fully coming soon, and of which you are the 'harbingers' and 'forthbringers' of, has also been 'sending off' a vibration, which has always been there for those sensitive enough to feel it. This has been present in the form of visions or dreams, but it also means that the energy that I represent has always been available for those capable of energetically holding it, whatever time or place that they live in. This is because I am simply an aspect of the archetypal force that I represent, the archetypal force actually belongs to the Divine, of which you are a part, and which is always accessible to you if you have the capability. But we are coming to a time now, where it will be much easier to access this archetypal force, because outwardly it will be more available, and so it will be mirrored to you much more easily.

I am Sarah and these are the words which I wish to say today, Blessed Be, Blessed Be, Blessed Be, Amen."

*by Yeshua and Mary Magdalene

Sarah and the times of the year

Have you noticed how we are creating a new spiritual calendar? The Sirius portal, Lions gate, as well as bringing new (and old) meanings back to the solstices and the cross quarter festivals of the year.

We also have some special days in May between the 24th-26th where she is honoured by the Romani people in Saintes-Maries-de-la-Mer in the Carmague in France. Years ago, when I had first 'discovered' her, someone told me that Sarah (as the daughter of the Magdalene and the Master Jesus) was the patron saint of the Romani people. 'Really' I said, 'Is that really possible, they really believe that?' Feeling amazed that this apparent 'secret' (of Mary Magdalene and Jesus having a child) that had been hidden to the rest of us, was something so vital and powerful and sacred to the Romani gypsies, that she was their patron saint! And I was assured that this really was so, that they believed Sarah was the daughter of the Mary Magdalene and Jesus, and this is what the ceremony at St. Maries de la Mer is all about. (This is the town in France where there is a story that Mary Magdalene landed on their shores after fleeing Israel.)

Over the years, a couple of Romani women have written to me (after seeing the Ascended Master Sarah Facebook page I've made) to say that they appreciate seeing her being acknowledged and honoured in this way, which makes me think that this is true, otherwise I imagine they would be quite offended by me saying something untrue, such as 'Sarah is the daughter of Mary Magdalene and Jesus'.

Whatever 'the truth' is, I really love this story.

Many years ago in my twenties, I had a couple of years of psychosynthesis psychotherapy, and one of the more joyful themes that emerged in my meditations was of me being a Romany gypsy woman, and having a pretty good life full of joy and dance and a fierce passion for life! (There was also a very handsome gypsy man in these imaginings, of course, lol!) I don't know whether this is a past life, or a part of my psyche that relates to these feelings of ecstatic dance, but it doesn't matter so much to me anyway - they are a precious part of me, that I hold close.

Sarah has been very hidden, invisible even, definitely misunderstood - and for many people, if they were to be told about her, they would be derisory and possibly even insulting. So there are some familiar themes here with the history of the Romani, and how they have been treated. Also she is the 'Holy Family gone rogue'! She doesn't fit in with the 'acceptable story', but is a misfit, a rebel, and even an outcast! Again, these themes fit in with what we see with the gypsy people....

Samhain came up as another important portal this year for the Ancestors (more on this in the Ancestors chapter, and 'Do it now' channeling in Chapter 8)

Channeling about Christmas

There is a portal in between Christmas and New Year, (and even going up to Epiphany on January 6th) that Sarah talks about here.

"Welcome, I am Sarah. Indeed, we are entering into the time of Christmas or the Winter solstice. There are many challenges around this time of year; weather-wise in the Northern Hemisphere, stress-wise for many people around Christmas and family, around material things. And yet there is also this opportunity of creating moments of stillness.

Imagine now, one of these moments of stillness is starting to appear. Perhaps you could see it as a bubble or a spark of light somewhere inside of you, maybe in your heart centre. Imagine now, one of these moments of stillness, is starting to appear. Perhaps you could see it as a bubble or a spark of light somewhere inside of you. Maybe in your heart centre and imagine with each breath, it glows a little brighter and imagine that the way you feel inside can perhaps not be linked to anything that is going on around you, but instead, to the divine spark inside of yourself – the piece of you that is always the divine, always divine truth, always divine peace.

Breathe into this part of yourself. Know what it is you, even as your earthly personality is also you in all of its delicious imperfections and wonderfulness. Your divine spark/self has come here to love all of you, all of the things that you are, no matter how imperfect you might judge them to be. And so, it is at Christmas or the Winter solstice at this time of year there are special challenges. Because of this year's events, you also have many, many special challenges, but this place inside yourself, which you can reach more easily by calling in my presence. I am a bridge, I am a connector, I am a catalyst.

Just imagine it's there, this beautiful spark of divine light. Breathe it in, breathe it out into your body. Accept its gifts of love and divine peace and know that all is well, all is well, all is well. Repeat this to yourself often, especially when things in the outer world seem to be anything but. All is well, all is well, all is well.

Call on my angels whenever you have need. Call on me when you need some support, some insight, when you need to know what is real and what is unreal. I will be there.

I am Sarah and my blessings are upon you each and every moment of your day. Blessed be, blessed be, blessed be. Amen."

Spring

Sarah's energy comes up very strongly in spring, indeed she is very aligned to spring. Both in the early days of spring, where a lot is going on under the surface (but you can't see it), and later on where we see the huge burst of growth as spring bursts forth.

"Open your hearts and breathe me in, I am there, already, lying dormant, waiting to be awakened. My energy can be seen as the bright green of nature, the colour of spring, new leaves growing on the branches, abundant growth." (channeled excerpt from Sarah's little book of healing, page 9)

This channeling came from an interview Lea Chapin did with me in the month of April.

"Welcome, I am Sarah.

My blessings are upon each and every one of you. As I speak from this side of the earth, spring is truly upon us and all of the blessings that come with it, the chance of something new – new life, new growth. So, I am a good person to call upon when you have new projects in your life that you perhaps feel need a little bit more power and umph. I will gladly come along and give that energy.

I have the power of bringing spirit through to the manifest world and this is not my power in truth but rather an aspect of the Divine that I am an archetype for, I am a face for, an energy colour – whichever way you want to describe it.

You can call on me even to help your garden grow out in nature. You can ask me to bless the water that you pour on your house plants.

You can bless the water you drink to help you grow or your children grow, or your pets grow in those times where change is needed and perhaps you wish for the fresh verdant energies of spring.

I am Sarah and I am here specifically as mankind blooms into a new era of growth. It is time to cast off those old chattels, those old beliefs especially the guilt and the blame and the resentment and anger and bitterness. It's fine that it's been there. It's ok it was right for the time. But now, now something beautiful and wonderful is coming for humanity. All things come in right timing, right time, right place, right being, and you are in this cusp now – this turning point. Can you feel it as I speak? Can you feel those blossomings' starting to occur in each and every one of you? Those of you who have ears to hear, the light within you has already sparked, has already grown so much.

My mother the Magdalena, she will come to you and help you heal your wounds. She will hold you when you are in pain and suffering and give you so much love and compassion. And my father Yeshua, he will light up that spark, he will fan the flame, he will make it brighter and help you have clarity to comprehend divine truths. And I Sarah, I will help you bring it all together. I will help you fully, fully embrace your humanity and fully, fully embrace your divinity. You have come to be all that you are and so it shall be.

Blessed be, blessed be, blessed be.

I am Sarah. Those of you who have come here to work with me, you are ready to hear my call and so it shall be.

I am Sarah and these are the words which I wish to speak this day. Blessed be, blessed be, blessed be. Amen. My blessings are upon you."

The Equinoxes

Sarah has special blessings for us, especially at the Equinoxes - her energies help us to come into oneness! Sarah INTEGRATES!! On the Equinox, where the energies of night and day are in equal measure, we can also come into greater balance and therefore wholeness. Call on Sarah to help you balance your feminine/masculine, dark/light - all of your polarities, and all THAT YOU ARE. She will help you with what you need, just ask ..

"Welcome, I am Sarah.

Whichever side of the world you live on, you are in a process where the seasons are changing. There is a moment of stillness, where one thing becomes another thing and, in this moment, you can call forth through your sacred power, balance for yourself. And in this balance, comes Oneness and Divine Wholeness, Divine Fullness.

Right now, you are receiving so many codes, energetic information, that is re-informing your DNA, your energy body. You are becoming something other than what you are right now. Of course, you are always the same eternally now with your eternal spark, your divine spark, hailed at the centre of yourself. This divine spark is the reason why you ARE. Without that, you would not be here, you would not have a physical body and be walking about the earth and that is truly what you are, your divine spark... an aspect of the divine.

But right now, the physical form that you wear, your vehicle for this physical manifestation, is undergoing great change as many and most of you know already. This is a process of 'lightening', that is coming in for you now - you will start to feel lighter and more able to connect to your spiritual sources. First will come the downloads and the codes. Then will come the clearing, to clear the way, the cultural conditioning, the past life problems, blocks and traumas, the family dramas. These will then be cleared.

I AM Sarah, and I tell you that these are amazing times that you live in. Yet you cannot find this from looking outwardly, into the outer world. You must learn to look inwardly, connect to your divinity that is inside of yourself. There you will discover your treasure. There is your gold and your diamonds, the butterflies, the trees, the flowers. All of the beauty inside of you, will help you see the beauty without.

I AM Sarah and these are the words that I wish to speak to you this day.

Blessed be, blessed be, blessed be, Amen."

Easter Channeling

Every year, Sarah's energies come in so strongly around Easter! Of course, Easter is a tradition of the old religions, going back into humanity's distant past, and belongs to the ancient rhythm of the earth herself...

"Welcome, I am Sarah.

Each year on the tide of spring, Easter is reborn. After the full moon, a death process occurs – dying to the old, so that a new life, fresher, brighter, stronger is recast. The fasting process that was traditional assisted this, and it would still help now to take lighter meals in the time leading up to Easter, focusing on fruits and vegetables… (and as always drinking plenty of water!) The process of dying to the old is not an easy one - support yourself in this process.. be kind and compassionate to yourself… And around Easter, you have the opportunity to take on another body of light… to be resurrected – dying to your old self and becoming a higher version of your light body self. These are the light codes that come in for you every year at Eastertide. I am Sarah and my blessings are upon you. I can support you in these processes, call on me, and I will walk by your side, helping you see the light as the light, and the dark as the dark, as you skillfully weave the dark and the light together in your role as Alchemist of Spirit & Earth. I am Sarah and my blessings are upon you, each and every moment of the day, Blessed Be, Blessed Be, Blessed Be, Amen."

Sarah's Temple of the Sacred Flame

Sarah's Temple exists on the Earth, as a vibration – and is being built within the New Earth Grid! (See glossary.) To help the vibration strengthen and gain more integrity, we can manifest it on the Earth within our own Sacred Spaces. We can also connect to Sarah's Temple of the Sacred Flame by being there together energetically in quantum space!

I was given a vision of Sarah keeping a temple where there is a central point where a flame is eternally lit. (She also keeps the same flame lit eternally in her Ashram.) The flame is Sarah's Flame of Unity.

Sarah's Temple of the Sacred Flame holds the part of the Ascended Earth and Ascended Humanity that isn't physically in manifestation yet. It's waiting for us in the higher dimensions to bring it into Unity & Oneness once again. We are directing this process from a denser level of matter than has ever been done before – and for this process, it is necessary for us to learn how to be quantum masters of matter!

Some of us are called to be Priest/esses for Sarah; flame-keepers, and weavers of Earth energies and Cosmic forces! It is in our Ancestral line, and our lineage and our heritage calls us to this path. As an Earth Priest/ess of Sarah, you learn how to work in co-creation with the Divine Forces to manifest this Temple upon the Earth. To find out more see Links!

You can also receive a free activation for Sarah's Temple; come and join us at our Facebook group Sarah's Temple of the Sacred Flame, as well as reading more about Sarah's Temple and the priest/ess work we do on my website (see Links).

Preparing for the way ahead...

Sarah's flame exists in oneness, but can be separated into certain aspects. (Just as we are individuated aspects of the Divine!) In the teachings she has given me, we work with the white flame of Divinity, Sarah's violet flame, and Sarah's green flame of manifestation (life).

There are node points on the planet where Sarah's flame (or aspects of them) are present. These are on the Tor in Glastonbury for example, also in Malta, Denmark, Hawaii, and Egypt, and other places as yet unawakened... These places were activated and awakened through Sarah having planted seeds there in times gone by, and there are more yet to discover!

This comes from a reading that I did about the Sarah's Temple of the Sacred Flame asking for guidance on manifesting it here and the path ahead.

The way is being cleared quicker than we probably can imagine.

Sar'h asks us to focus on the Divine within ourselves..

To help & support Archangel Raphael comes in – we can call on him.

We're forming a new collective group now with the advent of Sarah's flame.

We need to support each other through some challenging times ahead.

Archangel Michael comes in to remind us of our amazing strength, courage, initiative & force. We are not alone.

This is the untrodden path we are on, we need to be brave as we walk in the darkness, and then Sarah comes to light the path ahead.. Her flame is here to light the way.

Learn to trust your Higher Infinite Self. TRUST. All is well.

'Embrace your physical form & let your body move in whatever way it wants'. It helps to dispel fear & doubt; dance, walk, sing, run – get up and MOVE..

Sarah's flame is preparing us for the way ahead. As we bring in and ground each aspect of her flame, so we are initiated.

Spirit are preparing us for the Paradigm Shift ahead!

We are the Priests and Priestesses, the ones opening to the light, and preparing the way. We are One!

Chapter 6

Sarah's Teachings

The Yellow Thread

*Yellow is the colour of the mental level — and of teachings and the intellect! Also of the sun, and things bright, warm and happy!! Yellow is uplifting and inspiring, and this is exactly what Sarah's teachings do! She wants to empower us, to lift us up, help us find our confidence and self-worth. She **wants** us to be happy and feel good about ourselves! Through her teachings, Sarah shares her wisdom; she shares the clarity of understanding that she has achieved. The simplicity of her words belie the depths of experience and wisdom she has reached in order to be able to impart her words of truth so effortlessly!*

This is my favourite part of the book, because each of these teachings has an immediate and practical use! Yesterday, I read the 'what can I do for myself in love' channeling in the afternoon, and then later that day, I was putting my son (who has ADHD and autism) to bed, and I was looking forward to reading him 'Farmer Boy'. Except he didn't want that one, he wanted another one. Lately he has really been challenging about getting his own way, with everything, and to say I'm weary of it is an understatement, because many of the things he wants to do, are just not manageable. Also, I really struggle with changing a plan once I've made it. I don't actually know why, it just seems to be wired into my personality. So there we were, both really tired, bedtime, at an impasse. I took a deep breath, 'What would love do?' I asked. 'Choose another book'. There it was. Another option. But not because it was 'the right thing' to do. This wasn't a decision I had made with my mind, it had come up inside me. Love had answered. And because it had come up inside me, it made it easy to do. No struggle! We read, 'The Book about Moomin' and 'Snow Bears', and I got to do silly voices. No conflict. Lovely!!

Be Happy & Full of Joy

This first channeling is such a delight and is short and sweet! It's got me listening to comedy podcasts while I do household chores, much more fun that way for me!!!

"I am she, I am she, I am she of the woods, she of the light, she of life. I am there amongst the trees, in the leaf, in the bud. I am in all things. I am life, I am life.

Where is your life, where is your love? Where is your heart, what does your heart spend its day doing? Does it laugh, does it sing, does it play with anything? Or is it sad, is it low, does it drag itself through the day, wondering when all will be laughter, all will be joy? Come sing with me, come dance, I am here, I am here.

Come be happy, be full of joy. Do what you must, but remember most important is to laugh and play, then the energy around you will be vibrant and full of sparkle and light. Make some time to play, to laugh, to sing, don't leave it until after everything else is done, because everything else is never done. Make some time, something small, do what you will, laugh and play.

Say to yourself, 'today I will laugh, if only for a moment, I will see the funny side of things.'

Start small, grow large!

Blessed be, Sarah."

What Can I do for Myself in Love?

This is such a simple teaching (as Sarah's teachings tend to be), but it is so beautiful! Every time I read it, I think, 'why don't I always remember this, it's so simple, and SOOOO obvious', and of course it is obvious, and of course, we forget. But imagine if we had been brought up to do this, and it was part of our habitual behaviour patterns. Imagine it was part of everybody's habitual behaviour patterns, wouldn't that feel lovely to be in a society that responded in that way :-)

"Welcome all, I am Sarah.

Today I would talk to you on the nature of Divine Love, how this is a quality which you can learn to give to yourselves, from yourSelves! There are many situations in your world, that if you had been able to invite in the energy of Divine Love, would have been greatly eased. For example, if you think about the terrible pain between the nations of Israel and Palestine, the wounds that have been caused. Justice will not heal this rift, nor patience, nor strength. Only Love.

And so it is in your own lives, the worst pain that you find there, the most terrible things that have happened, can only be healed by the power of Divine Love. At these times, when pain is all around and you don't know what to do, or how to respond, turn inwardly into yourselves and ask yourSelf what Love would do?

It might be that you need to remove yourself from the situation, or tell someone that because of the love you have for yourself, you cannot allow yourself to be in such a situation any longer. It might be that you need to go away and make yourself a bowl of soup!

But if we respond to the trauma and conflict in our lives, in this way, with love for ourselves, we are always acting from Love, instead of rage and pain, and this Love can be more real inside ourselves than what is happening 'out there', and you can infect a whole situation with the Divine energy of Love!

If you ask yourself, 'what can I do for myself in Love?', then you are not shouting or adding to the trauma. It may be that it comes to you, to explain how you feel. But doing it from Love, you can be calm and careful of yourself, because you are looking after yourself, and meeting your own needs to be loved and no longer in trauma, pain or shock.

And the Loving thing to do in each situation will be totally different, and Love will always give you the answer that you need. And only You can give these things to yourself and no other!

In finding these things inside yourSelf, in finding this Divine Love, you are bringing the Divine onto the earth and into your everyday reality and existence, and all is well, all is well, all is well!

May blessings shine down upon you each and every day of your lives!
Blessed Be, Blessed Be, Blessed Be,
Sarah."

Do the Things that You Love

I love swimming, not so much the act of swimming (I do a kind of lop-sided breaststroke), but being in the water. I've been swimming in the fjord more and more over the years, as time and energy has allowed, and this is something that brings me so much light and good energy! When it comes to doing the things that we love, there are so many things that could be added to the list, – just add the things YOU love to the list!!

"There is a place inside of you that becomes full of light, when you pray, when you sing, when you meditate, when you dance. This is a way that you can refuel yourself, to keep yourself full of light. When seen from our perspective, from the higher planes, we see you as light, and so think on those things that will draw down this light into you, & make them a priority for yourself.

It is very easy to become immersed in the mundane world and to see that all around you - but in truth you are a being of light, and need to 'feed' yourself this light, because it is not yet readily apparent in the world around you. One day, when the earth has achieved her next stage of ascension, that light will be apparent all around you. It will be readily available.

But for now, you need to take steps in order to obtain this higher, finer quality of vibration of light for yourself. This is because those parts of yourself that wish to make themselves manifest on the earth plane now, are vibrating at that higher level, & cannot do so (manifest) without your direct intervention. This is because, as I have said, they need a steady and stable foundation of higher vibrational light which is energy.

So don't think then of spiritual practices as something which you 'have' to do, but realize instead the quality of life that this can give you. As you do the things that bring light down into your earthly body, then the higher parts of yourself can manifest and become one with your earthly nature, creating something very beautiful, and you will feel much expanded joy, health and abundance through it.

Feed yourself the light you need, doing the things that you love. There are many ways to bring down higher light through your earthly self; meditation, prayer, singing and chanting and dancing are but a few. You could add being in nature, painting, making love, creating poetry or music or so many things. Many healing practices pave the way for the higher light to flow through. These things are very simple when seen from a higher perspective. Pray to the Divine each day to create through you & to give you Divine Inspiration, & then remember to act upon it!!

You are a child of the Divine, and just need to lift yourself a little higher to bring yourself where you want to be. The act of lifting yourself higher, will enable you to go more deeply into living from your true Self, here on the earth. These things are done little by little; a little each day, & will over an extended period of time have great results.

So, remember to consciously plan into your daily routine a 'spiritual practice', whatever that is for you. It doesn't matter what it is, just that you have one. If you already have a practice, then look into it, and see if it is the right one for you, whether it needs fine tuning, or adjusting or increasing & adding to, or changing altogether. If you focus your awareness upon it for consideration, you will see what it is you need to do, what feels right.

As each person creates these finer, higher energies around themselves, and through themselves, so you & they are becoming beacons of light. Beacons of light made matter and manifested upon the earth. As more and more of you act in this way, you resonate in sympathetic vibration with each other around the earth, which magnifies the vibration. So It is when you come together in groups, the magnification is multiplied exponentially; but also just all of you individually being here together on the earth plane at the same time is creating a foundation of higher, finer light upon the earth that allows for the Divine and all of the beings of light, to achieve more and more of a miraculous nature upon the earth.

I am Sarah, and I tell you, all is well, all is well, all is well.

Keep on with your individual endeavours, and do not feel they are not important, or contributing in any great way. It is the little things that make the big changes, those small & tiny things that you do each day are magnificent in God's eyes & I bless you for them."

Blessings Are Upon Us

I love this next channelling. Sarah taught me this teaching by repeating over and over again at the end of channellings, 'Blessings are upon you, each and every moment of your life'. And I would think, 'are they, are they really Sarah?!' I certainly didn't feel blessed, but instead felt I had an extremely challenging life! But I could feel that she meant it, and didn't mean it as a way to try and 'pep me up' or make me see the bright side. She meant it really as a literal truth, in a very factual way! Gradually I've come to the understanding that everything that happens to us, has something within it that brings us closer to the Divine, there is always a blessing within each and every situation, but often we have to get our 'blessing glasses' on in order to be able to see them. And we can do this by asking Sarah to help us see; you could say something like,

'Dear Sarah, please help me to see the blessings in my life, each and every day, and in every moment of the day, so mote it be, Amen.'

Try it!

"Welcome all, I am Sarah.

It is my joy, to be here with you this evening. Welcome, welcome, welcome. My heart expands to you, with such blessing. I pour it forth upon the earth, & so can you.

So can you pour forth your blessings, upon yourself, upon those you love, upon those you see suffering. Do not think for one moment, that these blessings go nowhere, and do nothing. Your thoughts, your blessings, your intent, your heartfelt emotions mean everything. It is a beautiful thing, to be able to bless each other, to stand and see your brother or sister in difficulty or despair, in suffering, in anger or in rage, and to know that you can bless that situation.

I would say this about blessing, that you are bringing forth, through that blessing, the most divine nature in that situation. This might mean in a situation where there is suffering, that your blessing creates a little doorway for some compassion to come through.

In a difficult situation, where it seems there is no way forward, that Divine Grace can shift and change the subtlest things, so that things can move & flow once again.

Of course, it is true, there are many beautiful things in your lives, that perhaps your eyes are not open the widest to see, and that because of daily routines, the pressure of time, and the difficulty of certain situations, it may feel difficult to slow down and step back, and to see the beauty & the blessings that are there.

It may also be, that you don't see blessings that are present in your life, because you don't realise that you can have those things. That you don't see the possibilities that exist for yourself, that you have, shall we say, a blind spot to those things.

In this way, we can say that perhaps you don't always see the good and the possible!

So, what can be done to rectify these things? Well, of course you can pray! You can pray & ask to see all the blessings that are in your life. You can regularly send blessings to others. You can have the intent that the power of blessings, runs through your life - and is a force therefore of bringing the Divine that is inherent in all things, more out into the world....

Those blessings are always there in every situation through your belief and your intent, you can bring them to pass here in the physical world, which is where you are as spiritual beings, here in the physical world. This is the Divine's creation, where the Divine is made manifest. The Divine is inherent within all things, at all times, in every place – there is no place where God is not.

This is a wonderful spiritual practice then to take on. To say to yourself, 'Blessings are upon me, each and every day of my life' ...and so it is with us all. And then to ask to be shown how that is true & to practice seeing it every day in every way in all things.

As you open your heart to this practice and this way of being, so blessings will visibly shine forth upon you, because you are looking for them, and practicing how to see them, and know that they are there, even in the darkest corners.

May blessings pour down upon you, each & every moment of your life. All is well, all is well, all is well. Blessed Be. Amen."

God is bringing you home to yourSelf

Sarah steps forward now as an Ascended Master guide to show us how to master this skilful balance of light and darkness. And she is saying that as human beings we are ready to balance the polarities within ourselves, and we are at the forefront of learning this skill of bringing unity consciousness to our day-to-day life.

We have the hard work of letting go of our old ways; often through being forced into this process, by our old lives simply not working for us in any way anymore - or simply by not being able to move forward until we clear the way), standing amidst the wreckage of our lives wondering what the hell is going on, and then through allowing divine grace to intervene, the new shoots can begin to form, often growing up through and around the broken pieces of our lives, to create something completely new.

Never doubt then that Sarah's energy can feel catastrophic and painful, something that can mainly be appreciated positively in hindsight, and can give new meaning to what would otherwise be seen as disastrous. In truth, this feeling of catastrophe, is our ego's reaction to our old safe lives being pulled apart, the ones that were keeping us stuck in our limitations, and stopping us from growing.

"Welcome brothers, welcome sisters, welcome all!

I am Sarah, come to tell you of your beauty and the wonder of the world!

Do you hear my call, my call bringing you back home to yourselves? There have been many times in your lives that you have heard this call, but not always known it for what it was. Yet the call it was!

But God does not weary or grow impatient, but instead looks for the opportune moments in your life, where you are most likely to hear the call.

The call back home to yourSelves!

Often the call sounds like alarm bells to you, as it is those times when things are breaking and shattering all around you, that God is calling out to you!! God calls out to you at these times because it is a window of opportunity to reach into the confined thinking of your ego and create a new vision, a new perspective, a new way to be and to do.

When all is going well, and you are happy and content in your life, there is no reason to change, no reason to search for a new way, and so no new growth is achieved. When all is shattered and broken, you have the greatest momentum to move forward, and if there is nothing left to mend, then it is well with you to start anew as you have no other option!

This may sound like the greatest cruelty, but you came here to grow, not to be comfortable! Your egos like to get themselves to a place of feeling comfortable, and then to stay there as long as possible; no matter that the situation does not suit the needs of the soul, which wishes to progress and grow and evolve.

Oftentimes, the situation suits the needs of the soul for a while, while you are learning some lesson or skill, and when it is time to move on, the ego becomes stuck in its sense of safety and comfort and drowns out the voice of the soul.

Then your Higher Self, which is your individuated spark of God, and how God manifests itself in the physical world, finds a way to loose you from your self-imposed prison, to which you have become comfortably accustomed and frees you from yourself by creating a situation in your life where something has to change!

Perhaps a man or woman walks in or out of your life, through death, love or hate. Perhaps something happens so that your eyes are opened and you can no longer see the world through the distorted vision that you did, and are forced to confront the reality of the situation with clear vision!

There are many ways for God to reach you, and each of you can think of your own situations where life has been blown apart for you. But can you also see that this is a blessing for you; that God's love is so great, that he is reaching out for you in these moments, calling you home? How can this be, you may ask?!

In all your moments of your everyday life, your comfortable existence, your level of consciousness is on the vibration of the ego, and you are not listening to your soul. When your life falls apart, and crisis comes, you are driven into a state of shock. Your heart is broken open, and in that time, there is a space for grace to come in, which is God. Your customary deafness has gone, and all of your senses are acutely aware of what is going on around you, and where you are. Your ego defences have gone, shattered, and you are not sure where you are, or where you are going!

This is a wonderful space in which to grow something new, for God's voice to whisper in the darkness, and because you are lost and alone, frightened and afraid, you can hear that voice whispering to you in the wind, as your ego lies trembling in a corner, unsure of the next move, having lost confidence in itself!

And wherever that voice whispering to you may seem to come from, whether it's an inspiration from a book, or the trusted voice of a friend, a passing comment from a stranger, or even a thought plucked out of the sky, you are more likely to listen to it, because in the midst of your crisis, you sure as hell don't know what to do!!

And there, there is this new opportunity, this new thought, that was never there before, and perhaps you wouldn't have ever considered before, in your comfort and your ease, your place of stagnant stuckness where you were existing. But were you truly alive?!

God is your friend and wants you to be happy and joyful, full of love and life!

But also, just as a friend holds the hope that her dearest friend will leave her alcoholic husband or his cheating wife, so God holds the hope for you, that you will always be growing into better things, and not staying stuck and stagnant where you are!

Of course, you can choose to make these changes without inviting in crisis and discontent, you can ask for Divine Guidance and listen to those small whispers in your ear showing you the way to go.

But sometimes, just sometimes, the risk seems too great to the ego to leap into the unknown, and even the greatest of us here on the physical plane are human beings with all our frailties and fears and worries, and being comfortable is no bad thing, and something quite natural to want! And in these times, God will lend you a helping hand, by forcing things a little!

So, when crisis and strife enter into your life, give thanks to God for the blessings being bestowed upon you, but make it very clear that you want to know what they are!! Then the suffering can be worthwhile.

Many a woman will gladly suffer labour pains for the joy of seeing her child, and all of us have laboured and worked to give birth to the things we want to create and manifest in our lives. And so it is with our greatest moments of loss and grief, heartbreak and pain.

We are working and labouring and struggling to bring out the best in ourselves, because God would only employ such drastic measures for the most important of things, so you be assured that if crisis is in your life, there is a very good reason for it!

Perhaps you are meant to learn how to love, or be loved. To trust or be trusted, or whatever it is that will benefit you the most right now, and bring you home to who you truly are.

Love, peace, strength, joy, prosperity, abundance, harmony, health!

God is bringing us home to ourSelves, if we could only see what is meant for us to learn, become and be. And we can. You can.

Learn to see as God sees, see the blessing in every situation, trust that everything that happens in your life, is leading you back home to yourSelf, to God. This is the path to enlightenment."

Of course, this isn't the only way to Sarah through crisis and dire events, but it is a way to connect very strongly and powerfully with her energy, should you just happen to come across her when these things are happening in your lives.

Sarah's message tells us that we are not doing something wrong by having dark and light in our lives; in the eyes of Sarah, everything in our life is a blessing… This is a wonderful practice and really useful.

Everything that happens in daily life can be taken as expressly being there for our greatest good, which means that we can ask (what feels like) the negative in our life what it is there to teach us.

For the most annoying/difficult/stuck things in our life, one way of doing this is to ask ourselves the question 'if this event/issue/person was there for my highest good and greatest learning, what benefit could I be getting from it right now?' and see what answer comes. It can be easier to write it down. We don't have to accept that the situation is for our highest good when we ask ourselves the question (which is just as well!!). This is why this exercise can work so well, as we receive insights that we never would have imagined!!

Sarah's gift to us is to shine the light into the darkness, to give us the higher perspective and the spiritual gifts that are inherent within every crisis and difficulty of our lives. These difficulties are in fact the most beautiful gifts we can be given, if we just know how to look.

Being Loved

When I read this next channelling, the biggest thing that comes through is that energy of being loved, just perfectly loved, not for doing anything, just for being. Many of us have experienced this as babies, or in loving our own babies. Even if we haven't, we have the memory, often in our subconscious, of being loved this way by the Divine. When we get down deep enough in ourselves, we KNOW it is true, even if perhaps we can't feel it consciously. The more we work with this practice, the more conscious the memory becomes. It's a lovely channelling and practice. There's mention of 'coming home', and to me that means 'coming home to mySelf', i.e., consciously reconnecting to the Divinity inside of me (which I am always connected to) so that I can know it, feel it, and BE it! Amen!!

"Welcome all. I am Sarah. Today I would speak to you of many things, but really, they are all one. Just as although you are all many, you too are all one.

I have come to you today to speak to you of love. Of the love that is most simply held in your hearts, of the love that is there as a memory, the memory of being perfectly loved, perfectly held, of nothing else in that moment except that perfect sense of love.

Can you feel your hearts stir in memory, held in the depths of yourSelf, can you feel the warmth of that love, long forgotten now by your conscious minds, but held there nonetheless in perfect harmony, perfect peace, perfect love.

This is the love that the Divine has for you, just for you, that love you can feel, and every time you love somebody else, perfectly or imperfectly, you can do so, because your soul remembers that first time you came into existence and were loved, for being ……. exactly that, you were loved just for being, and you didn't have to do anything, or be anything or say anything clever, or be the best in your class. You didn't have to be better than the rest, you didn't have to be anything at all, because you already were ……. Perfect, whole & complete.

And this memory is held within each of us; with our intent, and with Divine Grace, we can find it there, and once that memory is found, what does it matter if we are not the cleverest, or the best? We are perfect exactly as we are, else how could we be loved so perfectly?!

And so it is, when many babies are born into the world, that they find themselves loved in this way. The essence and energies of the pure creative force of the universe, is in them, and around them, and that baby knows that it is loved, just for being exactly the way it is. And when the baby is loved in this way, so for a moment we have emulated our Divine Creator, & in that moment feel the bliss & ecstasy of **loving perfectly** that is our divine heritage.

And so it is, that with those around us, we forget little by little, how to love perfectly, we allow more of our mind's desires and wants, to dictate how we love… Looking sometimes for the perfect person to love, or hoping for the perfect child, or the perfect boss, the perfect parent, the perfect friend. And we forget that in loving, our highest goal can be, not loving the perfect person, and so bringing us bliss, but instead, loving perfectly, loving in the perfect way, loving simply for being. When we can love another or ourselves in that perfect way, simply for being, then we have come into alignment with the Divine Source, and stand reflected as our Maker.

And as with all things, the first step is to practice!

So, you could practise loving things just as they are. You could say to yourself, today I will practise loving myself just as I am. And just for that day, or that morning, have the intent of loving yourself. Notice the moments when your love for yourself fails and stutters away, and at that very moment, double the love you have for yourself, strengthen your resolve, and you will notice how helpful it is.

And when you do this practice with yourself, you might find that in these very moments when you are feeling cross with yourself, it is because you are struggling or suffering in some way, feeling less than, or worse than, and really quite suffering. Imagine how the Divine who loves you perfectly might respond to you in this moment, what would the Divine say to you and how would that feel. Have the intent of loving yourself, even if you feel anything and everything but love, (and of course, I would always recommend reassuring yourself with a 'all is well, all is well, all is well!)

And this intent allows a doorway to open for Divine Grace to come through, and you might find that your self-condemnation becomes that very doorway that the light of the Divine can enter through!!! And with that intent of loving, understanding can occur, and in the understanding, a healing can take place, and in that healing a new perspective can come in and take the place of the old, outworn habits of self-criticism.

Do the same with your loved ones, & just at the moment when they are being their most annoying to you, double the love you have for them. Bring your attention, your awareness to yourself, observe your annoyance and have the intention, the resolve that you feel twice as much love for them. Notice what changes, what shifts there are as you practice this more and more & what behaviours change.

With your loved ones, your partners and your children, observe how bringing love to bear does not result in repressing your true feelings, but that in speaking your truth, or in acting as you believe you must, love is coming to bear as well.

So if you would like to be as one with the Divine, then a mystery, a secret is that you must bring yourself into vibrational alignment with the Divine, and this is one way that can help you to do so, by intentionally acting as the Divine, and so little by little day by day, you will become more and more into alignment with the perfect pure vibration of the Divine Source.

Some might think it would take a lifetime or even many, many, many lifetimes to reach such lofty vibrational heights as these, but I tell you that in this time, and this place, and in this moment all is possible. Divine Grace is all around you of such incredible magnitude that even the very smallest effort, the very tiniest intent, will propel you forwards in such leaps and bounds that before you could never have imagined that you could reach so far, or climb so high or feel such bliss.

These are special times, and they are yours to seize the incredible opportunities that are existing right now, just for you, this is why you are here, why you came here, to remember who you are..........

Don't waste away your life, thinking enlightenment & ascension are only for the few. They are not, they're for all of us, all of us here on this earth have the potential for enlightenment, and a great proportion of us can achieve that in this very one lifetime we are living on this earth. Of course, many of you have the advantage, being old souls who have gone around the block a few times..........

So, what are you waiting for, don't you want to return home?!

All is well, all is well, all is well. Whether you achieve enlightenment within one lifetime is not the important thing for an eternal being! Any desire, any intent, any work or effort you make will move you closer to your goal, so why not start now & seize the opportunities held in this moment?

And just imagine now, how it feels to be held in that Divine Embrace, how good it feels that you are loved, and all is well, all is well, all is well. With these blessings showering down upon you, I give you my love, and bid you farewell.

Blessed be, blessed be, blessed be, Sarah"

All is Well

This teaching is possibly one of the most used of Sarah's teachings, and yet I don't think I have shared this channeling publicly for many, many years. It was published once in a UK spiritual magazine, 'Paradigm Shift', and then I don't think it's seen the light of day for a decade or so in its entirety! I've pondered upon the way it came through – from the Angelic realms. At the time, I think it was the best way to receive the teaching; through the dispassionate, purely objective and Divine Wisdom of the feminine aspect of Melchizedek.

Without that 'dispassionate-ness', there are sentences that could seem, well, a bit cruel if I'm honest. Or could perhaps make me want to tell God/ess to 'F*** off!' if I was in the middle of a crisis. But I think this teaching is not meant to be read in a crisis, but rather the teaching is to be read, stored away, and then when it's needed, we pull out the 'All is Well' practice.

When I read the channeling now, every time I see the word 'highest', I am also seeing the word 'deepest' as the counterbalance, or the other half of that truth. I think I can do this now, because in the 13 years since this was written, I have moved 'deeper into the centre of my being', which is a wisdom of the Divine Feminine. The 'highest' corresponds to the light within us, the Christ consciousness, or the Christ Flame, and the 'deepest' corresponds to the love within us, the humanity, which is the Magdalene Flame, the Divine Mother.

When this was initially channeled through me, I wouldn't have been able to understand the meaning of the 'deepest' part of my being, being able to respond in this way, because I hadn't done it yet! In actuality, the 'highest' and the 'deepest' are the same thing, seen each from a different place. Those of us who work with Sarah, are being called to experience both sides of the polarity; the Sacred Masculine, and the Divine Feminine, and then also the Divine Truth, that where one is, the other is also. That in truth, they are Oneness, and never apart. It just depends on how you're looking at them!!

I have personally used this teaching over and over again, for example, through my Dad's terminal cancer, through my family breakup, through my own health challenges. When the s**t really hits the fan, and I see only darkness (metaphorically speaking!), this is the practice that I pull out. It works. It always does something good when I use it.

"Welcome all. I am Lady Lucia, Queen of light, the female face of the Archangel Melchizedek. From the Angelic realms henceforth I come, to sprinkle radiance and light upon you all.

Within the polarity of your world do you live, and so where one exists the other must be. Great light brings forth great darkness, and great darkness brings forth great light. In the midst of suffering lies the key to the gift of compassion. One brings forth the other, when the keys are used to bring forth the highest vibrational potential. Why else would you feel compassion if there were not the suffering to bring it forth?

Turn not your face away then from the darkness of the world; use it as an opportunity to bring forth light. Do not overwhelm yourself with suffering and pain, do what you can, stay in tune with your own needs, your own light. We must all work as to our own needs, our own light, listening always to the voice within. But this I would say, if all turn away from negativity, who will be there to bring the balance? It is not 'healing' of which I speak, although this is one way to understand the need to bring forth the highest potential, but more allowing another perspective in.

Imagine if, in each situation in the world in which there was pain or suffering involved, imagine if all that was brought forth in response was love. There would the darkness stop, balanced once again by the light. That if the suffering of an individual increased through illness and disease, they were proportionally surrounded by that much more love and assistance. Each situation then which mankind would traditionally think of as 'bad', would then become an opportunity for the light.

This is what we attempt to do from the angelic plane. When mankind is in trouble, we gather all around to give our aid. And if you are never in trouble, how will you learn how to call forth that help to you, to learn that it is there? The help is there, just for you.

When the darkness intrudes into you, and you feel it all around, that is because you have become sympathetically attuned to the vibrations of the dark.

At these times, it is well to remember that in each moment, all possibilities exist, the possibility for dark and the possibility for light, and that all you need do is refocus your attention on the divine reality that 'all is well', and of course it is, how could it be any other way, your true selves, your real selves are all at one, you are all the Divine, and your lives here on earth are as a film or a video playing in which you get to choose in each and every situation how to respond. If you believe in the darkness, then that is what you will become.

So, remember, the next time something is happening in your life that concerns you, breathe into your heart* and affirm 'all is well' with each breath in until you feel yourself lifted into a higher place.

If a wrong has been done to you and you feel perhaps hurt, angry or betrayed, breathe into your heart centre, affirm all is well until you feel the possibility that this might be so, and look at the situation afresh with new eyes & see what this opportunity may hold. Do you need to speak your truth, to be a warrior for the light? Can you use this opportunity to show yourself how much love and commitment you have for yourself that you are prepared to nurture and protect yourself by making a stand for yourself?

If a loved one is in trouble or suffering, and you feel the Divine has turned their face away to allow such troubles, such suffering, breathe into your heart and affirm 'all is well' with each breath in, until you feel the possibility that this might be so.

You could ask and pray for support and help to be able to withstand the suffering of your loved ones, so that you may remain a beacon of light when all seems dark.

You might pray for greater understanding if it is yours to be had, and understandings and illuminations may come, that this is the wish of your loved one's soul and higher self that they go through this experience for the highest good of their spiritual growth, that whilst their physical and emotional bodies are for the moment going though pain, their souls are learning beautiful gifts which will be with them for eternity.

Who are you to say that this should not be so because you struggle to stay with their suffering?

If you are watching the television and you see terrible suffering there, you could throw yourself down into darkness thinking it is all wrong, or you could turn your face away. Or perhaps you could stay with the belief that the Divine's plan for the earth and for humanity is built upon a rock, and that whilst you see out to the world from your own eyes, you do not have the entire plan presently at your fingertips, and that despite outer appearances, it is possible that all is as it should be.

If you have reached a point of resilience within yourselves, and if you feel you can hold the divine truth of 'all is well' in your heart, when you witness great suffering taking place around the world on the television, you can simply observe the suffering and do this practice of breathing into your heart centre, breathing in 'all is well', and then breathing that energy out into the suffering of the world.

There are always many ways to see a situation, and on each level, all of them are true. If you wish, your goal can be, always to see the highest possible perspective in each situation.

If you can remember to remind yourself that all around you is the Divine, that you are the Divine, and that you are a part of the Divine's plan here on earth, then with each challenge you are confronted with in your life, you will be able to remind yourself, 'all is well', and lift yourself up from any despair or whatever your own individual dynamics might be; to once again connect to the highest possible potential in that situation, and once again open to all the divine opportunities for you to express your own most beautiful light here on earth in response to this challenge.

If you can know deep in your heart that despite outer appearances, 'all is well', then this allows you to respond always from your highest places, your highest selves, and is a most beautiful gift to learn and be given through divine grace. You don't have to know how 'all is well', or even entirely what it means, but simply have the intent that through breathing this into your hearts and stating that it is so, you might come to know this Divine truth, through Divine grace, with every part of your being.

All these things you have come here to learn, do not worry that you do not know them already, encourage yourself in each tiny step you make every day, breathe into your heart, knowing all is well."

it is suggested that for greatest effect, you breathe into the 'Hrit Padma', see glossary for more details.

In Sarah's Presence

To be inside Sarah's space is to get very real inside of yourself! In her presence we start to connect to everything that is inside us. This can feel very grounding. I often cry when I connect to her presence, because of all the things, often small things, that I have been holding back. We often keep ourselves 'away from' stress or painful and difficult feelings. In Sarah's presence, we become more whole, more integrated, more real. Of course, this is our natural state, but many of us have moved away from this due to our upbringing, cultural conditioning and wounds from this and past lives; we have developed ways of separating ourselves from our natural feelings and our truthful thoughts. 'Lightworkers' have a tendency, sometimes without realising it, to 'escape up' to get away from emotional pain. So, when we come into contact with Sarah's presence, we can feel quite heavy in our

bodies and in our being, as her presence moves us back towards our natural state of being. Which in this physical incarnation is to be a spiritual being incarnated on the earth, and in a state of Oneness and Integration. We often practice bringing in Sarah's Presence in the meditations we do with Sarah, in our Priest/ess groups and online in the Facebook groups.

All is God/ Journey into darkness

This emphasises many of the points made in the last channelling. I love the passion in it!

"Blessings be upon you. I am Sarah.

Darkness is a time for you to develop your strength, overcome your fears and light up your life. Until the darkness comes, what little will you know of these fears? When it comes, batten down your hatches, go into the quiet spaces, fill up your reserves with food and water, as you may not be going out for some time. Be with what you need to be with. Say hello to what is there. Try not to judge, to dismiss, to cast away. It has come to tell you its story. And it deserves to be heard.

We are drawn ever towards the light, back home to ourselves, but we do this by going through into the darkness, those darkest places in ourselves, where we have hidden our most shameful secrets, our deepest pains, those things in ourselves which we wish never to see again, never to feel or hear or even know about. And yet they are there, waiting in the darkness, waiting to be owned, and honoured and acknowledged as part of ourselves.

We could see these parts of ourselves as our children. Those children born out of wedlock, and born of rape and brutality and war. Do we leave them as orphans? Neglected, unfed, uncared for? Kept back in the shadows so that the decent people might live a life uncast by their reflection.

Or do we say, come, come, come out into the light. Come bring, your pain and your suffering, bring all that you are. We are ready to hear you!

This is my gift to you, of love and light, beauty and darkness, all together, all whole, all as one. To love what is there, what is. To love it as it is, in all its putridness, and deformity and decay; in its ugliness, and terror and intolerable pain. To love whatever is there, as yourself, as God, in all its entirety.

All is God. And from the rich, damp and dark, fertile places can a new life arise. Born from the darkness, released from the very fetidness that was so foul in shadows; the vileness taking on new life, new love as it becomes the very medium for growth into the light that was always longed for, the journey into enlightenment that you craved.

Look, look into the darkness.

For I tell you this is the primal matter of creation that will give you the spiritual growth you long for. It is your fuel, your unformed clay waiting to be given shape. It is your mud from which the lotus will reach up and be given unto perfection.

See what it is there, let yourself be with it. Let your hearts be full of joy even as you undergo the sacredness of the journey into the shadows.

All is well, all is well, all is well.

You are God ever expanding, ever being, ever growing; light and life, death and darkness, all are one, all are part of the same journey of creation.

All is well, all is well, all is well. May blessings be upon you, each and every moment. Dedicate all that you are, all that is in your life, to God, to your inner divinity.

All is well, all is well, all is well. Sarah."

Interdependency

Sarah's overall message is of integration and oneness. Although this message is short, it shouldn't be thought of as inconsequential. Sarah has always showed me humanity as a circle, each of us a point of light in that circle, each of us having our own unique and perfect place in the circle, and together making up the whole. We all need each other in so many different ways. Balance as always is the key. Interdependency, not neediness (overdependence) or independence (separation).

And although Sarah is balanced, whole and complete in herself (as an archetypal force) she still needs people! Her human self in her life as Sarah needed people, and she suffered when those needs weren't met, just as we do. We are not supposed to do everything on our own. Each one of us holds the perfect piece of the whole. No-one else can do the particular thing that we, each as a unique being can do. Sarah is always impressing this on me, the beauty of reaching out to others when we need them, and allowing them to give their unique gifts to us – and how much joy that brings to all!

"Welcome, I am Sarah.

Blessings are upon you this day as you bravely open up yourselves to more beauty, more joy, more love, more excitement, more inspiration, more magic, for many wonderful things are coming to you even as the challenges also keep coming. Help each other, support each other, be strong together.

Do not be afraid to reach out to your friends and family and your support groups that you have. Reaching out to those people who will understand, who know the reality of life on earth, with all of the things that you are going through.

Be grounded, be real. Love each other.

My blessings are upon you each and every moment of your day. I understand your difficulties. I understand your sufferings. I love you.

I am always here for you. Whenever you need me just call. Blessed be. Blessed be. Blessed be. Amen."

The Dalai Lama says this about interdependency,

'Things are highly interdependent. The very concepts of "we" and "they" are becoming irrelevant. War is out of date because our neighbors are part of ourselves. We see this in economic, educational and environmental issues. Although we may have some ideological differences or other conflicts with our neighbor, economically and environmentally we share essentially the same country, and destroying our neighbor is destroying ourselves. It's foolish.' (from Illuminating the Path to Enlightenment.)

It is 'us' that are living on the earth as the human race – not 'us' and 'them'. We are One.

Co-creating with the Divine

This next question was asked by the host during a podcast interview with me and Sarah. I love the answer that Sarah gave and the beautiful teaching in it – it's one of my favourites! When you read this, really take the time to do what Sarah is suggesting, and come and write your experience on one of the Facebook or Instagram pages that we have – we'd love to hear!!

Q: *What is really going on at the moment? What is the bigger picture behind the global fear, the fear mongering, the restriction, the lockdowns, the mandatory masks and now the push for the global vaccination programmes? What's really behind this?*

"Welcome! I am Sarah.

Thank you for calling in my presence on this day so that I may share this light of oneness and integration. As has been said, it may seem as if this is a time of darkness to many on the earth, challenging it is certainly, but there never has been a more necessary time for each of you to co-create from the space of your heart. So, if you go inside to your heart now, right into the very, very centre of your being and send out an image of how you would like the earth to be and one really good way to find this out is to look at the earth as it is and notice all the things that particularly affect you, all of the things that emotionally distress you.

Now each of you has to co-create in your ways, your own unique way. Each of you has your own unique purpose so take those things that particularly emotionally distress you and then ask yourself: what would the polar opposite be? What would the positive affirmation be of this negative feeling, of this negative situation that I experience in the world?

Now say that over and over again inside your own heart and imagine that that affirmation is growing and glowing in energy, coming stronger and stronger and sending off a beautiful light into the world. Now this is one small thing that you can do each day or each time that you experience distress about the world that you are living in. Take a few moments to send out from your heart, from the intelligence and the power and the love of your heart right at the centre of your being. Take a few moments to send this out and experience the shift in yourself and know that you are adding to the world's healing and when I say the world, I mean the earth and I mean humanity.

Now let me see, what else can be said upon this very important subject for the times you are living in at the moment? The world is always kept in balance and again when I say the world, I mean manifest creation. You are living in a world of polarity and things must always be kept in balance. This means that if darkness increases on the earth, so must the light. These are the laws of the universe that you live in.

Everything is always kept in balance and there are specific deities and light beings who work towards this.

Now then, imagine the amount of light that must be coming in at the moment to counter the distress. Perhaps the Divine plan is greater than can possibly be imagined and that all is well, all is well, all is well.

I do not mean this as a platitude, I do not say it contritely, but it is important to keep yourself connected to that level, even whilst allowing yourself in your full humanity to experience all of the emotions that you need to feel about your situation. It is important not to bypass what you feel in your body but to allow it to express it and to love it and then to bring in the higher, the Divine— all that comes through you from your Higher Self and from the divine beings that are around you.

I would like to send out a blessing to each of you now and I will just take a few short moments to express some sound and some toning and this blessing holds the energy, the quality of the integration and the oneness that is your next divine step on your path of humanity. So if you feel comfortable and if you so wish, imagine you're opening up your energy body now in your heart to receive this divine energy of Oneness and Integration as it comes through.

I am Sarah and my blessings are always upon you. You may call upon me and I will be a sister walking at your side, catalysing your process and bringing blessings down upon you.

I am Sarah and these are the words I wish to speak this day. Blessed be, blessed be, blessed be, Amen."

Be honest and true to yourself

These two channelings talk of the courage and bravery that is needed to be honestly yourself!

"Welcome I am Sarah! Blessings be upon you, my presence is with you. Encourage yourself absolutely. Be honest with yourself, always scrupulous. Be brave, notice where you make mistakes, or would like to do something differently. But allow yourself to be as you are.'

Know YourSelf

I love this fabulous channeling from the Archangel Michael, so strong and powerful, and is totally aligned to Sarah's teachings! I've always felt that he is a part of the 'Holy family' although I've never read this anywhere, but that's how it is in my head anyway!

"I am the Archangel Michael, and I come to tell you of the courage that will be yours, as you walk this path of the heart. Many eons ago, when men walked with the angels, so it was that we could discuss these things among you as brethren. Now in these times, things are a little different, and our communications often stay at the outer edges of your energetic aura, looking for a way in, a way to take hold, because I tell you, with all true communication that is spoken from the heart, these things are not just words, they have a form, a shape, a life even.

And so the communications we choose to express to you, are not just idle thoughts flitting through our minds, but carefully crafted divine truths that are understood by the one who is giving in its every depth and breadth, and every which way possible.

So are divine truths best imparted, by one who has learnt that truth from beginning to end and back again. And so, some of you find yourself learning things on earth in great depth, and in great detail, and so it is, that when these lessons have been learnt far past their superficial mind depth that is contained within the left brain (part of your logical thinking/memory); so it is, that in illustrious illumination, you know a thing so well and in such depth - because you have *lived* it every which way, and learnt it from beginning to end and back again, that you can impart these things to your fellow humans, and even to unseen spirits of nature and others that share creation with you.

And so it is, that I Archangel Michael, choose channels and choose to tell you of subjects which are in my sphere of expertise. I am known as the hand of God, wielding truth and justice with my sword.

I am a fighter, a warrior, and I have great honour and nobility, just as many of the world's warrior classes have chosen to emulate.

I am a warrior for God! Think not that passivity is the only spiritual way.

I hold the power of fire in my hands, and I wield it through the sword of justice, and take dynamic action where I see truth being slayed in the world of men. And so it is that on the path of the heart, a way home to the Divine, I too have my part.

A warrior for God must also know themselves, must slay untruth and injustice which lays within their very own heart. Because this way of the warrior, honouring truth and justice, can be turned to the inward path, and the principles are the same. Be ruthless and fearless in finding out the truth within yourself. Take no prisoners on your path to discover all that is divine within you. Do not dilly dally on your path, wandering this way and that, but keep your clear focus on the goal ahead.

The Divine itself.

We Angels can look on the face of the God directly. You must see the Divine as reflected in a mirror. But you can listen to our message of hope, that the universe around you is as the divine made manifest, and if you know how to look, how to listen, you can find the Divine there.

Today, I have come to tell you of courage. As with all things, courage exists as an energy, and has its own frequency, its own vibration. Naturally within yourselves, your own ego tries to protect you, to save you from suffering and sadness, a noble aim within itself, but one that ultimately keeps you from ever finding your true Selves.

When you can muster enough courage and care for yourself, when you are brave and true, clear and resolute in yourSelves, you can say to yourself, gently whisper to your ego, 'It's OK, all is well, you don't have to protect me anymore, you've worked so hard and so long now, and it's time for you to rest, all is well, I am here now, I am here.'

And calling on your courage, you can direct the world, the universe, to help you uncover the last vestiges of your hidden selves, all that remains in the subconscious awaiting healing, and your courage will see you through, and keep you warm, when the feelings and memories that may arise would make you cold with their sadness and rage, but you can, with the way of the heart, call on the love of the Divine Mother to see you through, and offer you hope and comfort in your time of despair.

And I, Archangel Michael, I know this energy of resolute unwavering, of staying faithful to my cause, and carrying out the work I have committed to do, despite the suffering that may seem overwhelming at times, and I offer this to you now.

I offer you this hand of unwavering courage, that will burn bright even in the darkest of nights. For it is that time now for you, for those of you, who would integrate the last of themselves, and overcome the illusion of the self, to be born anew into the Divine Self, re-created in the alchemy of the heart, a new path forged ahead.

All is new, all is new, all is new.

My hand never wavers because I have absolute certainty. I have absolute certainty that this is the way to the Divine, and the prize is so great, that no suffering could be so great as to make it not worth its while.

And so it is with you, when you cry out in despair and misery for me to help, I will always be there, showing you the way forward, shining my light upon you, and showering the radiance of fearlessness and resolute conviction for walking your path.

I can, with objectivity and knowing as I do, the ultimate goal, the ultimate prize, which is all that is real, and all that is true, I can, easily and effortlessly burn with the fire of hope and illumination, showing you the way home to yourSelves.

These are the words which I would share with you today, I, Archangel Michael, warrior for God, showing you ways to slay illusion and suffering so we may walk once again together as brethren, and humanity can be restored to its proper place.

I give you blessings of fiery light upon your path.

Blessed Be. Blessed Be. Blessed Be.

Archangel Michael."

You are a Brave Pioneer

"You are expanding yourselves into new states of being; humanity is growing, changing, evolving, and you are at the very forefront of this expansion! This change has never been undergone before, you are pioneers! Courageous, brave and curious! Courageous and brave, because your courage and bravery will see you through your doubts, worries and fears. I will help you to discover your own individual ways of working with them, recognising that they are an integral part of the process, and that by working with them, there is much to be learnt from them, many gifts of wisdom they have to impart!' Courageous and brave, because you are stepping into the unknown, 'going where no-one has gone before', and taking humanity into previously uncharted spiritual territory."

We are Already Home

'Welcome. I am Sarah. Today I would speak to you of manifest creation; of the world in which you live. Throughout history, there have been many ways of thinking of manifest creation; each has had its use and its own appeal. Within each idea there has been something useful for mankind to work with. But now we are approaching a time where we know deep in our hearts that the manifest creation which we see all around us, is no different from the transcendent God nature which we know we will return to when we are out of this life. It is time for us to stop longing to go home.

We already are home!

Everything else is an illusion.

There is nowhere we need to get to, nowhere we need to get away from, nowhere to run to.

We are already here.

Everything that exists is of God.

All else is illusion.

It is time for us to know this in our hearts, so that we can manifest it in our lives, and live in accordance with Divine Truth, which is All That Is. Of course, there are many deeply held beliefs and energy structures of the mind that exist within each of you, that have been sitting there for eons, happily living out their existence through the world of illusion.

But I tell you this, the day is approaching fast, where all illusion will fall away, and all that is real will be as clear and as apparent as your own reflection in the mirror. This is happening here on the earth, not in another life or another dimension, but here in physical reality, in physical life, in all of its day to dayness.

All is well, all is well, all is well, you are a child of the universe, a child of the Divine.

You are loved beyond measure, beyond compare.

All is well, all is well, all is well.

Let the illusion fall away from your eyes, and as it does, honour it by feeling the pain that it caused you to feel those things. They were felt by you. So it was, and in the feeling of those things, so you can let them go and watch them as they fall to the ground and return from whence they came.

The chains are becoming unbound.

Nothing will remain, all is well, all is well, all is well.

You can imagine to yourself, 'If I believed that everything in my life was of God/Goddess. That there was nowhere different I needed to be, do or change, what would I want to do today?!!' And see what comes to you. Call on me when you do this, as I can shine the light of the Divine a little closer in your eyes, helping you to see all that is real, and removing all that is unreal.

There is nowhere we need to be, get to or away from.

All is here, all is here, all is here.

Blessings are upon us all, each and every moment of our lives. Blessed Be, Blessed Be, Blessed Be. Amen.'

Dance with Life

And lastly, I want to leave you with this last gem! There's a lot to unpack here, and it's worth re-reading it again and again - as it is with many of Sarah's channelings.

"Welcome I am Sarah!

Dance! Dance with life! Dance as if your life depended on it! Dance to BE here. Dance to the tune of your OWN drum.

Live your life, as though it were a DANCE. When you feel sad, do your sad dance, full of grace and beauty, but sad nonetheless. When you are happy do a HAPPY dance, full of joy and fun and playfulness perhaps, bringing joy to those around you.

Dance brings out the beauty in all aspects of life, dance expresses the nobility, the grace, the raw terror, the frustrations and the gut-wrenching sadness, even the ugliness… dance expresses it all. It doesn't try to change anything, it doesn't judge, and neither should you.

Live your life AS IF you were dancing. Find the poetry in what you do, the humour, the meaning in the everyday…… just as the dance would do.

Movement is part of your sacred expression. To help you express your life (as it is being lived through you), you could imagine (or better still actually do it!) a dance pose to your current situation, or your feeling state in this moment. Would it be a dramatic move, or would it be a quiet and inwardly reflective gesture?! You could do a dance of your day and its events, or a dance of fury and rage, or a dance of thankfulness and gratitude. You could dance to express yourself (of what you are feeling right now), and a dance to take you where you want to be (so that could be a dance to conjure up the gratefulness inside you). You simply start with your intent. Write down, 'I will dance to express how I feel right now', or 'I will dance to help me find the peacefulness inside me', **

Sometimes in life, you dance alone, other times you dance in a group, or in a partnership. Sometimes the dance consists of stepping on each other's toes and you move on! Other times, a dance rises up of incredible grace and beauty that comes seemingly out of nowhere, and takes you completely by surprise, and then is over just as quickly as it started, leaving you a little out of breath and startled.

Some dances you know very well, others are not so familiar! But a comfortable, familiar dance can one day suddenly become difficult to dance to. It's just not your rhythm anymore! And a new dance has to be found.

If you love to dance, imagine this, imagine you are transferring that love you feel when you dance, into your life. When you are dancing, don't you want to keep going? Even when you are tired? Doesn't it make you want to keep going, keep moving forward, backward, sideways?!!

The dance never stops, never dies, it just changes.

I am Sarah, and I tell you that dancing is what you're doing. You are in every moment, expressing life through you. You are creating each moment, as that life lives through you. The life that is lived through you comes from source, the way that you dance it, is your choice, your decision, your power.

This is the dance of your life.

Let your body move!"

*** you could also dance to invite in the energies of Sarah, and allow them to move through you, or to dance with them…..*

CHAPTER 7

Weaving the Oneness

The Golden Thread

Many of us in modern times, associate gold with a masculine sun. However, the old Norse saw 'Sol/Sunna' as a sun goddess. The Spanish name 'Solis' (also derived from the Latin root 'sol'), which literally means sun, was once received as a name for Sarah, and is interestingly a gender-neutral name.

Gold is spiritually associated with higher ideals, wisdom understanding and enlightenment; it is generous and giving, compassionate and loving, sharing that wisdom, knowledge and wealth with others. Optimistic and positive, gold adds richness and warmth to everything with which it is associated, and illuminates and enhances whatever is around it! In our world of polarity, we can still bring our consciousness into a state of oneness, and shine this inner golden quality out into the world!

In this chapter we look at duality and oneness. Not an easy task for our left brain thinking, linear as it is, but perfectly felt in states of right brain consciousness and divinely so!

Here we talk about the Sarah codes** and how they are helping us to create the Rose Sophia Christ consciousness - and we also talk about the polarities that we struggle with; the light and the dark, male and female, heaven and earth. Ultimately, and in a state of integrated consciousness, we can see that they are all One, when the Divinity within us becomes conscious. No longer buried in our subconscious as it is now, the golden nugget buried deep within us is projected out into the world around us - and reflected back as Ascended Masters, Beings of Light, Gods & Goddesses. One day we will see that these are all aspects of ourselves, and we will be able to live and own them as we walk the New Golden Earth.

This is the wonderful paradox of life on earth, to experience the duality, the many aspects of the Divine that we see in the world around us, and to appreciate each for its own unique beauty - and then, as we are now doing, to return to a place of unity consciousness, where we are also and at the same time as experiencing the duality, being aware of the oneness that is in all living things.

** The Sarah codes are codes of light that act upon our energy bodies each time we connect with her, and work on us so that we integrate all that we are; divine and human, dark and light, male and female.

'Has Sarah been working with us through the ages, and has her interaction with us changed (i.e., in the way she communicates with us?' (Question is from a live interview.)

"In all honesty, the energy that I carry has been slumbering in regards to humanity in the collective unconscious. The divine masculine and the divine feminine as understood as coming together in the sacred marriage, was created as a powerful energy matrix, that was also anchored here on the earth (by the Master Jesus and Mary Magdalene.)

The oneness that I represent (as an archetypal force), was planted here within that energy matrix as a seed. It was not the time for it to flourish then.

When a great thing happens in the space time continuum, there are always echoes going backwards and forwards. This is because time actually exists in physical manifestation, and exists as one whole piece of 'material time', all woven together as one fabric, one tapestry.

Powerful events, which have happened during the course of earth's and humanity's evolution, are always sending off these echoes as powerful vibrations, through the tapestry where humanity is living and existing.

My time**, which is coming into being now, and of which you are the forerunners or harbingers of, has also been 'sending off' a vibration, which has always been there for those sensitive enough to feel it. This has been present in the form of visions or dreams, but it also means that the energy that I represent has always been available for those capable of energetically holding it, whatever time or place that they live in, because they are able to reach through the mists of time to the place where my energy will be in manifestation.

I am simply an aspect of the archetypal force that I represent. This archetypal force belongs to the Divine, of which you are a part, and which is always accessible to you if you have the capability. But we are coming to a time now, where it will be much easier to access this archetypal force, because outwardly it will be more available, and will be mirrored to you much more easily.

I am Sarah and these are the words which I wish to say today. Blessed be, Blessed be, Blessed be, Amen."

** *by which Sarah means the time when her energy (the archetypal energy of oneness which she holds) is being held by the collective consciousness of humanity, and not just by her, and is fully anchored on the earth.*

Sarah Integrates!

I love this channeling; I can feel the magnetism within the words themselves!

"Welcome brothers, sisters, welcome all. I am Sarah, who watches from above and yet is within, I am she who moves in the darkness, and whispers in your dreams, I am that voice calling you home. I am the unseen until the very moment when you are ready to see, and then you can see that I was there all along, all along……

I am darkness until I am light, in the shadows until I am seen, invisible until I am known, transcendent and yet in physicality… Within and without, above and below, all things are as one, and my energy is that of oneness, of unity.

Work with me, and all parts of yourself, all parts of your being, scattered across space and time, will be called home, called back into oneness. My energy holds a magnetism that none can resist, a magnetic love if you will, that creates an irresistible force, calling all things back home to themselves. All those parts of you scattered across space and time will find a way, a homing beacon, back home to your souls…

And your bodies will find that they are irresistibly attracted to your souls, that they **have** to embody all of your soul being, as the powerful magnetic force that I carry of integration, calls your body and soul to be together, your physical body, powerfully grounding your soul here on earth.

And your soul's longing too, to be fully present in that divine spark that manifested you here in the beginning, to know that divine fullness of being within all of yourself, here on the earth; your soul's longing for home…

My energy can assist then in your work, in your efforts to bring parts of yourself back home to yourself. It will also help call into being those things and people in your life that are separate now, but are the missing pieces in your life.

As my light and my love resonates through your being, the magnetism playing upon the light of your soul attracts into being those situations that will call about all that has been lost and now needs to be found, people, places, parts of yourself and of your soul, dreams, memories, past lives, all of these things that are patiently awaiting the cosmic order of time and space.

I can be that force of acceleration for you, if you are ready for the challenges that it will bring with it, the lessons and learning, and necessary action to be taken in your lives upon the earth plane, the necessary discipline of living the Divine Truth here on earth!!... My path is not an easy one, and yet it is one of love and hope, healing and integration.

May blessings rain down upon you, each and every moment of your lives.

Namaste, Sarah."

Sara-la-Kali

Sarah is revered in Saintes-Maries-de-la-Mer on the coast on France, as the patron saint of the Romani people**. Here she is called Sara-La-Kali, which is French for Sara the black, and she has a much-loved grotto in the crypt of the church. The town was interestingly once called Ra, and has been a sacred site since prehistoric times. Once people came to worship at the sacred spring, which was dedicated to the Matronae, and in times gone by, temples dedicated to Midas and Artemis have both stood here. Now on the 24th May each year to honour Sarah, her statue of dark wood is taken in a procession down to the sea to re-enact her arrival in France. https://en.wikipedia.org/wiki/Saintes-Maries-de-la-Mer

I have a deep love for the energy of the black Madonna, and the dark aspects of the Divine Mother. As a sensitive and channel, these energies are something that I experience physically. When I channel this energy, it comes all the way over me in a very physical way, and part of me becomes them, as I embody them. I feel that the dark goddess is part of me, I feel her in me, I know her, and I love her passionately. She is me, and I am her! Sarah too has this quality. She comes to us in this aspect when we need to 'get real' with ourselves - those times when we are trying to hide from the dark, when we don't want to feel the pain, or when we are running away from those things we need to face. She shows us who we are, and takes us through the darkness into the light.

**This is not the same as the Catholic Saint Sarah, the wife of Abraham, whose feast day is on August 19th.

"Blessings. I am Sarah. Sometimes I am called Sara la Kali – 'Sara the Black'. This is rooted in myth and mystery and holds a key to the archetypal energy that I portray and which can be accessed through calling on me.

All that I am, and all that is, is part of Divinity's creation. There is nothing that is not of God. All is God. Each part of Divinity's creation holds the key to the light, because God is light; transcendent, formless, uncreated.

I am that which is created here on earth, the darkness; primordial matter. To reach the light of God, transcendent and formless, is to go through me, the darkness and manifest creation of form, matter and all being. But where I am, God is.

In the form, is the formless and so I am the potential of union in all things, bright and dark, good and evil - all serve the purpose of divinity, all things are there to serve the purpose of reaching in to find the light, or to find the darkness, until light and dark are perfectly balanced.

And in that perfect balance comes the occurrence of union, and the transcendent power of God (which is neither light or dark but is all) is released in its full potential, made visible and accessible here in manifest creation, the splendour revealed.

Within yourselves, the union and balance of perfect light, perfect dark, are the conditions met for the sacred lotus of the heart to open, the Hrit Padma**, connecting you to your Divine spark; and so revealing the light of your Higher Selves, your original Selves, so that you can

live here manifesting the light of God, your original Selves, fully upon the earth.

And so, to those of you who continue to work with alchemizing your lives, I say hold all that you do sacred, honour yourselves and the journeys that you are on. You are bringing in the light of the Divine with every effort to raise your vibration, with each attempt to live in your truth, and discover the light of the soul that is within you, and what you have come here to do.

Look for the sacred in all that you do, breathe into the sacred lotus of the heart, ask it to guide you, it is your inner Divinity, wrapped in the shrouds of darkness for now. With each breath into this sacred space, your energy, and conscious awareness causes the sacred soul to reveal itself a little more, and does this by shedding the layers of fear and doubt, anger and betrayal, confusion and uncertainty; look into your lives and dedicate all that you do not feel is 'of the light' to your sacred journey and continue to work with these things, doing all you are inspired and guided to do.

All of these things are a shedding of the wrappings and coverings and will result in the spontaneous revelation of that which is at the heart of your being, your Divine Self. And in the same way that it is possible for a labouring mother to guide herself to celebrate each contraction as being one step closer to reaching that of her heart's desires, her beautiful child held within and to rejoice in it, so it is possible to celebrate and give thanks for the painful and difficult challenges which are present in your lives, because they are bringing you one step closer to God, which is your very Selves.

Each challenge you are presented with, all that is in your life that is not as you would wish, all of this is given to you by God, so that you can find the gifts hidden within; the gifts of love and truth, warmth and compassion, strength and joy and so finding the light by going through into darkness.

Praise Divinity for giving you these things, because this is how you are taken into the light!! Rejoice in your own difficulties, your own suffering, because it is showing you the way back home to yourselves, showing you what needs to be shed, released, transmuted and transformed. Rejoice in the power of your own Alchemy, and give up expecting the difficulties not to be there, or that there is something wrong with you that they are there; everything is perfect exactly as it is. Hold the intent to give up all judgement, and just be with what is, ask it what it has come to teach you and let it reveal its perfect light.

Believe in yourSelves, that you have the power to be who you truly are. See your goal there shining at the end of your pathway. Do not waver, but hold it there with unrelenting intent. It shall be so!!

Through the holding of perfect balance of light and dark, you have learnt your own power and what you can do; alchemists you are and the workings that you do reverberate across the earth, nothing is separate, all is intertwined. Just by being, just by doing, just by holding that intent, you are sharing the transcendent light of God, with all of humanity.

May blessings pour down upon you, each and every day of your lives. Namaste. Sarah."

** *See glossary.*

Healing with Sarah & the Angels

Now you'd be forgiven for thinking that 'Healing with Sarah & the Angels' belongs in the 'Healing & Sarah's Angels' section, and yet, here it is! Although it technically is a healing system – because healing means 'making whole', you will see that it is another energy to the healing work that is in the healing section, and perhaps more represents 'our next step'. Indeed, Sarah is our next step, she is our future!

This is how 'Healing with Sarah & the Angels' is described in the healer manual,

'The word 'healing' means to make whole, or holy, and this is exactly what this system of healing is doing. As you read on, you will come to see how Sarah has come to teach us how to directly integrate the Higher and Lower Selves together, so that they are no longer apart. And how did this happen? I'll tell you a story…

In the beginning, times such as Lemuria, souls existed in a state of light density, they were able to very easily be whole and integrated, because they were not far down into density as we are today. The Divine vibrations of oneness, love, joy and so on were there all the time in our 'beingness', without effort or work. There are different explanations about why this ended, but end it did.

We fell further into matter. The higher, finer particles that make up our Higher Selves couldn't follow this far down into density, so we became separated, and we forgot…

So now we come to today.

We have come a long way since then and we are much further around the circle now. We have come to a place where it is time for us to reintegrate with our higher finer particles of our energy body once again, and come into full integrated consciousness with them. People use different words to describe this phenomenon, you can add your own here…

It is time for us to become 'whole' again. To remember who we are. To be fully integrated with the Universal Light Force Energy that is all that is. To be fully integrated with our Divinity.'

Now Sarah has come to help us do this in a number of ways. Each of us has our own path. Those of us who are esoterically minded will find esoteric ways of doing this work. Others will do it on other levels, emotional, physical, mental. But Sarah is here as an archetypal force. She is radiating out the energy of Unity and Integration to the world, and the world cannot help but respond!

In her healing system we see the incredible brightness, the whiteness of Sarah's Angels, so different to the cool dark subterranean energy of Sara-la-Kali, and yet they are both aspects of Sarah! She is a most fascinating Ascended Master to work with. She is in all of the Spheres!

Sarah's Flame

The way that Sarah acts upon our energy bodies is through the flame of Unity. This is how the power of the Divine works through her, and impresses the archetypal force she represents on the earth and humanity.

There are different ways to work with Sarah's flame. One way that we have used in 'Healing with Sarah and the Angels' is to work with three healing aspects of Sarah's flame - the white energy of Sarah's angels (and which also resonates to the divine spark held within each of us), Sarah's lilac violet flame, and then Sarah's energy of green, of nature, lifeforce and manifestation. In reality all of these energies exist within the whole, but it is incredibly useful to work with them as aspects in this way. But working with Sarah's flame in oneness, 'the flame of unity' is beautifully wonderful!!

"Welcome all, I am Sarah.

This evening, I bring you blessings in the form of my energy. As this flame pours out and overlays your own divine spark, so you are drawn and magnetised more and more towards being yourselves. This is humanity's greatest lesson now, to simply be more of themselves, to find and discover and tap into what is within each of you; your own unique individual essences and this is my gift. My gift to you is to make you more of who you already are. This is the path to dynamic peace, balance, integration, happiness, prosperity, abundance; all of

these things you long for. And this is the path, not to simply know these things, not to simply know that you are love and find those things that make you full of joy, but also to feel it within every particle of your being, to live being in that joy.

So much has been cleared and so much still needs to be cleared in the Collective Unconsciousness of humanity, in each of the Ancestral lines. But in this clearing, will you discover all of these wonderful beautiful divine gifts? The light is held within the darkness and all is well, all is well, all is well. But this next phase of your evolution will unlock much of what has been hidden before and it may seem that the darkness just seems to come up evermore and be evermore present and you may wonder, is this really how things are getting better? But then, as each step is made and each progress is made, you'll feel lighter and clearer and more centred and more yourself and you'll know all is well, all is well, all is well and then when the challenges come up, actually, it won't seem so difficult. You'll take them in your stride as you become stronger and more of who you truly are.

I am Sarah and I have come here to assist humanity in its work, and I am forever at your side and I am always here to add my presence and power should you wish it. I am working through all of those who call upon me, coming through you and to you, in a way that is physical. Through each of you. I am manifesting this Christ flame, this new energy that is coming here now. This Unity Consciousness, Oneness.

Blessings are upon you, each and every day of your lives.

Blessed be. Blessed be. Blessed be. Amen"

Ascended Master Sarah is a Wayshower

Sarah has been my Ascended Master teacher since 2006, and I sometimes feel a bit envious of other people when I hear they've been 'told' by Spirit to do such and such! I've tried to get Spirit to tell me what to do, but to no avail! Instead when I ask for guidance about what to do, I get given suggestions about how I can work that out for myself! This lifetime seems to be about me having to take responsibility for how I steer my life. This doesn't mean that I'm not trying to 'steer my ship' in accordance with the divine's will, not at all - it's just that Spirit, and in particular Sarah is of the opinion that it's about time that I learnt to do that myself! Even while I write this, I'm laughing at my own humanity, because truth is, if someone tells me to do one thing, I'm likely not to do it, because someone told me to! I've always been this way, and can remember my mum sighing and saying to me (after yet another bad decision) 'Well, you won't let anyone tell you what to do Rachel.' But!! I learnt a lot from making bad decisions in my youth, and like many spiritual type people, I have a natural inclination to not 'do what everyone else is doing', which can be troublesome at times, but which puts me in good stead for finding a third way (not doing what everyone else is doing, neither doing the opposite, but instead allowing a third way to emerge) that resonates with the New Earth and the 5th dimension! This is where Sarah comes in to help.....she is a *Wayshower*.

"Welcome, I am Sarah, and I come as an Ascended Master teacher guide or some would say, mentor. This is because I come to show you how to find that Divinity inside yourself. This is the last step, as it were, on the way to becoming masters yourself. This is the time now, for many of you in humanity. The oversoul of humanity is directing this last process, and although it may seem outwardly that all is chaos, from the point of view of the direction of evolutionary growth of the oversoul, there is an overall ripening and maturity that is affecting many thousands of souls right now. If you could see this phenomenon as colours, it would be a pearlescent rainbow of colours of pink and green, orange and blue, yellow and lilac, ivory and red....

I think that deep in your hearts many of you know this truth, but it seems hard to accept in the face of the 'proof' of what is going on around you in the world, and even in your own lives. Yet this is the path that has been laid for you, the path that has been laid by what has gone before, (*meaning that we have to work through what has already been manifested*) and now, as you come into your own mastery, you are learning what to do, and how to be, in order to step into that mastery yourselves. Each of you has a part of the divine plan within you. Each of you, makes up the whole. That divine plan is always shifting and changing in response to what is being manifested, and in that divine plan is the solution or should I say, the healing that is required. Within this healing is what will bring balance. So, where there is confusion, clarity can be brought. Where there is hatred, love can be brought to bear. Where there is sadness, joy. It is not so terribly complicated, is it? But what is much harder, and takes much more effort, is the learning of how to do these things! And how else would you do them, if you weren't in the perfect classroom where you are being forced to learn these things? (Necessity is the mother of invention!) When life is just 'good enough', it usually isn't uncomfortable enough to force one into making the effort to change, learn, transform and grow.

And as the darkness increases in the world, so does the light, because this is a world of polarity and so always keeps a balance. **Within me, there is no separation**. Within me, is held the archetypal force of oneness as it can exist upon the earth plane. Within me are the codes for how this oneness can be brought upon the earth plane, the plane of physical manifestation, and not just as an energy that is available on the higher dimensions. My father and mother came together in the sacred marriage, and from that union, a matrix of energy was born, you can imagine this as a sphere of light, (of pearlescent green) that holds the codes for humanity's next level of evolution. I, Sarah, hold that matrix, that sphere of light, and all who come into contact with me, come into contact with that light, which then in turn acts upon your lightbody. I am Sarah, and I tell you that the time has come for you to learn the hard lessons. Not because you are being punished for your sins, but because you are **ready**, and are ready to step up to the next level of your humanity. In this stepping up, there must be an acknowledgement of all that is within you, your darkness, your light, your divinity – and in this acknowledgment, which creates a 'beingness', this being able to be with all of the things that you are, then something else can come into being – and that is the '3rd way', something that is 'a being' born out of oneness.

I am Sarah and I have come to tell you of my news, that you are ready to hear, and that I am ready to speak. My circles of power resonate across the earth, even as your bodies soak up that which is needed. I am here to walk by your side. Blessings are upon you, each and every moment of your lives, Blessed Be, Blessed Be, Blessed Be, Amen!!"

Sarah's Evolutionary Blueprint embodied the male and the female in Oneness

'Lady Sarah, you unite and integrate the masculine and feminine energies of your parents, but when embodied, did you physically express this unity by having a hermaphroditic genotype/phenotype?'

"Welcome, I am Sarah. There are many mysteries upon the earth that humankind will come to know, and the mystery of the male and female forces is one that has come in and out of consciousness of many cultures & in many times. There is a great difference in perception as to what constitutes the male and the female, dependent on the time in history and the culture one has existed within. And yet these forces are real and apart from any perception, existing in their own right; the perception being only an interpretation of those very real forces. This is humanity's work then, to understand these forces for your own spiritual development, which is the only real goal that there is; as you develop spiritually, so you develop on the other planes as well, mental, emotional, physical. Never is one stage of development separate and apart from the other. It may seem so at times, if you look at one individual's life, or one stage of a culture's time; but always when these things are seen from the collective, as a whole piece of work in unity, as we can do here from the vistas of Spirit, then it can be seen that that stage where it seemed that only physical development was occurring or for example, only mental, was simply a time when that speciality of development that was occurring, simply needed that level of focus to the exclusion of all other things, to support that great development that was going on at that time. God's perfect plan is built upon a rock, and the Divine is always aware of all things happening, in all times, & in all places.

Which leads me back to your question? In this time of creation humanity is expanding into unity consciousness; yet this consciousness is currently based upon the physical reality of the individual separation of male & female, *(meaning we live in a physical world of polarity)*. Always one longs for the other, because it knows that it is only half there. This occurs until the development starts to happen on the inside, i.e., a person looks within themselves and sees that all of these forces are existing on the inside of themselves and are available to them from the depths of their soul. Nothing is missing. All is within.

The human race, on this level of its evolutionary path is meant to carry on developing within its current physical form of male and female, whilst at the same time learning how to honour the complement to itself, and yet from time to time there is born some individuals here and there that carry both genes of the sexes. In this way, these individuals help anchor and ground the reality of male & female existing as one on the level of the physical, which is a denser and slower form of vibration than the layers of spirit above. In this way, it provides a foundation for the higher work to occur. Not higher in the sense of better, but just in the sense of the speed of vibration. It is the same with those who are in one body and long to be in another. Through their challenges, which are many, they can discover within themselves, a sense of peace and completeness, by completing the changes within themselves that something deep within them dictates. This peace & completeness is partly from fulfilling their deepest heart's desire, but also from a resonance of unity consciousness. Although they have carried the changes out on the physical, there is also a sympathetic result on the other levels and layers, like a stone thrown into still water, it ripples out through the layers of the energetic body, and into infinity.

As for myself, I have had, as have you all, more than one life. In these lives, I have followed a path of learning and destiny which has created the energy form which stands before you today. I have had a path which has allowed me to hold this form of unity consciousness, passed onto me by my father, made possible by my mother. I hold this energy as a blueprint around me, and within the energy of my soul. It is of course an energy of the Divine, yet it is possible for it to pass through me, because of it being in my soul. I am here now on the earth in the etheric planes, this is another great mystery, and has been made possible by the works of many lightworkers across the planet making it possible for my light to be held here in this way. Being able to move in the etheric plane now, means that I can affect things more greatly, and connect with others in a much deeper sense than I would from the realms of heaven where my soul resides.

However, it was not necessary for me to incarnate in a physical form of male and female during the lifetime where I took on this blueprint. It is an evolutionary blueprint for humanity and holds the seeds of energies which will cause this unity consciousness to blossom within each of you. When enough numbers have been achieved that hold this unity consciousness, then the whole of the human race, will in one fell swoop be overtaken by this wave of oneness, and be swept into the arms of integration. At this point, humanity may start to shift to a higher form of physical expression, but as in evolutionary terms of the physical, this will take many many generations to complete, informed by the new energy of unity held within each person. The physical body will then be less dense, but really it is the consciousness that is the key. The physical body is simply there to support that consciousness, and will adapt to the best form for that to happen.

In these lifetimes where you are now then, it is important to remember that the key and the plan is held within each of you. If you have a strong heart's desire to be something or do something then try to love yourselves enough to make it so; God's perfect plan for you is built upon a rock. Love will conquer all, and help you see your way through all the challenges, limitations and difficulties that face you. At humanity's current point of evolution, the adoration of the God for the Goddess, and the Goddess for the God has yet to be achieved on a global scale, but will be a part of coming into unity consciousness. In oneness all things have a natural harmony and a natural balance that seems to simply find itself. These energies will start to sweep the planet more and more as the time goes on and will 'make it so', engendering that harmony and balance as it goes.

Each of you holds the seed within you for unity consciousness, and if you are in a female body, you can develop those masculine attributes within you on the mental levels so you are a pair of scales in balance, or if you are in masculine incarnation, you may develop your feminine intuition and be in balance too. There are many and endless ways to create and seek balance within yourselves, using all these levels of existence, mental, physical and emotional. Your soul is the one that will inform you of what path it is for you to take, so you can be your highest expression upon the earth, and bring you the greatest joy and happiness. That is why it is so important and so emphasised now for all of you to find ways of knowing what is within, whether it is through art, therapy, or psychic and spiritual development. The temple of the oracle at Delphi is known for the aphorism, 'Know Thyself', and this is why. All the keys to your development, and thereby that of the human race is within yourself, as each of you develop, so you speed up and assist every other human's development on earth. You cannot always see these things from the level of the earth at where you live, which is why it is a great spiritual quality to trust that everything is happening perfectly and that knowing this will help you to live more peacefully.

I am Sarah and all is well, all is well, all is well,

Blessed Be, Amen."

Chapter 8

You Are The Power!!

The Pink Thread

Traditionally the colour of nurturing, emotional healing, and harmony, pink encourages us to care for ourselves and others. But I would like to suggest that pink has another layer to it; that sometimes 'nurturing' means that we have to stand up for what we believe in, because the world 'out there' is doing some pretty shitty stuff to us or the people around us!

Pink is the power that generates our ability to 'do what needs doing', and works through the Daughter archetype - and it is a Divine spiritual power coming from the Divine Feminine. Read on to find out what this means!

The Daughter Archetype

Pia Skogemann, a Danish Jungian analyst, has presented her ideas about the emerging daughter archetype as she sees it in our modern society, https://piaskogemann.dk/%e2%80%8bthe-daughter-archetype/

Sarah comes to us as Daughter, and in our present day, this has special significance in our spiritual and evolutionary journey. This emerging archetype restores the Daughter, the young woman to a place of meaningfulness, power and strength. Just as we see in films such as the Maori story of Kahu in the 'The Whalerider', these daughters have a role to fulfill in the regeneration and renewal of our spiritual heritage; even becoming female saviours, such as Katniss in 'The Hunger Games'. In 'Frozen' Anna and Elsa work through the Divine Feminine challenges of having magical power and the wisdom to use it wisely, as well as learning how to work with the powers of emotions (and as many witches know, magical power and using your (unrepressed!) emotions are both parts of a good spell!) Through their emotions, their passions, their ability to be vulnerable and allow themselves to be seen as angry, as grieving, as being wounded, these young women are able to say what needs to be said, and do what needs to be done. They act on those feelings, even when those around them criticize and punish them for it. All of these films are expressive of the Daughter archetype, just as Sarah is. She is still wild and free. And yet the Daughters are motivated from a place of love, and of caring. It is power with compassion.

In the first chapter of our book, Sarah's name is changed from the passive 'princess' (whose stereotyped image is to look pretty, be quiet and get married) into 'Sarah the Great One', which gives a meaning of being a mother of All Nations, and of having power for the good of all. Like Sarah, all of these daughters, Kahu, Katniss, Anna & Elsa, show their 'inner sovereignty' (listening to their inner authority) through their bravery & courage in their integrity to do what they think is right. Far from the image of the helpless maiden waiting to be rescued (think Rapunzel or Sleeping Beauty), the young women are using their instincts, talents and abilities to create life-changing events for themselves and others. They are NOT keeping the status quo.

As with the goddess maiden archetype, the Daughter has everything she needs within herself, she is independent, pro-active and self-sustaining. Daughters and maidens do not have the experience of life, they can be hot-headed and impulsive without the restraining wisdom and patience of age. But – we all need to find the daughter within us (even the guys) if we are to manifest our own wildness and allow ourselves to have the freedom to express those parts of ourselves (especially those that are not culturally recognized, condoned or accepted) that need to be expressed in our lives – lest we otherwise suffer a spiritual death. We need this part of ourselves because if we overthink our impulses, or make them wait too long, they can die and fizzle out. Sarah is a Daughter, and she is FIERCE!

When we can find that Daughter quality inside of ourselves,* we find our Power!!

*and integrate it in oneness with our Divine Wisdom, our Divine Masculine, and our Divine Feminine.

Walking the path of Sarayei - Sarah by my side

When I work with and call on Sarah, I see her walking by my side, ready to extend a helping hand when I need it. This is how it has always been; not because I imagined it that way, but because it came to me that way. And I think it comes to me that way because that's how she is! Not in front of us, leading the way, but there next to us as our equal. This equality feels very real to me, and holds within it the truth that we are all Divine Souls, all equal at the level of who we truly are, and on this level of manifest creation, we are simply on different places of the path.

This is not to say that I am downplaying Sarah's role in the universe, or that I am up-playing my own, rather that I am acknowledging that 'I am' (a spark of the Divine) and that my 'I am' is absolutely my own responsibility!

Sarah is a friend, a sister, a light in the darkness, and to me she is my mentor. In a traditional sense, Sarah is also my spiritual guide, but that isn't a term that fits comfortably with me. I work with Sarah and the teachings she gives me so that I can find more of who I am. Sarah empowers me to tune into Divine Will myself, through being mySelf. It's hard work, and sometimes takes me a very long time to find the answers that I'm seeking.

Always Sarah is there supporting me every step of the way. When I don't know what to do next, or I feel I need help in handling a situation then I turn to Sarah, who will give me an illumination, an inspiration, a teaching or a practice which gives me the help I need.

She never 'tells' me what to do, and I never ask for the answers of what 'I should do'. I usually ask for what it is I need to know that will help me the most (or just go 'help'!!). I strive to find out what 'I should do' (ie, Divine Will) through feeling into what it is very deeply, and this often means clearing a great deal of issues out of the way.

Through feeling into Divine Will and believing in it (God's perfect plan is built upon a rock!!), I am manifesting the will of the Divine here upon the earth. The image of Sarah walking with me whilst I do this brings me great comfort; to feel that Sarah honours me enough as an adult not to take responsibility for my life (in so far as 'telling' me what to do), but also cares so much for me, that she is always there by my side, makes me aware of the great love that's there for me, for all of us, as we take our first tottering steps towards creating a new way of Being here on the earth; the Age of Aquarius.

"Every time you connect with my presence, every time you think of me, I bring you more into alignment with your own truth. My presence soaks into your very being, altering even the cells and DNA within you. I am that which makes you more of yourself, which is the essence of your soul. Each time you connect with me, a little more of all that is not of the Divine (or of yourSelf) is sloughed off, and falls away. I will take you deeper and deeper into the layers of your being, which of course also takes you higher and higher, as both these things are one and the same (as above so below).

My presence therefore is life altering in this way. As you become more and more yourSelf, you cannot help but make changes in your life. Those things that were there because of expectation, conditioning,

avoidance, lack of focus, or whatever it was, have to fall away once you are vibrating with the truth of your soul. They cannot stand to be there any longer.

And what can you do as this process takes place? As I know, this is a difficult path to walk.

You can love yourself. You can perform an act of love each day for yourself. When you feel you have some spare to give, you can also perform an act of love for others. And of course, performing an act of love for another can be seen as very similar because we are all one. But for now, I would say perform an act of love for yourself each day, until you become conditioned to it. Then you will find that it is more natural for you to perform an act of love for yourself as a way of beingness, so it is something that is your habitual pattern, and something which you will do all day, instead of one little incident per day. Yet to start with, performing an act of love for yourself each day, will do very well!

Make this your practice then, as you start to become ready to move on out of this course. This is what I would ask you to do, and what I would leave you with. It is a sacred task, you could say, that I lay upon your shoulders. Do it for me, because I ask it of you.

Each day, at a time that is good for you, ask yourself what it is you can do for yourself as an act of love. Ask yourself three times and then go very very quiet inside yourself and see/hear/feel what comes to you. It may be that you think of something very small, that you're always meaning to do for yourself but never quite remember to do, or it may be something a little more grand. Sometimes it may feel impossible to do, and you may get nothing. It doesn't really matter, there is no right or wrong here. What is important is that you do the practice, in this way, you are laying down the pathways of practical self-love. But when you do get a response, accept whatever comes to you, and above all honour it. Make it a priority. If you do forget, notice the omission, forgive yourself and affirm to yourself that you are learning to love yourself. It doesn't really matter what it is, because it is more the attitude that you are learning that is important. This is the gift of the practice, if you can learn how to act towards yourself with an attitude of love, you will be very much closer to God, and therefore your Divine Self. Such simple steps you can walk, a little one each day that will bring you closer to your soul, closer to all that you long for. So do it for me, because I ask it of you, draw on my presence before asking & I can help lighten your way.

I am Sarah and all is well, all is well, all is well. Blessed Be. Amen."

I AM the Wake-up Call

When I read these words on the page, it's as if Sarah's voice has become an orator, addressing a huge crowd of thousands with a tremendous speech! Every word is clearly enunciated, spoken very meaningfully and with great care. She really wants us to GET THIS, to start to understand...

"Welcome sisters, welcome brothers, I am here! I am here amongst the buds and the blooms, I am the new life quickening in the soil, I AM the glory of Father/Mother God in all its beauty.

I AM, I AM, I AM.

I AM THAT I AM.

Do you see the beauty that you are? Do you know the beauty that you are? Do you not think Divinity is beautiful?

You are Divinity who has forgotten from whence it came, but it takes not the beauty away, nor makes it invisible!

I have come to remind you; **I am the wake-up call**!!

Remember, remember, YOU ARE the Divine made manifest upon the earth. You are ALL THAT IS! It is only that you have forgotten that it is so, and in the forgetting your consciousness has become blank and reflects at the level of the ego, which is your earthly tool for life made manifest on earth.

You are what is held in your consciousness, and if you hold God there, knowing that it is so, then <u>shall</u> <u>it</u> <u>be</u>!!

Just imagine for a moment, what it would be like to be God made manifest on the earth?!! How would it feel, how would it be?! What would be different about your daily life, what would you be doing, who would you be with, what would you look like and sound like as you went about your daily things?

At night, when you slept, what kind of dreams would you have, being God?!! What levels of health would you have, and abundance & prosperity, love and joy, peace and harmony? How would your relations be to others and to the world?

How would all this be, knowing you are still you, your individual personality on the earth, completely unique, never to be repeated in exactly the same way, (just like each individual snowflake is completely unique), but also knowing you are God, that we are all God, that everything that you see around you is God, because God has created all, and there is only one power and one presence in the universe, and that is God.

All things come from God! Everything is God!! You are God!!!

I am God's voice calling you back home, not so as you should leave the earth, but to be here and be with God, who is your true Self, your true home. God speaks through me, because I too am God, and his will is mine, and I raise my voice to bless you all with God's mercy, God's love and God's truth, and my Circles of Power resound across the earth!

I am Sarah! All that is!! And all that will be!!!

May blessings pour down upon you, each and every day of your life, may you see all that is!

Blessed Be, Sarah."

Empowered to be YourSelf

Sarah is super empowering, and I love her so much for that; it's one of the things I appreciate most about her. It might not be the easiest path, having to learn how to do things yourself, taking one more step and then another towards mastery – slowly, one step at a time… but it is one of the most satisfying and, can I say it?! – empowering!!!

"Today I would speak to you about empowerment.

About what this means, and what it can do for you. Why it is so integral to the spiritual path.

Empowerment means the ability to move through your life being yourself. You are empowered to be yourSelf, and are able to manifest this in your words, thoughts and deeds.

You are empowered to be all you can be, all you would be, all you should be.

You are empowered not to be anything else.

You are empowered not to be what your mother wished you should be, or your school, or your culture, or even any part of you or of others that is ego driven.

You are empowered to be the highest part of you, which is of course, your true self, *everything else* being just the practice on the way, but really *everything else* being what teaches you, in the end, just what your true self is!

So, the practice of empowerment entails getting to know who you really are, spending time with yourself, finding out just what and who make you really happy, truly joyful. And then of course, there is the practice of allowing yourSelf to truly, actually enjoy all those things that make you truly & actually happy. Because as we know, it is quite possible to be doing all those things that make you truly, actually happy, and not to allow yourSelf, or give yourself any enjoyment whilst you are doing them!

Empowerment to be yourSelf is then the path to joy and happiness. Knowing that you have the ability to give yourSelf your deepest heart's desires, and not just knowing them, but then going one step further and powerfully bringing them into manifestation.

But first we must hold court with those parts of ourselves that do not believe in knowing and manifesting our deepest heart's desires, and talk to them, find out who they are, and why they came, and how we can help them to shift and change, and heal and transform into the highest possible vibration.

Often it is just the simplest thing, to shift and change one tiny perception that has been held within, and the whole concept can just come tumbling down, and then you are free, free to be just who you want to be, yourSelf!!

Imagine then, that the Divine has a perfect plan, and each of us holds our own perfect piece of the plan. The plan is never the same in each moment, but is continually manifested through all of manifest creation, (including us), and then recreated in each moment. The plan responds to all that has gone before, constantly readjusting itself, reprogramming, responding to the new opportunities that now exist because of what has gone before, and a core programme in the plan, is to bring each of us closer and closer to who we are 'supposed' to be, our Divine Selves, our Original Selves, our true selves.

Much of the plan at present, is devoted to this one core programme, to us, and all of manifest creation, actually manifesting divinity at the highest possible level, to actually manifesting the divine plan in its original perfect form. And for this to take place, there are many karmic creations, which are perfectly designed for us to learn why we shouldn't do that thing, (a little like a child, if you keep banging your head on that wall, it's gonna hurt).

The lesson can't be taught for us, the only way is for us to learn it for ourselves. So that when we act in anger and hatred, we create anger and hatred, we create suicide bombers in response to acts of oppression, we create divorces and affairs and separations, we create toxic waste upon the earth.

Imagine then an earth, where we all knew exactly who we were, and how to give ourselves our deepest heart's desires, and allowed ourselves to be in love and enjoyment whilst having our deepest heart's desires!!

That would be a world then, which is living out the Divine's plan, the core programme of constantly having to learn who we truly are, now obsolete, all that energy no longer being used up by showing us the truth, but instead, us all living out our truths, in love and joy.

Empowerment then is the path to nirvana, to the garden of Eden and to heaven here on earth. Applaud yourSelves on your successes and even on your failures of finding out who you are, and how to give yourSelves your deepest heart's desires. Your intent is everything, it will take you where you need to go, and your failures will teach you how to be successful, indeed success would not come without the failure. When you 'fail', when you have given yourself enough time to get over the initial shock, look at what you have learnt from this, what this 'failure' has to teach you, what hidden part of yourSelf has now been revealed to you. Is it possible that a part of you, which has been judged as wrong, has arisen to sabotage the efforts of what you thought you were 'supposed' to be by the moral values which you have been taught but are not your own?!!! Your failures hold the seeds of your success, and everything you need to know, is mirrored in the world around you - by what's in your life, by what isn't in your life, by the people around you, the feelings that are invoked in certain situations and by others, by your dreams! Take the time to listen, to watch, to observe, it's all there for you to discover in your own time, and in the right way for you!!

And when you do find out who you are and what you need, and when you have transformed the parts of you which block the manifestation of these things, then you are truly empowered, just by being exactly who and what you are in the world! And by being exactly who and what you are in the world, you are manifesting the Divine's perfect plan, for you and the whole of creation. Imagine the knock-on effect, of a person doing just that, all that power milling around in the collective unconscious, waiting for the next person to have a go!

Empowerment is simply this then, the ability to be who you are here on earth!!"

Those of you reading this book, are very likely special, gifted, magical, healing, divine, and with all likelihood, you have also gathered from the society that you live in, that you are weird, strange, different, don't fit in (insert your own words here..) To that, I would like to reply with this quote from Clarissa Pinkola Estés, a Jungian analyst and magickal storyteller who speaks with the spirit of great wisdom. From her 'The Dangerous Old Woman' series, comes this quote,

'If you were born gifted you will never ever live a normal life. Normalcy is the enemy of giftedness! And the giftedness, what is it? It's the soul! The soul seeing, the soul hearing, the soul sensing. It's living through the ways and the means of the soul; as opposed to the ego only, or the over-culture only.... If you are gifted, you will never, never live a 'normal' life... but a radiant one.'

Be yourSelves, be radiant!!

Your True Self

"Blessings, I am Sarah, all is well, all is well, all is well.

Today, I would speak to you of your True Self.

What is your True Self?

Many of you know instinctively inside yourself exactly what this means, but perhaps if you were asked to consciously explain this meaning, it would be a little harder to say exactly what that is!!

Your True Self, is your personality self, as your Divine light wishes to be shone upon the earth in this incarnation.

It is your ego self, shone through from every side by the Divine light inside yourself.

No shadows, no blocks, nothing hidden away in shame or fear, only your beautiful self, as you were created by the Divine to carry out its plan here on the earth.

Each of you is a perfect part of the Divine's plan, each of you is exactly as you were meant to be; perfect in every way.

Ah, what a lovely thing it is to behold this perfection and beauty inside each of you. Perhaps you can imagine it now, and open a little more to that which is within you…

It is so beautiful, so perfect, that to behold; it is pure bliss, joy, ecstasy!!

What a blessed thing indeed.

Collectively, humanity is moving now towards a time where you are throwing off the shackles of your inherited limitations, your generational dynamics that have made you wrong, simply for being what you are, and the call is coming, for you to be yourSelves, be yourSelves, be yourSelves…

You can hear it, so many of you, that are being called out of the shackles of your lives, that have kept you in the wrong job, the wrong marriage, the wrong town, the wrong country, the wrong life.

You can hear the call, and hear it calling you forth so loudly until you can no longer sleep, or rest, or be well, or ignore any longer that which sings to your heart, 'what is your true heart's desire, what is it, what is it?'.

And without even knowing what it is that you are being called to, you are stepping forward towards that call.

How brave, how true – what pioneers you are, those that heed the call of your soul to be Who You Truly Are, (even though some of you are in fear and pain) to be your Divine Selves here on earth.

And every little step that you take to heed that call brings you closer to your GodSelf, which is humanity that has remembered how to love, and show love through the humanity of your bodies, your personalities, your emotions here on earth, denying nothing, accepting all that is; Being Love!!

So, who is 'Who You Truly Are'?!!

It is those things that come up inside yourSelf. Those small things that you love, that mean the most to you. Those things that light you up inside, and say 'do me, do me'. This is you being you, in this earthy, physical lifetime. Getting to know yourself, and what it is you truly want to do, is the most important job of your life, here in this one lifetime on the earth. This is how Divinity implemented its Divine Plan here on the earth. It went, 'OK, so I need this to happen, let's give this person over here, the desire to do that, and to really notice what's going wrong here', 'and this bit is a really big job, let's get a whole group of people to have the desire to sort that one out', and so led and guided by our hopes and fears we have the ability to sort out the world, one little hope and fear at a time. When I say fear, I mean the parts of the world that you notice are really wrong, and probably, quite probably depress you quite a lot. You have the capacity to notice the wrongness, because the Divine (which you have to remember is You!!) has given you the ability to do something about it. Not the whole thing, but one small thing that it is within your remit to do!!

So Who You Truly Are in this lifetime, might be the person in your family who notices that there is a dynamic in the family that means it's very difficult for everyone to show love and affection and you are so hurt and wounded by this, feeling that you're not loved, that you go away, and find a path of healing where you learn to accept love, and how to show it, and then maybe once you have practised it and become really good, you might just get the opportunity to take that back into your family and get the chance to do something different, and in a moment where normally you would get to feel a lack of expression of love, you get the chance to show that affection outwardly to someone else, and so change their experience and yours too…

YOU are the change you wish to make.

If there is something that you notice is wrong in the world, and particularly bothers you much more than those around you, I would suggest that, this is for YOU to do something about!! That this is an opportunity for you to discover for yourself, what you can change in your own life, what new skill you can learn, that will afford the world an opportunity to have one less instance of this problem!!

For example, if you are heartbroken about the ecology of the planet, discover all the ways that you can live lightly on the planet, and utilise your skills for this end. For example, if you are a social networker, organise local clean up events, if you are a writer, write a blog about it to raise awareness, whatever it is that you are, and whatever way it is that you do things in, find some way to express your need to help. There is always something that you can do, from the large to the small, from a few minutes given to it, to a whole lifetime's work.

Your true self, also knows what it is that makes your heart sing with joy, it knows what you want and sings of your heart's desires.

Start listening to yourSelf, it is telling you what you need to know!!

All is well, all is well, all is well. Blessings be upon you, Sarah."

Believe in YourSelf

"Welcome all, I am Sarah.

What is relevant and informed for you to hear right now are those things which are most pertinent to your life, those things that will matter in this moment, rather than what will be.

And what is pertinent for you right now, is that you believe in yourself. In yourSelf.

Much of what the higher self is trying to say to you, is dismissed as whim or fancy, and often when you have a reading with someone else, you find that what has been said to you, was what you knew already, what you had already felt inside yourself, but hadn't taken so seriously, until you heard it through another.

What then is this dynamic?

This dissolution of the self, whereby what is heard and felt inside the self is dismissed and ignored, whilst the energy of the self is kept on day-to-day matters, and the process of doing what it seems needs doing, or is supposed to be done?

For many of us, it is how we have been taught to be, not in so many lessons, but by example of those around us, who we have watched and learnt this way of ignoring what is inside us, and taking our direction from other authorities, and also by what we have said and felt when we were children being dismissed and put aside as unimportant.

This looking to guidance from others is a process that exists all around us in a myriad of ways in this society, from having an understanding of what is the law, to finding out in a job what the policies and guidelines are of that institution.

We are constantly guided to find out from others what the right thing to do is, and so it is no small wonder to find that it becomes a difficult thing then to look inside, to see what is there, what there is for us to do when we look to a deeper truth, and access our own wisdom, connecting to our higher selves.

Of course, we can gain valuable insight and knowledge by consulting those around us in our society that hold great expertise, knowledge and experience in different matters, but then this should only serve to function as another tool to help us go inside then, once we have gained what we need to know, and feel what the right choice, decision or action is for ourselves.

This can be a whole new way to see things, to see and value others as the incredible help and resources that they are, but ultimately to know that the power for what we do in our lives, what we invite in, the actions that we take, the way in which we shape our lives, is ultimately up to us, that the responsibility is wholly ours.

That we have inside us, the most incredible guidance system, to do what is needed to do, the right thing for us, that we can feel and hear and taste from our higher selves all we need to know, and that if we feel called to go in a direction that we know absolutely nothing about - then we can call upon the wonderful resources of the world around us, all these people that are also the divine made manifest.

God being here in physical manifestation.

And so today, that is what I am saying to you – you can wake up to who you are!! And you can start to believe in yourself, in those impulses, thoughts and ideas that come to you over and over again as a dream or a wish.

You are the divine made manifest upon the earth; don't you think God knows what it's doing?!!

Do you think God needs to doubt its own ability to judge and know what's right for its own happiness?

Start to believe, just a practice, not even for real!

So, take those things that come to you, and then go 'OK, so if I pretend to believe to myself that I know what is good for me, that these thoughts, ideas and impulses are coming from my higher self, then I should really listen to them, right? And take them seriously and put into action what's come to me today?!!'

See what happens!! And if it works, then why stop!

Blessings are pouring down upon you, each and every moment of every day.

Namaste, Sarah."

This is another channeling on the same theme…

Thank you, Lady Sarah. Are there any questions that we haven't previously discussed that you feel would be appropriate to provide us with answers to? *(Question is from a live interview.)*

"Well firstly I would like to say that these are exciting times that you are living in now, and I appreciate that it can be a little difficult to appreciate that. However, I would just ask you to just step for a moment outside of yourself, and take a step back, and realize just how much amazingly magical divine potential there is in this current moment in the evolution of humanity at this point on the web of time. There is just the most amazing amount of spiritual help coming in and possibility for transformation.

So, I know some of you that are listening to this, your burdens are heavy, and the path is difficult right now. However, I would say to you, look for your tools, remember the training. All of you who are listening to this, have learned many, many things as you each come into your spirituality.

Do not think for a second, that you are powerless or that you can do nothing to change your circumstances or to change your consciousness particularly. You are at the point of learning self- mastery. You are at the point of coming into co-creation with the divine in a way where you are creating powerful creations full of light and full of love.

The world around you is changing. The earth grid is much, much different than twenty/thirty years ago and this is because of the work of humanity. So, don't think that it's all bad. Don't think that it's hopeless and there's no future when you are hearing about the climate change and the way that the politicians are behaving. Yes, all of those things are there, and they will even more powerfully bring out your gifts and even more powerfully bring out what is needed in opposition to it, to create the balance. The Earth is always trying to keep a balance. Creation is always trying to keep a balance. So, whatever comes up negatively, there must be a positive to it and then my teaching to you is about how to bring those two things together and bring them into balanced integration.

So, the last words that I want to speak to you, is to have hope, to believe in yourselves. You are a spark of the divine - each of you, and that's a really precious thing, and that's also something that I have come to teach more about so that you can feel that more in your everyday lives.

So, I'm Sarah. Thank you for giving me this opportunity to speak today. And I would like to do this again. It's the time, it's the time now, for these things to be said and for these words to be spoken and there are more people now who are ready to listen to what I have to say.

And it's outside of religion, it's outside of bloodlines. This is about here and now, and what we can do to work with earth and to work with all of the problems on the earth with the pollution in the seas and then. You know what all the problems are, I don't need to list them.

But you know, how do we work with these things, and that's what I'm here… That's what I'm here to do, to walk by your side, as sister, as mentor and teacher. I'm not a guide, I'm not here to tell you what to do, but I will help you and support you in finding those answers yourself and I will give you tools. I will show you energies that you can use, that will have a powerful effect on not just your lives. Actually, really on the world around you, actually really on the land where you live. There are so many things you can do, and I have come to teach you.

Blessed be, blessed be, blessed be, Amen."

The Heart of Your Joy

"Today I would speak to you of commitment.

Commitment is placing the heart of your joy at the centre of your life.

Finding those things that you commit yourself to is a paramount activity in a person's life, because to commit yourself is a serious intent, something where you are saying to yourself and to others, 'this is what is important to me, this is what I want to see grow in my life, and so I commit myself to nourishing this thing in my life, to focusing my energy, my intent and my love on doing everything that is in my power to see that it is so. And so if this thing does not succeed in my life, it is not because I did not show up, or make enough effort, or stay with it when the going got tough, but because that is just the way it is.

What have you committed yourself to?

What have you allowed yourself to commit yourself to?

Have you committed yourself to those things that you consider 'should' be important, or have you committed yourself to those things that really *are* important to you, those things that are the heart of your joy?!

Or perhaps you have not allowed yourself to commit to anything at all; fearing the very worst, that all those things that are the heart of your joy cannot be yours, that the universe does not support you, is not your friend, will not allow you to have your deepest heart's desires?!

If you do not commit to a thing, or a person, how can you hope to make that thing succeed and bring forth fruit, and joy and happiness?

How can you hope to make it flourish without you to water it with love and tenderness, undisturbed by the course of events and the ups and downs of life?

Commitment means that you will keep showing up, consistently, persistently, not in dribs and drabs and little bits and pieces here and there, but day in, and day out, even when you are bored and fed up, and more than a little ready to go and do something completely different.

So what is the heart of your joy?

What do you consider so important that you can apply yourself in this way, and really be there throughout the process of nurturing this thing in your life?

What is it for you?

Take some time to find out, to avoid finding one day that you have been applying yourself to nothing very much at all!

Take some time, make some space, sit down and ponder on the heart of your joy, so that you can then bring all of your wonderful focus, attention, love and energy to making it so.

Bring your joy into the world, after all it is why you are here!

You are the Divine made manifest upon the world.

God's plan manifests itself through you, through your joy…

All is well, all is well, all is well…. Namaste, Sarah."

Sarah is an Initiator for the New Age

"Welcome all I am Sarah.

My energy now is seeking to be more present in the world.

The energy that I represent is one that initially creates chaos and conflict but then takes you to the core of your being, your centre and your place of stillness.

This is the process that you will be led through when you are initiated into my energies.

For each of you it will be different, depending on where you are on your own unique and individual path, and each of you will have many different experiences, and receive different gifts, information, openings and awakenings.

I cannot say a definite 'it will be a 'this awakening' or a 'that awakening', because when we come so close to your core as we are in an initiation like this, it is your soul and your higher self that calls the initiation forth in the way that is needed.

I am simply the vessel that the initiation comes through. In this way am I empowering you to be more of yourself, which is a divine being of God."

Blessings from Sarah

"Blessings I am Sarah. I bid you welcome. Welcome to the fountain of blessings that I shower upon you as you read these words. And shower them upon you I do - have you any idea of the ability you have to create in this world, to co-create with the Divine? I know this is something that you hear very often, and perhaps get a little tired of hearing. 'Oh, another thing to add to my daily tasks' you think. 'Just what I need!' And yet this is not what I mean as such.

It's hard for you to see the whole pattern of the world. It's hard for you to see the flows of energy, the tides, the waves, as together you grow, form, dissipate, grow again. But you have so much more power than you realise to send out blessings into the world. This could be a part of your daily practice, in whatever way you wish. It could be as simple as sending out your love in the form of blowing a kiss out to the world! Many of you see so many of your unconscious projections coming back to you as you look out into the 'world', and this is not meant as a criticism. Not at all. This mirroring effect of the world is meant to be a way for you to more effortlessly, and easily be able to see the things that you need to heal and love inside yourselves. But what could be a way to counteract this difficulty of how 'the world' might feel a little heavy, is to send it some love and joy each day. You could do a chant for the world, light a candle for the world, if you like walking in nature each day – you could bring home a leaf, or stone, or whatever you find that day on your walk, and place it on your altar 'for the world'. You could place a crystal on your altar, or some blessed or sacred water 'for the world'. Really whatever the things that bring you joy, project them out 'onto the world'. Not only is it healing 'for the world', it also lifts your burdens and struggles a little bit too! The more that you can shift any heaviness you feel about 'the world', the more you can tune into the vibrations of the Divine, the Divine Resonance

– and the best way to do this, is not to try and achieve it all in one big event, but little by little, drip by drip. If you like when you do this, you could say 'Blessings for the world', and have the intent that you are sending them out…..

I am Sarah and these are the words I wish to speak to you this day.
My blessings are upon you,
Blessed Be, Blessed Be, Blessed Be, Amen.
Sarah."

Do it now!

This year Samhain came up as another significant portal. Sarah is a great supporter of all things magickal, and of us developing our spiritual and psychic abilities. Samhain is a time when the veil is thin, and we honour the ancestors. But for the time we are in history now, it's also especially important for us, to remember our ancestors who were the wise women and men, and were punished for that. We need to grieve for them, express our righteous anger and reclaim our family heritage!

This came through from 'The Elders of the Star Council' of which Sarah is one,

'We would speak to you today about the urgent matter of nature. When we say this, we mean YOUR nature! It is in your nature (collectively) to be healers, shamans, witches, clairvoyants and so on. It is human nature to be all of these things. Some have forgotten these truths. But you cannot, because these truths literally run in your veins. Literally, because you are descended from ancestors who were all of these things (ie. your family line before you), even though you no longer know their names. But we are telling you that they know yours, and are supporting you in these pivotal times!

The Divine has created each of you exactly as you were meant to be, so if you are a healer, then heal… do what you need to - take a course, or if you can already do it, then DO IT! These things (witch, shaman, psychic, healer, seer, wisewomen, healerman and all the others) are no longer a hobby or a dream. They are not what will be needed... one day (when society is more advanced, and will see your worth). They are needed NOW! Find ways of using whatever it is that you do. Fit it in around the life that you already have. Don't overdo it. Don't give yourself a breakdown trying to singlehandedly 'save the world'. Just do what you can. Just as you would if there were a place, or a people, or a country that was in trouble – you would quietly donate, or give your time in order to do the bit that you could do. It's the same thing that's needed for 'the world' right now – but perhaps the people and the society and what feels like 'the world around you' doesn't realise that 'what you do', is actually needed and valid, or even a real thing! But look inside yourself, and ask 'is what I do a real thing'? And the answer always comes back YES! *Listen to this* and don't worry about the world outside. In fact, stop listening to the world outside in order to find out 'what's true', or 'what's really happening'. It's more important now that you all start listening to *your own inner template* of 'what to do', and 'what's really happening'. The reason we're saying these things is because YOU ARE THE PLAN! Each one of you has been given a gift that together (with everyone else), when it is all added up, has exactly what is needed to shift and transform the earth grid so that the consciousness of humanity can in its turn shift and transform. In truth, things will become more and more uncomfortable until you realise that this is worth trying (ie. being yourself) because (in the end you'll realise that) SOMETHING needs to be done, and what have you got to lose (by trying)?!

To say that you are the solution to all of the world's troubles would be to lay too much on your shoulders, and of course that is not true. But in another way, it is absolutely true (when you take it as a collective truth that applies to everyone), because the TIME IS NOW for each of us to find out 'who we are', and what we 'came to do.'

Be positive & strong in times like these

This next channeling is from Mary Magdalene, her beloved Mother. Sarah is who she is because she stands upon the shoulders of her Ancestors, and her Divine Heritage. Their wisdom is her wisdom, so it's not such a surprise that 'her' teachings often come from those around her. She builds upon and adds to, what has already been given. I've found that the teachings come through from the person or being that best holds the energy that is being expressed in the channeling, so that we can absorb that too, as well as the words! This channeling came through specifically for the pandemic in 2009, but I think it applies to any 'times like these' (we know what they are when we're in them!!) When I read it through, it feels like it builds on and adds to 'All is Well' with some good old-fashioned common sense! And I can feel Mary's energy flowing through as I read her words!

"Welcome, I am Mary Magdalene, I come to offer you my grounded truths, grounded wisdoms, and grounded thoughts. In times such as these, where so much is unsettled, it is good to return to the simple things of life and ensure you are care-taking of yourself to the most excellent degree. You may wish to expose yourself to the media & the thought-forms of fear, in limited quantities, so that you are not overly irradiated with distress, but also stay tuned to the realities of the situation.

There is much that can be done by turning once again to the basics of life, much to absorb yourself with. Take a few moments now to think of how much attention you are paying to these basics in your life. For example, are you going to bed early enough to gain the right amount of sleep that you need? Have you made the time in your weekly schedule to properly exercise your physical body? How much sunlight have you received, and what kind of lunch did you have today - did you take time & care to prepare your food?

Think now, of how much more time you can take to make these simple tasks even more pleasurable for yourself. For many of you, this may seem like a backward task, as on the earth plane, it is usual to be thinking of how all these things may take less time! And this is often so amongst the more spiritual quarters, as if time taken up looking after the physical body is something to be endured rather than enjoyed!

But this is a good time of year to be thinking of these things, as the mind and body are awakening fully again after the winter months, the senses are returning to their full potential and activity is rife! What will your activity be, will it be mindless panic brought on by the world around you? Or could it be an opportunity in your life to slow things down a little, to consciously return to a slower pace, make the activities in your life something to be enjoyed, rather than rushing through them so you can enjoy yourself after?!

This slowing down, allowing yourself to be absorbed in what you are doing, seeing how relaxed and calm you can be in each moment, and noticing when once again, you are whipping yourself along in the rush of the day, and then just simply slowing down once again – this slowing down, is a wonderful antidote to the fearful thought-forms which are being generated right now.

They allow you to see things in a grounded way. When you rush through the day, your feet hardly touch the ground, and this is true because in this way, you have become ungrounded. You are not connected to the fullness inside yourself and the sensations of your body living here on the earth, but are disconnected from what is grounded and true and sensible!

So keep in mind these simple things if you can, remembering not what less time can you spend looking after yourself and those around you, but what more time can you take to make these things even more special, in the most simple of ways, and allow your mind in calm creativity to take luxurious moments enjoying the freshness of the outside air.

These things I would suggest in these days of uncertainty and drama, allowing yourself to be as comfortable as you can, until the seas have calmed once again and you feel more sure of the route you are taking.

These are my truths, the truths of women and mothers who know that a good meal and a good night's sleep can do wonders for the spirit of the soul, and even more so when the calmness becomes a way of life, instead of an interlude between panics! These are wonderful things to learn and to practise at times like these, and offer you a great opportunity in your development.

Stay in the centre of your being, and ask yourself 'in this current moment is there anything for me to fear?' Stay attached to the reality of the situation, rather than the projections of catastrophe and strife. Take note of what is said and suggested and then return yourself to the simplicity of caretaking yourself.

Make everything you do, every action you perform something which is helpful & nurturing to you, and when you have to do those things which don't seem so, do them in the way which is the most helpful and nurturing to you. Keep yourself positive and healthy in mind and heart, knowing that you are kept within the love of the Divine Mother at all times and see yourself and your loved ones in your mind's eye as safe and well. Affirm to yourself that all is well, and that you are strong, calm and grounded.

Blessings are upon each and every one of you, each and every moment of your lives,

I am Mary Magdalene. Blessed Be."

Your Emotions Are Your Power

Anger seems to be a difficult thing to manage in our society. When I trained as a hypnotherapist back at the turn of this century, I couldn't even find any hypnotherapy scripts that dealt with anger and offered a helping hand.

We have lost touch with the purpose of anger, which means that it gets repressed, which means that it comes out in unhealthy ways! The best therapeutic thing I ever saw about working therapeutically with anger was a documentary on television about men in a US prison working in an anger management programme, set up by volunteers. I watched it with my husband, and we cried nearly all the way through. It was a fantastic programme, so much wisdom in it, and the work those men were able to do on their anger issues was amazing.

Sarah advocates for being in our full power, for fully feeling all of our feelings, and we can't do that if we shut away our anger as not being socially acceptable. This isn't the same as taking our anger out on everybody else though; we have to own our anger, and use wisdom in dealing with it. Here is Pele again, a deity naturally qualified to speak on this subject!

"I am Pele. Goddess of the volcano, of the lava flow, of evolution. I have been fortunate enough for my mythology to have survived the changes which have taken place on the islands of Hawai'i. Many of the ancient ones have been forgotten. Much is spoken about me. I am popular for those who wish to feel more passion in life and I am, in the stories and myths about me, portrayed as a fiery woman; those who displease me through wrongful behaviour, soon know how I feel! And in the stories and the myths about me, I am often portrayed as a woman who is not frightened to express her anger!

And it is this that I would speak to you about. Anger is much judged, harshly judged. It is part of the human emotion, part of your power in fact. All of your emotions are designed to bring to you, some aspect of the divine, in co-creating with the divine. And anger has been designed for you to feel energy, when those around you are abusing your boundaries in some way, or doing some wrongful action.

However, what is often forgotten, is the divine balance of blending anger with love. These are the things which I would speak to you about.

Not judging your anger, but recognising that it is a powerful quality that will motivate you to speak up for yourself, to stay in your integrity. But as I said, it is necessary at these times to call on the power of your heart centre, to stay heart-centred. And even though, you may speak to that person in anger, stay loving with that person, stay within your loving integrity.

Anger unspoken, anger unexpressed, is detrimental to your health, will block up the flow of divine energy within you. If you feel angry there is a reason. And of course, be mindful of it, of course don't go around shouting at everybody because you feel angry! But acknowledge that anger, allow your mind to decide what action to take, speak with love, stay in your integrity. But don't quell that power, that was never meant, that is not part of the divine plan, that that power goes unused. It's there, it's for the highest good, work with it, learn to love it. Too much is anger hated and judged, and becomes a negative force within the body, within society, and is acted out. Learn to love your anger, and work with it. And use it for the highest good, it will direct you to which way you need to go in life, to the paths you need to walk, to the changes you need to make.

And this is one of the things that I have taught the Hawai'ian people since time immemorial, how to stand in their power, but stay within their heart centres.

I thank you for bringing my energies into the world. It is a great blessing that you perform these acts, for not only yourselves, but for the whole of humanity.

I send you my love and blessings, that you are doing this work. And they shower down around you now. Mahalo nui and aloha. Blessed Be."

The Way of the Heart

The teachings of Mary Magdalene and Sarah could be described as the 'Way of the Heart' because the heart is at the centre of all of their teachings...

"The life that you require needs to come from the heart. If your life is not fulfilling you, it is because you are not living from this place. Yes, you must find your place in life. Yes, you must live in the everyday world, and work and deal with all the thousands of things that are involved in everyday life.

But... you can do all this, living from the place of the heart.

Only your heart knows what it is you need to have a fulfilled life. What does it mean if you live your life doing all of those thousands of things that need to be done, but your heart is not fulfilled? It means that your life becomes an empty, meaningless experience.

If you have purpose then, fulfilling all of those things can become a joy, because they are in service to your truest heart's desires. You must ask your heart, 'what do you want to do'?

You must find out how to do those things, and make them happen. Everything you do then will be in service to those things that bring you joy.

If you have to work at a job that is more for the money than for the fulfilment, but it brings you those things that make it possible for you to have your joy, then it is given purpose. It may be that you need to change your life completely, or it may be that you just need to add one or two things. It may be that a shift in attitude is what is required rather than any outer thing.

I am Sarah, and I can help you in this chosen task. I can give you the inspiration, the support and the help that you need to move forward on this path.

All is well, all is well, all is well.

Blessed Be. Sarah."

What Can I do Today..?

Just good old fashioned sense this one, but such a good practice!!

"It is time for you to fall back on your own resources and see what it is you can do to help yourself. Opening yourself up to possibilities that there are possibilities is a good first step, and one which you need to take through the use of your positive intent.

Right now, each day you can ask yourself, 'what can I do today to help myself, what do I need?', and so in this way, by allowing yourself to experience your felt need, possibilities can arise that fulfil what it is you require.

Right now, it is hard for you to see the possibilities that can open up for you, because you are still in a place of lack, of feeling separate and alone, which is something you are working with right now – asking yourself 'how can I be integrated within the culture that I am within?'

These are all good questions and ones that will lead you to create your own place in the world; finding where it is that you want to be…

There are many challenges for you in being here, many opportunities.

Keep asking yourself, 'what good can I find in today' – or 'what good can I find in this?'

Keep looking for what's good for you and so within that inherently believing that there is something good in what is happening – that within your situation there are positive potentials waiting to unfold, even though they might not be apparent to you right now!

Act 'as if it might be so' and see what can come up! In each moment where you feel lost, without the structure and call to fulfil 'a job', you can ask 'what would it be good for me to do right now?' and listen quietly inside to see what comes…

Firstly, focus on coming into right relationship with the world, i.e., the people that you meet is a very important focus for you, and one in which is the possibility for you to open up to the world in a whole new way and to have it opened up to you similarly (and so even as it is you that will open up to the world, it will appear to you that the world is opening up to you)

All is well, all is well, all is well, all is well,
Blessed Be, Sarah."

Seeking wisdom and acknowledging your self-worth with Grandmother Anna

"Welcome. I am Anna, Grandmother of Jesus.

I work in conjunction with this family of light. None of us are alone or separate. And so, it is with you all. None of you are working alone or separately, although it may feel sometimes as if you are. This is not the case; realise that you too are in a circle of the family of light. You are never alone.

What I would say to you today is, to realise the truth of your deepest heart's desires. Realise the integrity of your aspirations and truly honour the worthiness of your goals. Feel yourself standing within this circle of light now, this family of light. Feel yourself reach out and hold hands with those on either side of you. Feel the power and strength of that circle - you do not battle alone. You are not alone.

Feel that light, flowing into you from the left, from the right, all around, all around, all around. You are not alone. You are not alone. You are not alone. Feel how that energy, that love, that light, coming from this family of light, grounds you, energises you, makes you feel even more yourself.

Acknowledge your own worthiness, acknowledge your own worth. Honour yourself. Be proud of who and what you are. I am! I am proud of who and what you are, and I see how you stand true in a world that is not easy for you to be in.

I am Anna, the Grandmother, and as such, I speak with the wisdom of the years. I speak with a wish to give you strength and succour to those of you walking this path. And of course, I wish you well and send many, many blessings your way in these challenging times which you are in. But remember, you are not alone, you are not alone, you are not alone. You have each other and you have all of us. We are here for you and our blessings are upon you."

And finally, these last two channeled messages came through as 'Sarah's message for the week', and are rather nice!

Freedom

"Give up the responsibilities that you don't need to take on as yours, because a time is coming when your biggest responsibility will be to ground down into your own essence and truly manifest what is there. I AM Sarah and I tell you that you are walking into important times that you will remember for the rest of your life. Important times, where you see the light of the Divine truly manifesting in your life and it becomes more than how it is now."

'Welcome All, I am Sarah. Allow yourself to tune into the rhythm of life… Your own life. Listen to what rhythm your heart is beating to.. your life blood. There are so many ways to instill duty, structure, order onto yourself, and yet? Does it work, or does it impose more rules, more ways to suppress the life joy inside that wants to be expressed? If you want to rest, then rest. If you want to work the whole day, then work the whole day. You were never meant to work 9-5 from Monday to Friday, that is not the rhythm of life, that is the rhythm of the industrial society. Do what you can, within the limitations of what you have to do. But remember, it is not your structure, but rather one that has been imposed upon you, so don't feel guilt or shame for not 'living up to' this artificial construction. You are at heart wild and free. Take your own moments where you can and enjoy them. Don't be ashamed. Throw shame into the fire, let it go, and be free!'

Look beyond what you see

"Welcome I am Sarah. Blessings to you this day!! What you see is very much dependent on where you look! Now this may seem a very obvious thing to say, but you know that many of you have spiritual sight, but do you remember to use it?! Mindfulness meditation is one way of doing this and bringing in that extra layer of perception as a discipline, but really this is just a formal way of looking with your extrasensory sight. How to bring it in more often so that you can add this to your day? Remember to breathe, take a breath. When you start to think about what you have to do next, take a breath, breathe deep, allow yourself to soften and relax, hold a crystal if you wish, or step outside for a breath of fresh air if these things help you. Let go of any tension in your body and simply allow yourself to be 'spirit-filled'** for a moment. Doing this from time to time (especially when you are tense or very busy) will keep you more connected to your spiritual self, and so more able to see with your 'spiritual eyes'. I am Sarah and these are the words I wish to speak to you this day, Blessed Be, Blessed Be, Blessed Be, Amen."

**With the words 'spirit-filled' came the sensation of opening up from the top of the crown all the way down – having an energetic posture of softening, relaxing and opening all at once, and simultaneously being filled with spirit/energy throughout the whole self."

Chapter Nine

The Ancestors & The Future

The Black Thread

Maybe you're wondering why black is included here? Well, all aspects of the divine have their positive and negative. Black is not always such a popular colour in 'spirituality', and yet we like to use it a lot in our everyday life, for example, in our clothes and in our homes!

Black is the colour of grounding. In some ways it is the foundation that we stand upon; it is the colour of matter. To be an Ancestor, you could say that first we start with the energy of Black, and then build layer upon layer of colour, tone, vibration and experience upon it, until finally we end up with a glorious array of colours on our tapestry of Ascension. But without the Black, there is nothing to anchor it to. Just as the cloth enables the tapestry to be woven to it, so the vibration of matter (the Black) allows our lives to be lived and our soul tapestry to be woven. Without the Black (matter), none of this soul journey could have taken place in the first place.

Matter is the unformed clay – and we are the potters! It is our job, to take it and create beautiful pieces of art, (or whatever it is that we want to create upon it!) By bringing in the full spectrum of colours that we can lay our hands on, in each lifetime!

Black is a Goddess colour! As we see in Sara-la-Kali in her aspect of a Black Madonna, Sarah has also become Queen in the realm of matter, meaning that she has transcended the illusion of the dark and integrated it into the whole; weaving in the light and the Godself, All is in Oneness. The manifestation of matter is a Divine Feminine attribute, as we see in Lakshmi/Narayani; as we see in Sarah.

Black is the female Yin, to the white Yang. In darkness, there is also peacefulness and rest – as opposed to the overstimulation of the light. The 'colour' Black is literally the absence of colour, and white contains all colours!

Before our current daytime system, each new day would begin when it became dark; as many tribal and earth-based spiritualities understand, life and creation begins in the darkness, not in the light. The tiny shoot from the seed would shrivel and die if it was exposed to the light too soon, it needs the softness and vibrational quietness of the dark in order to grow and become strong before it is ready to emerge – but always the inclination of the plant is to grow towards the light! And so, it is with us, created in darkness, our inclination is always to grow towards the light. Without one or the other, black or white, creation could not exist. Everything is needed – All is Welcome Here!!

In Western society, we don't have a strong culture of working with ancestors anymore. It's something we have forgotten. As a healer I have worked with healing the ancestral line of myself and other people for many years, releasing traumas, negative beliefs and so on. Then a few years ago, I started to do 'name work', working with runes. This is a technique I developed to work energetically with the letters of your name using runes. With the first name, the soul energies come through. With the last/family *name, the ancestral energies come through! I was completely surprised to discover that we have Ancestors with a capital A. These are ancestors who are coming through on a higher spectrum, a higher vibration. All of us are multivibrational, and the more integrated we become, the more aware of become of our own higher energy bodies (higher selves!) The healing work that I was doing previous to the runes, was working with the ancestors on the lower levels, but the name work showed me how much more there is to our Ancestors!*

This next channeling comes from my 'Sarah's 12 step program to Ascension'! (See Afterword.) The first step is the Ancestors.

Ancestral lines & DNA

"Blessings. I am Sarah.

Today, I would wish to speak to you of the Ancestors and Ascension. I say the Ancestors, with a capital A, to highlight the importance of them, but also to give them the respect that they deserve, and to acknowledge their accumulated light and wisdom. There is a tendency, still, in western society, to think of 'ancestor worship', as something that belongs to crude and undeveloped cultures, and although I am not suggesting that you start to 'worship' your ancestors, I am suggesting that you start to realise what an untapped wealth of help, support, wisdom and resources they are!

All of you who have sensitivity, an interest in spirituality, healing gifts, psychic gifts, empathic abilities, or spiritual gifts, do so because you have been born into specific ancestral lines. In the beginning, each ancestral line was charged with responsibilities, and the necessary powers and gifts for those responsibilities to be carried out successfully.

Although mankind has lost awareness to a great extent of these family lines, and even more so, of the duties and responsibilities that are attached to them. There is often a sadness for the 'lost knowledge', and although this can be understood, it is not necessary, because the knowledge is carried within each one of you!

You carry the codes and keys within your ancestral DNA, and you have the ability as spiritually gifted individuals to read these codes and keys, and more than that, to tap into their power and potential. Sometimes, it is a blessing that knowledge has been lost, because maybe your ancestors understood it in a corrupted form, through the lens of a corrupted society, and then when it is revealed again, often through the work of many years of one person's lifetime, it is coming out now in a purer form.

As much as possible, things have been preserved that needed preserving, either through historical objects, through the stories of myths and legend, or even fairy tales and children's stories, or through archaeological discoveries that draw (the correct) conclusions. But you must always assume that the information you are being led to, is the correct information for you at the time.

Where something needs to be brought out, and is brought out in the way mentioned, by a particular person who devotes many years of their life to that one thing – then this person, will have had a past life lived in that particular subject, so carries the knowledge on the soul level, but then will also have been born into an ancestral line, who were the actual people who were living the subject in the past. For example, someone who has chosen on a soul level to reveal the mysteries of the magical tradition from the past, will have DNA that links them to that tradition, and also will have had a past life, or past lives of accumulated knowledge. In this way, that person knows the information 'in their bones', but will also get the inspirations and inner knowing that their soul can give to them. Do you see how useful it can be to have both? In this way, spirit and soul and body can all work together in harmony, which is the way that soulful works are accomplished. The body knows a lot as well! It knows where to be, and how to move you to it; it knows how to move you towards the people of the right vibration as well!

This is the time for all the strands to come together. It is no use to have a high spirituality, if you do not know how to ground it, to earth it, and to make it real, and this your ancestors can help you with! Your 'soul purpose', which so many of you 'know', with that deep knowing that it is very important for you to live this - and not the lives that have been prescribed to you by either your family or the culture that you have been brought up in; this 'soul purpose', may also very well be called an 'ancestor purpose', because whatever your soul wants to accomplish will have been carefully planned to also take into account whatever it is that the ancestral lines you have chosen to incarnate within have been designed to accomplish. You see how you are already part of a great plan? And perhaps it might sound a little complicated?! But really it is not. You have been given the right body to accomplish your spiritual task, because it is actually in the DNA that the codes and keys exist for you to have or develop your psychic and spiritual gifts that you need!

But how do you find out everything that you need to know?! Well, firstly by doing all of the things that so many of you are already doing, the meditation, the yoga and chi gung, the high vibrational eating, the learning how to feel and follow your intuition, and so on and so on. You don't need to do all of these things, there are so many so that each of you can find the ones that bring you the most joy and the greatest results for the least effort!!

Secondly, you can call on the help of Mary Magdalene. She knew how to release the hidden information held within the physicality of her body, which includes the emotional layers. If you don't already know your soul purpose, then you will find them locked away in the desires which you have hidden from yourself! However near or far you are from learning this knowledge, the only way to come closer to them is by taking one step towards them, and then another, and another. Even if you already know your 'soul purpose', and are living it every day, and focusing your intention and energy towards it - you can still benefit from focusing on this understanding of the particular qualities of your ancestral line, and the original duties and responsibilities that were charged to your ancestral line, it will be a very useful thing for you to understand these things, and give your life a deeper meaning, and also a deeper appreciation for your families.

Now I know that there will be a few of you who perhaps come from very difficult family situations, and have maybe even found it of great benefit to remove yourself from those families, and I am not saying that you should return, or have any contact. No, I am not saying that at all. It must be understood that because you are living in manifest creation where POLARITY is how the divine creates itself, then polarity itself causes a great many spiritual learnings and lessons. Each soul must experience the full polarity of each situation it encounters (this is not exactly true, but it is the closest I can get to teaching this to you, but you need to take in the 'spirit' of the teaching, rather than taking it as literally true). For example, if you have a lifetime of being poor, then it will 'round out' your soul learning to have a life where you are equally wealthy as you were poor. When it comes to ancestral lines, the same is true. So, if you have a family line which has been charged with the responsibility of wisdom, where there has been a great and kindly sage, there must also be an ignorant and foolish leader. In this way, the family line develops the understanding of what these things mean, and how they affect the manifest world.

But perhaps it would be better to call these duties a 'sacred task' that has been laid upon them, and so see it as an honourable thing - but you could also understand it as a debt that the family owes as payment for the gifts that they have been given! Take whatever way works for you!

Going back to the ancestral lines, if we look at polarities, we can talk about wisdom/ignorance, kindness/cruelty, hate/love, anger/peace, and I'm sure you can think of many more as you contemplate your own

family history. But what I am saying, is that however harsh your family situation possibly was as you grew up, then there exists within your family ancestral line, the opposite polarity for you to tap into.

Also, there is an 'ancestral oversoul' that you can connect to, so it is not necessary for you to try and find the 'right ancestors' to connect to for information or wisdom. You simply need to connect to the 'oversoul', (you could see this as a collective, if you wish, a little like communicating with a council of wise ones, which can direct you.)

Some of you may connect particularly to an ancestral line of women or men. This can be very powerful to experience a line of your forefathers or foremothers standing behind you and supporting you in your soul destiny, all of whom have a collective experience shared with you – an example could be a family line of medicine women or men.

What has also been generally forgotten is that is often a very specific gift that exists in the ancestral DNA (sometimes this knowledge can be found in the folk tales of your ancestry, or in stories of your grandparents/great grandparents), as each of you is part of the divine plan that makes up the whole, it very much makes sense for a particular person to carry a very specific gift – there is no need for everyone to be a 'jack of all trades' in the spiritual sense, and for that gift to be something that they do extraordinarily well! There is very limited understanding at this present time of what each of you are psychically capable of, far more than the average person's understanding of what a 'clairvoyant' can do, and this is going to start expanding out very soon now, as more and more people 'tap into' the wealth of resources that are available in their ancestral lines. ***

You are also tasked with creating balance in your ancestral line**** Now this is not the heavy work that it may sound like! This is because at your point in the history of evolution of the human race, phenomenal forces are pouring in to assist. Right now, you are at a point of 'raising vibrations', (meaning collectively, as the human race) but before that happens, your house 'needs to be put in order' (house meaning your body/ your DNA or ancestral line.) So right now, the focus is very much on preparation work, for yourselves individually, for your ancestral lines, and also for the earth and her energy lines. It doesn't need to be done perfectly (just as when you are readying your house for guests, you clean and tidy up with the time available that you have!) but it just needs to be done 'good enough'!

But these phenomenal forces that I am speaking of, are for example legions of angels, dragons & unicorns, planetary consciousnesses, and all of the powers from the different kingdoms of stone, animal, and the elements of fire, water, earth and air, and so on & so on. You are the intermediary, you are the shaman, you are the one standing in between spirit and earth as a conduit. If you focus your attention and your will on balancing your ancestral line, it will be so, because now is the time, and this is the divine will. This is why I am saying to you, even for those of you who have distanced yourself so far from your family line that you would rather not think about them, even for you, do this work, because a sacred duty was laid upon your family line, and you have the opportunity now to do a good thing, that will relieve not only the past, but all the future ancestors as you stand in a great circle together, (and as you do this, what are you all focusing upon? – I tell you, it is love for each other, and the great spirit at the centre of that circle, which is what we are all created from!)

This circle of your ancestors, has a huge wealth of experience and knowledge which you can tap into, that are directly related to your soul purpose. You can also ask them to help and support you, and they will be able to help you in ways, that otherwise they would have been unable to if you had not asked! These ancestors know the traps that it is easy for your lineage to fall into; they also know the strong points and will have many tips to give you. What an amazing resource this is for you!!

I am Sarah, and these are the words which I wish to speak to you this day. I hope this has been helpful for your understanding and development, and you are welcome to ask questions and receive answers to the best that they may be given.

My blessings are upon you, and your sacred work. Blessed Be, Blessed Be, Blessed Be, Amen!"

*** It is not necessary for you to have been part of your 'ancestral line' from a past life for it to be relevant for you in this lifetime, or for you to work with it. If you are reading this, then you are being called to connect more strongly with the ancestral line that you have been born into, because it will benefit you, and also because you can benefit it with helping to balance the energies within it. Some people are incarnating on the earth at this time (from other star systems) as 'guests' into the ancestral line, and may only have one incarnation, but they still have something to offer and vice versa.*

**** The current upsurge in numbers of people wanting to find out their ancestry through companies such as 23andme.com is coming from this wave of energy coming up from the collective unconscious that is attracting us towards working with our ancestors. Even just thinking about our ancestors through sites such as this, and even without us doing any 'spiritual' work, is connecting us more powerfully to them, and allowing them to step in and contribute a little more!*

***** As far as I understand it at the moment, your ancestral line includes all of the different strands of DNA that have been brought together to make what makes you 'uniquely you', and that your 'ancestor purpose' will also be unique to you, within the greater context. However, our understanding of these things is very basic right now, and it will be interesting to discover what each of us finds out!!!*

These words which Sarah speaks in one of her very first channelings, (you can find the whole channeling in Sarah's little book of Healing.) It *feels to me like this is what she is referring to, the codes and keys which are 'hidden' away in our DNA!*

"My father, performed many miracles.

I am here to light up your hearts so you can perform those miracles yourself.

Remember who you are!

You are the Divine made manifest, the divine clothed in the wonders of matter.

It is time to awaken, time to remember; you are not the consciousness of your body and your mind, they are the physical manifestation of you, each of you is the Divine, birthed into manifestation, given individual consciousness.

I have come to help you remember what you already know, to empower you to be the perfect and divine beings that you are!"

The Importance of your Ancestral line

In this channeling then, Sarah has linked our life purpose to our ancestral lines; our souls deliberately choose the ancestral lines that will give the soul the potential to fulfil their purpose!

Sarah, what can you tell us about ancestors? Please can you tell us more about the sacred roles each lineage has been given and how we can tap into them now for support. *(Question is from a live interview.)*

"Blessings, I am Sarah. Each of you comes from very different distinct ancestral lines. Right at the beginning of time at the beginning of creation, each of your ancestral lines were charged with a specific purpose, with a specific role or job to do and then in order to fulfil that sacred task, you were given the gifts and the functions through your DNA that were needed to fulfil these tasks.

Now because you are living in a world of polarity, your ancestral lines have had to live through both polarities of being able to carry out these tasks and then not being able to carry out these tasks because this creates the fullness of the learning. However, now is the time for you to understand and have more consciousness about the role, the function, the tasks, and the jobs of your specific ancestral line. This might not be visible from looking at your nearest family members. In fact, I can almost prompt you that this is the case - so how can this be achieved then?!* You can do it through meditating, you can do it through (if you have the ability), tracing back your energy lines right back to the beginning. You can also work with those people who have some skill in this area, and who are able to support and assist you. You can also ask the universe for signs; you can also do an oracle card spread for yourself. You can also use whatever tools you have in your toolbox. It is more that you have the awareness that this is so. (*Sarah means that by having the awareness that your ancestral line has particular gifts, then the universe will start to put ways in front of you, so that you can discover what they are.*)

Many of you talk about your soul purpose and of course your soul has an essence, your soul has lived through lifetimes and lifetimes and lifetimes and lifetimes gathering experience, gathering skills, some of which you will have brought into this life as an energy field around you.. Yet I would say to you, *do not forget the importance of your ancestral line*, the ancestral field around you, your DNA gives you powerful and specific gifts that your soul wants you to express in a unique way and here again we have another integration. We have the soul, the spirit, the physical body and the DNA coming together in oneness, coming together in unity and this is where the greatest power is, this is how you can manifest all of these things on the earth in your lives and in your jobs - not stuck up there on the higher levels but happening right here right now, being the piece of the puzzle that you are.

I am here to inspire you, to light that fire of inspiration within you, and now that seed has been planted, you can go away and see what comes to each of you and it will be so!

Blessed be, blessed be, blessed be, Amen."

(See Online Classes for the Sarah class which I taught for working with these Ancestral energies).

Sarah & the Star Babies

This is from an interview I did for the Sacred You podcast with Anjuna Sara'n Magdalena, where she talks about her work with Sarah. It's not an area that I have worked within, yet as Anjuna talked about it, I immediately felt Sarah's Divine Presence running through the whole 'program'. I asked Anjuna if I could quote her here, so that this very important topic and beautiful work could be included in this book. (Find the Sacred You podcast and Anjuna's details under Links)

'Sarah is the future for me, also she's the one who brings the new Star babies through. She's like a Star Midwife, and she's preparing the women to Receive. As she's working through me when I do ceremonies with Sarah, it's all about light conception… It's a lot about working with the womb; it's amazing - and preparing the womb of the women. Because many wombs of the women are still infused or programmed with the old stories of partners and victimhood, and we know all that… right? And they really have to receive salvation from it, their babies, their star babies. And they have contracts with certain star babies, and I use this word 'star babies' because these babies, they have a really beautiful gift. I mean every soul brings a beautiful gift and we are all from the stars, but there is - as she has showed me, there is a whole new group of beings who want to come through. And this world has to be prepared, the woman has to be prepared, the parents have to be prepared… Sarah is teaching the parents how to become more aware and conscious, working really with all the forces of nature, and all the divine forces to be in service for the highest good of all beings. And receiving the star babies; because these babies who are coming & who are going to come through - they are already masters.'

The Land where you Live

In the next channeling, Sarah talks about the 'area of influence'! This is the area that you are energetically connected to, and varies with each person, depending on the individual and also the type of place and surrounding area of where you live. We work with this in the Earth priest/ess of Sarah training! Sarah talks about a process of cleaning up energy in your 'area of influence', which also is a process of deepening into the land energies. In doing this work, you can then 'be here' in greater degrees than you ever have been able to before. Sarah has given us many different ways of achieving this, which root us down very deeply into the land, and provide us with the strength and balance we need to take our work up to 'the next level'. This generally means working with the collective, and the earth on a more planetary level.

"Welcome all, I am Sarah! I would speak to you this day about the land where you live. Each of you has an area that you call home, and this is the area which you are now being called to work with. It is wonderful to travel and experience sacred places, but each place on the earth is a sacred place in waiting! Whilst it is true that a certain amount of time is needed before the earth's new grids become fully online, that doesn't mean that there is no work for you to do now. A large clean-up operation needs to be put in place for you to each clean up an area around your home. As you can imagine, there is much debris lying around energetically, and this is something that must be tackled, in the same way that physical waste needs to be tackled. But in truth, the cleaning up of the energetic waste is paramount to the cleaning up of the physical waste. What exists in vibration is what attracts the physical matter to come into form. If you clean a site of waste physically, but don't clean up the energetic waste that has caused it, then within a matter of days and weeks and months, the physical litter and pollution will have returned.

I am Sarah, and I tell you that each thing that each of you does, has an impact on the whole, and affects the entire web. You are all connected, one to each other, and what one does, sends out vibrations along the lines of light that connect you all in this great web/net of light. Each of you has responsibility over the area where you live, and there you are connected to your local elementals and land deities, and so you can much more effectively and safely deal with the cleansing of these areas, and so this is the place to start.

I am Sarah and I give you my blessings, blessed be, blessed be, blessed be, Amen!"

In this next channeling Sarah refers to her Ashram (see glossary) which is above Kilauea, the active volcano on the Big Island of Hawaii. The earth energies around Hawaii are exceptionally high, and the New Earth grid (see glossary), exists here in a much more pristine state than many other parts of the world. Hawaii has a vital role to play in bringing down energies for the earth for our evolution, and is a place with a high enough vibration for this download of energy to be possible to actually happen. There are also Hawaiian deities, such as Pele, the goddess of the volcano and lava flow, and one of her sisters, Hi'iaka who also can assist us and Sarah in this work. Pele, as goddess of the lava flow, is able to prepare us so that we are then ready to work with 'the next level', that Sarah brings.

Earth Engineers from Atlantis and Lemuria are Awakening

"Welcome, I am Sarah. I would speak to you about the ascension earth grids and what that might mean. Of course, these names don't mean anything in themselves, they are just ways to refer to something that you don't actually have words for. The ascension grid is an interface between yourselves and the earth. The earth herself has a very high consciousness; she is already 'ascended' one might say in her consciousness, and yet her physical body is somewhat 'behind'. This is the 'disconnect' that you have been feeling when you have attempted your journeys to the Ashram, each time you have to 'purify', not just yours, but also to an extent, the energy that is around you, so that you can 'reach' the energy of the Ashram. There is a 'disconnect' between the earth's consciousness and her physical body, and this is because of the lower vibration that has been created by humanity.* Each human being's body is made of the earth. It starts as a very high vibration, as high as the earth's consciousness herself. This is why newborn babies are so deliciously pure, because they start out at the same vibration of their own soul's light and that of the earth together. Then as they become more and more descended into the energy matrix of humanity, that purity is lost, and the vibration lowered. The earth also has many places of accumulated negative energy that have built up by people who have not been in 'right relationship', whether with themselves, or each other, or the earth. But being in right relationship (in the world today) is a big job that takes a lot of consciousness, because the 'built up' thought forms of humanity, are generally leading you astray, and into less healthy and more negative patterns of thought and behaviour.

But we are reaching a tipping point now, where it will be possible for 'the light' to start becoming more present and more dynamic. One of the reasons why it has been so hard for people to connect 'up' to the light, is because your 'software' on the earth is not currently sophisticated enough. There are talks of many different types of grids. Crystalline grids, Christ grids and so on. It is not possible for me to explain in technical terms using letters and words what these different grids are and their functions, for this you need light language, and of course, even to call it a grid is not technically correct, but we must do the best that we can, with the limitations that we have. As I said before, the ascension grids are an interface between the New Earth grid** that is now present in a rudimentary form, and higher levels of vibration. This interface, being built in co-creation with the divine forces such as nature spirits, angels and so on, will be able to exist on the etheric level (which is one step away from physical matter, and though not visible to the human eye, is actually part of the 'physical' realm). The ascension grids will make what is not generally accessible to the higher dimensions accessible (meaning that it will be easier to access, through the interface, which exists as a 'physical' thing, higher states of consciousness, such as peace, joy, abundance and so on).

What is being suggested is a web of light that is grounded down through each individual who is ready to receive this 'seed'. From this seed will grow this web of light that is interfacing between the New Earth grid and the consciousness of humanity. Each person will be able to spread that ascension grid out as far as it is they have influence over their local area, and this will differ from person to person and place to place. One way to describe this is to compare what happens energetically when you have a cat. Most of you who have had cats will know that cats are hugely attached to their geographical area. They have an area that is 'theirs'. They are generally not happy or feeling safe if they are outside this area. This is because 'their' area is defined by the cat stretching their energy field out over that entire space. To say 'aura' isn't exactly correct, but it is a function of the aura to put out an energy field in this way. Each of you has an energy field that goes out into the local area around where you live. You might not realise this, but it is true. For some of you, it might be as small as your own living area, and for others it might spread a number of kilometres all the way around you. (This is how you are 'connected' to the land around you where you live.) It also depends on how populated your area is where you live. It is the same if you have a cat, is it not? If there are a lot of cats in the neighbourhood, each cat's area tends to be smaller!

But some of you have been earthworkers and earthhealers in lives gone past, particularly Atlantis and Lemuria, and some of you have been trained, created even to be earth engineers. These are people who can affect the energy systems of large pieces of land, through working in co-creation with the divine forces at their disposal. Many of you are waking up now, and realising that perhaps your healing skills go beyond working just with people, and that you have an actual technical ability to create lines of light upon the earth.

Working with the area that your energy field extends out to, is a safeguard within itself. The basic function of this energy field, on an 'animal' level is to highlight any dangers to you, and to keep you safe. This is because, to whatever level you have attuned yourself to, within your 'field of influence', you will be aware of threats and dangers coming in, and problems in the energy systems. Indeed, those of you who have a soul energy signature of being 'earth engineers' will have an aura that will start sorting out these problems by themselves once they are detected. This is why you are unable to be in areas of severe negative energy or that have severe energy system failures, (unless you are there to work on a specific task), because your aura is then constantly trying to work to fix the problems and you become exhausted. It is really important then, that if you have the energy signature of an earth engineer, that you find somewhere to live where the energies are not too disturbed, and/or build an effective grid using crystals, for example, that create a 'good enough' energy bubble for you to live within.

On a higher level then, the function of this energy field of influence is to denote the area that you should 'take care of' and maintain to its highest level of functioning. This is what we would teach you now. It is time to remember. And as we teach you these things, that are really are a 'remembering' for each of you, rather than something you are learning for the first time, you will be able to affect and influence your area to a positive effect, and then we will be able to teach you how to 'grow' your ascension grid around you.

It is important that you don't overextend your field of influence, because you will not be able to energetically maintain it. If you overextend your field of influence, it will weaken your energy system, and the health of your own energy system and your local area will need to be repaired & re-energised again.

But you don't need to worry about these things, all of these things are very easy to learn, and will not be difficult for you to find out about. These things are so simple, once you have learnt them and they are part of your life, you will wonder how it was that you never knew them! But it is because, the time is now for you to remember these things once again. The energies have reached the correct level for your hearts, minds and consciousness to realise the obviousness of these things. There is no struggle here, only an 'aha'!

If you feel the call of this truth, then it will be easy for you to learn these things, because the energy signature will already be present in your energy field - this is like a programming. Any difficulties you have with the process will come from energy blocks, and as you know already, all these things can be overcome, given a little time and sometimes a little extra help from others.

I am Sarah, and I work with a council of 'elders' for the earth. These are simply 'people' (beings of light) who have the correct experience, qualities, tools and training for assisting the earth and humanity with their ascension. It is this council that will be providing the support and teaching necessary, and I am for the moment the 'face' of the council, which is also intergalactic (just as the earth is herself a being of light that has a body in this solar system.)"

*this split is closing all the time, and Sarah's Ashram moves ever closer to the Earth plane!
**See glossary.

There is a Light coming over the Earth

"Welcome I am Sarah. There is a light coming over the earth that can be seen as a dawn. Many of you can relate to the experience of having had a very 'long dark night of the soul', and now there is to be the first glimpse of the light. First of all, it will be as if your 'eyes' are imagining it. Is the light coming, or is it still night, and you will wonder, 'am I just imagining this glimmer because I am looking so hard at the horizon'?!! But no, you will know for certain that you are seeing the first moments of the dawn. Not the full coming of the light as yet, but enough to give you hope. Within yourself, you will feel a lifting of the heaviness that has been pressing on your soul. A certain point of achievement has been reached, a road will have been crossed, and you will know that all of your (collective) work has not been wasted.

But what does this mean in actual, pragmatic terms?

It means that now is the time for you to truly focus on clearing the world around you. There is a moment coming where the world you live in, the earth herself, will be ready to shake off her old costume and will want to put on her new attire (the New Earth grid*). But right now, there is too much magnetic discharge to allow this to happen. Too much human energy waste from the last eon is present upon the surface of the earth, and it is mankind's responsibility to cleanse and clear it. Many of you have successfully cleansed your own energy fields and now you are ready to move onto the next level of your evolutionary process (ascension), but you are held back by the contents of your house (the earth), which also needs the same level of cleansing that you have given yourself. This work has already been started by those who have been doing earth work, but this work needs to be done at a much greater magnitude and frequency now. The time is coming now not to focus on your own development, but to work with the areas of land around you, because you cannot develop further without bringing the earth into alignment with you.

It is not that the earth needs your help. The earth is herself already 'ascended' within her consciousness, but it is more that *this is your time now* to come into mastery, and rather than the earth doing this work 'for you', now is the time for humanity to 'step up to the plate', going beyond what you thought you were capable of, and realising that you are all Star Beings. The earth herself is part of the galactic cosmos, and so are you. Those who created the earth's current energy system, are present in physical incarnation on the earth again, in enough numbers for the next level of earth's evolutionary 'software upgrade' to happen again.* *You* are those ancestors who knew how to create the earth grid in co-creation with the earth and all of her kingdoms. *You* are the connector between the lower and upper worlds, between the heavenly and elemental realms. *You* are the ones who simply need to open up to physically receive the energies and the information you need for everything that needs to happen, to happen. But - you should not do this alone. It is too big a work for an individual. Do it in groups**. Do it in co-creation with the Divine and each other. Use everything you have learnt up until this point. Did you think it was all for your own spiritual development that you have come this far? No, it is not for the individual but for the evolution of the whole of humanity and for the Earth, for Gaia, and as you move and shift upwards, you will all move together, and the earth with you. And so it is.

I am Sarah and these are the words that I would wish to speak to you this day. Blessed be, Blessed Be, Blessed Be, Amen."

See glossary for explanation of the 'New Earth grid'.
**These groups can be physical groups or virtual online groups*

What should you do?!

"The Divine's plan is always shifting and changing, and in fact it is humanity that is an outward expression of that Divine plan. You are all working together as a collective, each of you with your own blueprint of the everchanging plan as part of yourSelves! You are the living plan! Inside each of you is a spark of the divine. It is how you came to be alive. If you are here, then you are part of the Divine plan!

And what should you do?! Well, simply those things inside of yourselves that want to be done! Each of you is perfectly programmed to hold your own unique and perfect piece of the Divine plan. These manifest themselves through your personality, your desires and wishes. Your life situation is always creating the perfect conditions for you to grow and manifest that divine plan. Your difficulties force you to grow and deal with situations that you would otherwise avoid. Nothing is wasted in the eyes of the Divine, and every situation has something in it that is fuel for your development and manifestation of the Divine plan for the highest good. I know some of you will be thinking of situations that you are very certain were or are not for anybody's highest good, and yet still, I tell you it is so."

Blessings for the Sea

Sarah is particularly connected to the sea, one translation of her Sanskrit name 'Sarayei' means 'the infinite ocean', and she has a strong affinity with water. We can imagine that the sea is the lifeblood of the earth, and it seems that this is what we need to work with first as a collective; it seems the most urgent.

The oceans and seas particularly need 'great groups' to help cleanse them - although we should start with the areas where we live, and then once we have cleared the energies there, we can gain great power and grounding in order to move further afield, such as working with the sea. This suggested order is because we are going to be working much more intensely and with greater depth than we ever have before. This work may sound intimidating to some who are aware of how much work there is to be done, and yet Sarah's response is that it will take us less work than we imagine due to the abilities and techniques we are co-creating with the Divine – we will see!!

The sea welcomes our efforts towards her healing. The earth has a consciousness, and our human bodies are 'of the earth'. Thereby in directing healing towards the polluted energies of the seas and oceans, we are simultaneously healing that aspect of ourselves that has caused this contamination on the earth. As without so within. And so we can heal this part of ourselves, either through our inner work or by work in the outer world, (a combination usually is the most effective!) As this part of ourself is healed, we will find more and more solutions to the healing of the earth and her seas - from the damage that we ourselves have caused. Therefore, it is not strictly the earth or the sea that need our healing, more that we are healing the aspect of humanity that has caused this damage upon the earth, and when this is healed, so can the earth be too.

"Welcome all, I am Sarah. I would talk to you today of the sea and of how it mirrors your own physical self. You are aware that the sea has become quite contaminated, and so it is with the water element of humanity. The emotions which have been left untended, create an energetic charge, and these waves of energy (which have built up over the centuries) flow over the earth and settle in certain places. The sea has collected a great deal of this 'leftover' emotional debris/waste, and the time is now & for the generations ahead for the clean-up process. One day the sea will once again have an energetic signature which is pure and sparkling, and when this occurs, humanity's energy body will mirror that sparkling purity. What a time that will be!! Such beauty, here on the earth.

All is well, all is well, all is well. The Divine's perfect plan is built upon a rock, ever changing, ever growing, ever creating, ever ending. All is well, all is well, all is well.

So do not think that there is little you can do, there is much you can do. You can start (if you aren't already) to acquaint yourself with the environmental issues that exist at this present time. You can make small changes in your life so that you yourself, contribute less and less towards these difficulties. But also, at this time, you can contribute greatly by starting to shift the essence of the sea back to where it belongs. It is hard for the places on the earth (including the sea) to keep their consciousness present when pollution and toxicity is present. Where pollution occurs, the consciousness of that place withdraws. Places on the earth where the consciousness is very present are places that you think of as 'sacred places' or 'power places'. Some of these are known, many are not.

But before the physical clean-up of the sea occurs, the energetic clean-up of the sea needs to be well underway. As always, change happens from the 'outer' or 'higher' realms first (which are not really outer or higher realms at all, but it suffices here to say so) and then moves down into the physical. These are the laws of working within the physical realm.

As with all things, this can be achieved most simply by 'bringing God into it'. By this I mean, calling upon the Divine to enter into that which needs healing. Intent is everything; method can be chosen according to personal preference!!

As a human, you can take it upon yourself to do this on behalf of humanity, and each piece of work that you do will spread out exponentially. Think not that your efforts are too small to be of practical use. Each part makes up the whole, and each piece of this work that you do will lead us all closer to that sparkling purity that lies ahead. Before beginning the work, imagine the earth as her beautiful, radiant self; pristine and clean once again. Feel how wonderful this is & will be, as we move towards that time now. Resolve to hold that possibility as reality in your heart, and to know that it is so, and that nothing is too great for the Divine Creator, that exists within each and every one of us.

All is well, all is well, all is well.

Deny not the anger and pain that may arise in your heart for the predicament of the earth and the suffering of the creatures that live upon her and who are dying even as we ponder on how we can solve these environmental difficulties. Allow them to be there, but then call upon the Divine to light up the way to healing for us all and for the earth. Bring the Divine into your heart, and allow yourself to be given hope. Simply ask for what you need, whether it is hope or reassurance or whatever it is you might need and then imagine yourself opening up to receive it, and it is so.

Use 'all is well' as a mantra, which you breathe in and out of your heart space, when you feel overwhelmed and that no solution can be found; that the world is too harsh a place.

But overall, believe in the possibility that it might be so, allow yourself to day-dream of a world where all is well, and how that might feel, how that might look like. Think on the things that touch you deeply in the world today, those things that sadden you, and then imagine how they would then look in a world where all is well, and pray to the Divine that these things might be so and for the highest good of all.

Blessings are upon you, each and every day of your lives,
All is well, all is well, all is well, Sarah."

The Norns, mistresses of the weave and of the Tapestry of Life, teach us that the past informs the present. We are the sum of our memories, and yet we are more than that. Memories can be shaped and changed. Traumas can become healing memories. Some things can be laid to rest. Yet there is another memory within the body. This is the memory of the Soul.

The body is imprinted with all that the Soul wishes us to know, understand and follow in THIS lifetime. It is your body that is your guide. When you have a thought about something, feel into your body and ask – is this true?! If your body lights up in response, then you have your answer. When you read these words, your body recognises what is true for you, or what isn't. When you see, hear or read the truth, your body has a resonating chime, and this is how you can accept those things you know as truth.

There is a trinity between the Divine Feminine (Mary Magdalene), the Divine Masculine (the Master Jesus), and the Divine in Oneness (the daughter Sarah). Sarah is bringing the teachings and the guidance of how to be in oneness in a physical life, even whilst (we live) within the physical laws of polarity.

She does this as Ascended Master, guiding from her Ashram, and also from the Etheric planes on Earth, where she is in (etheric) physical existence.

She also anchors her Archetypal force into the Earth grid by incarnating many pieces of her soul. The numerous aspects of Sarah's soul are incarnated here at this present time, and are enough to help birth and anchor this archetypal force - that comes to help humanity usher in the 'golden age', and to take up their new responsibilities as co-creators with the Divine. Most of Sarah's soul (which is vast) is not incarnated on the Earth.

…The picture that I get, is that tiny fragments of Sarah's soul are each able to take up physical existence as an incarnation, and that this is done

in this way, so as not to overwhelm the ancestral line of those families, or cause complicated difficulties to that individual person living that life, but allows for this soul to be integrated into the community and allow a life to be lived, whilst at the same time, grounding this archetypal force, and allowing it to manifest in whichever way that (incarnated) life/ person chooses. It also creates a web/net of light across the globe that means that change is inevitable, because a new 'colour' (energy) is now present amongst the weave, and things cannot stay the same, because they are not (the same)!

And then Sarah is impressing these words upon me:

"I am Sarah, and I tell you, all is well, all is well, all is well. Nothing is awry and all is well. Each moment is created in response to the will of the Divine, each moment perfect and preparing for the moment ahead. Blessings are upon you, each and every moment of your life, blessed be, blessed be, blessed be, Amen."

Afterword

The Orange Thread

In Sanskrit, the sacral/orange chakra is called the Svadhisthana, which means sweetness! This chakra offers us the possibility of experiencing the sweetness of life on Earth, through experiencing our sexuality, our creativity, sensuality, pleasure, emotions and our relationships!

Sarah's 12 Step Program to Ascension

For the last few years, I have been working with 'Sarah's 12 step program to Ascension', and just to make that clear – that's EMBODIED Ascension. Embodied Ascension refers to the process of us integrating with our Higher Selves, whilst living an earthly life! In my 20's, I had a plastic bunch of orange tulips that lit up when you plugged them in - now I'm not normally one for plastic flowers but something about them when they were illuminated, was so special, so magickal! I used to say that they represented a colour that we can't even see yet on earth, and that they represented the colour of my soul!! Now I don't know if that's true, lol, but I know that looking at the colour and light experience they created - they were plugging me in to some latent possibility that was so beautiful! Many years later, I think that it is this potential which each of us have, to embody our Divine Self, and be our Higher Selves on the Earth. Fully Human, fully Divine.

This illuminated orange colour also represents Sarah's Ashram, a place which represents the energy of 'the time when we are living in oneness with our Divine Self'. (If you sign up to my welcome newsletter, you will receive a free meditation/journey to travel there! See Links!)

This is a channeled excerpt from 'The centre of yourSelf' channeling from Sarah's book of Healing, and talks about this mission we have to integrate with our Higher Selves, and All That We Are!

"Today I wish to speak to you of how the Higher Self can inhabit your physical body and become more nearly the way in which through you can be in contact with nirvana, in fact of all of creation, all of the time. These are the mysteries I have come to teach.

Your body is your physical tool here on this earth; it is how you will effect change here on the physical planes. The ascended masters, the angels and archangels, all can assist and help from the realms within which we exist; we can gently persuade and create optimum conditions from within which the best possible chances for change and transformation can occur. But it is YOU that has the power to create the New Earth here in physical manifestation, and in so many more ways than you know.

You are upon your mission to become more of who you are, a Nara-Narayani, your Higher Self here in full manifestation upon the earth."

Sarah's Ashram holds the energy of us being All That We Are. It doesn't mean that we have to transcend the 'sweetness' of life, but to live it fully, tasting each drop.

We are the Weavers, AS are the Norns, as is Sarayei, Sarah, Sara, Sar'h, Sarah Tamar - the daughter of Yeshua & Mary Magdalene. They are the master weavers showing us how to Integrate all the threads of our Being - each one of us a perfectly unique and Divine Design full of Wonderfulness and Magick!!

And from Sarah,

"All is well, all is well, all is well!
My Blessings are Upon You!
Blessed Be, Amen,
Sarah."

And finally…
A little poem by me to Sarah
'If I was to say
how you came into my life
what would it be?
that one day I imagined you there
& so it was!
And you never went away!
…I've not thought too much about it
just got on with it
like I do with everything!

I wonder if that was a coping strategy of my Ancestral Mothers?
Don't think – just do!
A requirement for survival?!

So if I were to say
how you came into my life
and I told the truth….
then you came in a cloud of green –
whenever I closed my eyes, there you were

green, green, green.
I thought I was mad,
I thought I was stupid,
I thought I was WRONG!
And maybe I was
maybe I am!
Who's to say?!

But you being there –
Well, it helps me!
You've taught me things
I needed to know!!!

You being there
has helped other people…
You help them shine THEIR light
& you do it so well!
Better than anything I've ever seen!!!

So I don't care if you're 'real'
or imagined!
I don't care if others say
my channelings are cheesy
(well, maybe a bit!)
It works – you 'work'
for me 🖤
Blessings to Sarah!! Hooray!!
Amen.'
Written by Rachel 2020.

Just Before You Go...

You can find all of my books over on my author page at Amazon! (Just type in Rachel Goodwin to whatever your local Amazon is, and when the books come up, just click on where it says my name.)

Please consider writing a book review on Amazon if you liked this book, or share it on your groups and pages in social media – book reviews are like gold dust to us authors, it really can make the difference between someone buying a book or not buying a book. You can help me get Sarah's name out there! There are many who are waiting to be touched by her light!

If you write a review, let me know, and I will send you a special thank you from my heart!

Wishing you many Sarah Blessings!

Rachel Goodwin,

Glossary

Ascended Master: An Ascended Master is someone who has lived on the earth, and reached a point in their spiritual development where they don't need to reincarnate anymore! They have learnt what they need to learn by being here on Earth. There are many 'Ascended Masters' that none of us have ever heard of, and many more than we would imagine. Examples of 'famous' Ascended Masters could be Buddha, Jesus, or Quan Yin, as well as Mother Mary and Mary Magdalene. Others who became well known through the theosophical movement are St. Germaine, keeper of the Violet Flame and the Master Morya. The 'known' Ascended Masters are male or female, and have a recognizable face, because they have a specific role to play – a job to perform if you like, and carry out in accordance with the Divine Will. Sarah is a 'new' Ascended Master. She has only now stepped forward at this point in humanity's evolution… because this is her time--- She›s here to mentor us into the 'New Age'; to walk by our sides - not to guide us, but to show us how to find what we already know! Humanity has approached the time where we need to discover our own innate wisdom, and the Divinity inside each of us! We are stepping into our own mastery.

Ashram: The Ascended Masters are each said to have an Ashram somewhere on the Earth. An ashram is an Indian term, meaning a place where one strives towards a goal. Sarah's Ashram holds the vibration of the energy that she seeks to integrate back into the earth plane, in accordance with the Divine Will, and it is possible to do a meditation journey in order to visit there on the Etheric planes. (See the Links for the Welcome Newsletter to receive a free meditation journey to Sarah's Ashram.)

Glastonbury Tor: A sacred site in the UK, adjacent to Chalice Well where the Red Spring emerges, as well as the White Spring close by. Avalon and the Arthurian legends are tangibly present in this magickal landscape. Sarah has a Violet Flame Temple in Glastonbury, and her mother, the Magdalene has an etheric temple within Chalice Hill, (see Classes.) In the Magdalene's Temple, Sarah is handmaiden, as her mother is the great healer who prepares us to work with Sarah!

Higher Self: there are many ways to describe the Higher Self and Soul, and we tend to each find our own way of understanding, but my way is this. I see the Higher Self as the first expression of the individuated Divine Spark, and the highest in vibration. When I've seen the Higher Self energetically, it's very large, and only a small piece manifests within one person at a time. The next manifestation and lower down in vibration as we move towards physicality is the Soul. The Soul has a more earthly quality, and carries the 'soul purpose', meaning what we have come to incarnate to learn. Another way of understanding the Higher Self is as Spirit; in this way of seeing, Spirit is masculine and Soul is Feminine. (This is not literally true, but many artists and philosophers, have seen soul and spirit in this way, and there is 'a truth' to it, even while Spirit can be seen as an expression of Sophia.) The third expression is the physical body. All 3 expressions come from the original spark of the Divine, and are the same thing seen from a different vibration.

Hrit Padma: The 'sacred lotus of the heart' or 'sacred heart' is placed energetically in between the heart and the solar plexus, and in Vedic teachings is considered to be the seat of the Soul. It is where our Divine Spark is located. See also, the Threefold Flame.

Lightbody: Human energy field body.

Narayana and Narayani: In the Narayanaya Suktam, it is said that Narayana is Brahma, Vishnu and Shiva. Narayana is the the flame/divine spark that burns within the Hrit Padma. Narayana is transcendant and sleeps floating in a sea of inky black - but it is him who places the threefold flame/divine spark within each of us. Narayani is the feminine form of Narayana, she is within manifested creation. Another name for Narayani is Lakshmi. In the Lakshmi Tantra it says, "'There is no place where He exists without me. There is no place that contains me without containing Him...There is not a single place nor moment when it is possible for me to exist without Him, or for Him to exist without me." That they are separate is illusion, and Narayani is the divine feminine force that leads us to realise this Truth. Sarah holds these energies. Her 'human' face is that of Narayani, but she also holds the energy of Narayana – because that they are separate is only an illusion. This is Sarah's truth that she has come to help us realise, that of Oneness and Unity.

New Earth Grid: A grid is 'a network of lines that cross each other', for example, an electrical grid powers a town and surrounding area. The earth has energy lines in the same way that human beings have a meridian system. (A concept used in Chinese medicine to describe how 'Qi' or life-energy flows around the body.) These earth energy lines can be described as ley lines, song lines, and dragon lines. The New Earth grid holds high vibrational energies that are 'a stepped down version' of divine energy, and support life on earth in the 5th dimension (and above). This New Earth grid is a physical manifestation of the energies that exist in the Higher vibrational realms; the New Earth matrix made matter, as it were. A matrix of energies can be understood as a pattern or code of energies that operate somewhat like a blueprint. Sarah has shown me that when the New Earth grid is complete, we will be able to access the higher divine energies here physically on the earth. Currently we are able to reach these higher energies through meditation and spiritual practice. The grid is in the process of being built. As human beings exist in the 'middle world', and are able to connect above and below, we are a key component in the building of this grid. Gathering together at sacred sites (whether physically or online) enables Spirit to download parts of the New Earth energy matrix into the grid.

Paramatman: In Hindu philosophy, Paramatman is the Universal Soul. It can also be described as the Collective Consciousness, Absolute Reality or Truth. The Atman is the individual self – on an energetic level, we could describe this as the Divine Spark. As Sarah's work always deal with the polarities, she also represents the individuated spark aswell as the Eternal/Universal Soul. These can also be described as Narayani and Narayana (see above).

Soul: see Higher Self

Sophia: How do we define the indefinable?! Sophia could be described as the Divine Feminine consciousness. She is said to be the Holy Spirit – Divine Wisdom. She appears in many different cultural sources from ancient times to present day, and you could drive yourself a bit crazy trying to understand all the different references that have been made over time about Sophia! But the best way to know her, is to experience her yourself! Light a candle and ask Sophia to Presence Herself to you – see what happens!! (or for more information, read Caitlin Matthews book on Sophia in the Bibliography!)

Spirit: In this book, I am often using the word Spirit with a capital S to mean 'that which we are guided by'. In an animist understanding of the universe, all things are created by Divine Source; we can communicate with all things in nature, animals, trees, the sky, the land and so on. Also, things that are made, such as a chair, a picture, or a book has a type of consciousness. Spiritualism would refer to Spirit as being angels, guides, ancestors, ascended masters. We could just simplify it and say 'Spirit' refers to the invisible world of the Divine, gods and goddesses, and all light beings. The list of these is too long here, but if you communicate with them, and get divine guidance, then that's what I mean by Spirit!!

Threefold Flame: The energy of the threefold flame is available to us at the Hrit Padma. It is our Divine Spark. This energy is neither male and female, and yet is both. It is transcendent and immanent. This flame of the transcendent and the immanent burns within us; we are the flame! It has also been called Mahamaya and Narayana's Flame. Sarah holds this energy of the Threefold Flame. See also Narayani and Narayani.

Healing System with Sarah & the Angels

Want to go further and deeper with healing with Sarah?
You can receive initiations into Sarah & the Angels Healing System!

1st level – you are initiated into and attuned to Sarah's Angels white healing ray
2nd level – you are initiated into and attuned to Sarah's violet flame
3rd level – you are initiated into and attuned to Sarah's green ray of healing
4th level – you are given all of the symbols for using with advanced healing methods
5th level – you are taught how to initiate others into Sarah and the Angels healing system

Visit rachelgoodwin.dk to find out more
or to contact Rachel for class dates:

About the training https://www.rachelgoodwin.dk/healer-training/
About the healing system https://www.rachelgoodwin.dk/sarah-healing/

Links

Anjuna Saran Magdalena, *Divine Channel of the Christ Rose Lineage*: https://www.soullightbeing.com/

Louise Keoghan, *Sarah Healer & Teacher, contact her for Sarah healing sessions and training courses:* http://www.celestiallightalchemy.com/

Mary Tobin, *Voice for Mary Magdalene, read the Blue Rose Channeling here*: https://www.bluerosehealing.com/blog/melchizedek

Sacred You Podcast, *spiritual podcast with Rachel and guests*: https://anchor.fm/sacred-you

Website:

Welcome newsletter:

Receive a free journey meditation to Sarah's Ashram!
https://app.getresponse.com/site2/ascendedmastersarah/?u=hsajf&webforms_id=hlF8e

You can also sign up for the Welcome newsletter on any of our social media pages

Sarah & the Angels Healing System:

About the healing system https://www.rachelgoodwin.dk/sarah-healing/
About the training https://www.rachelgoodwin.dk/healer-training/
Find a Sarah healer https://www.rachelgoodwin.dk/find-a-sarah-healer/

Sarah's Temple & Priest/ess Training

**Sarah's Temple of the Sacred Flame and the
Earth Priest/ess of Sarah Training**

https://www.rachelgoodwin.dk/sarahs-temple-of-the-sacred-flame/

Facebook:

Sarah's Sacred Healing Circle FB Group:

Experience free group healing with Sarah & the Angels
www.facebook.com/groups/sarahssacredhealingcircle/

Sarah's Temple of the Sacred Flame FB Group

Receive an activation for Sarah's Temple of the Sacred Flame!
www.facebook.com/groups/sarahssacredflametemple/

Ascended Master Sarah Facebook Page

https://www.facebook.com/ascendedmastersarah

Instagram:

mary.magdalenes.daughter
https://www.instagram.com/mary.magdalenes.daughter/

rachelgoodwin.dk
https://www.instagram.com/rachelgoodwin.dk/

Online Classes

Rachel's Online School https://rachels-school-df9d.thinkific.com/

'Ancestor Intensive' – Healing with Sarah & the Angels
https://rachels-school-df9d.thinkific.com/courses/ancestor-call-healing-intensive-with-sarah-the-angels
Do you want to connect with the Divine Energy of your Ancestral Lineage? And work with the blocks and resistances to you manifesting and grounding these in your life?! Then this 2 hour intensive is for you, the time is NOW!!

'Growing your own Ascension Grid '
https://rachels-school-df9d.thinkific.com/courses/grow-your-own-ascension-grid
Ascended Master Sarah has given us the technology to build a matrix around our homes creating a sanctuary of 5th dimensional vibration for us and our families - that supports our spiritual growth as well as our Ascension process!

Mary Magdalene's Etheric Temple & 'Why Ascended Master Sarah now?'
https://rachels-school-df9d.thinkific.com/courses/why-sarah-now
Hear about Sarah's work and experience a heart healing meditation within Mary Magdalene's etheric temple in Chalice Hill in Glastonbury, UK.

'Net of Light'

https://rachels-school-df9d.thinkific.com/courses/sarah-s-net-of-light

A powerful Sanskrit chant at the beginning to clear your energy body and then a channelled meditation directly from Sarah to empower you with her 'Net of Light'. "You can call upon me and ask me to place my net of light around you. This is a little like the starry sky at night and it comes and sits around your energy body so you can just simply imagine it with little points of light in the night sky – a comforting cloak that helps give you some protection from the bombardment of the outside world and helps you maintain the energy integrity within your own light body."

'Sacred Marriage – Balancing the Divine Feminine and the Masculine'

https://rachels-school-df9d.thinkific.com/courses/balancing-the-divine-feminine-and-masculine-the-sacred-marriage

We will connect not only with healing work that needs to be done in balancing the Divine Masculine & Feminine within us, but we will also look at how you can keep this work going by spending just a few minutes a day.

'Sarah's Violet Flame'

https://rachels-school-df9d.thinkific.com/courses/sarah-s-violet-flame

Be attuned to Sarah's Violet Flame! Everything that needs moving up a level needs this energy - as a Lightworker, this is one of the most useful tools you could get... to manifest the New Earth and Co-create the Age of Aquarius!

'Sarah's Violet Flame Temple in Glastonbury'

https://rachels-school-df9d.thinkific.com/courses/sarah-s-violet-flame-spiral-temple-in-glastonbury-zoom-call

Ascended Master Sarah, daughter of the Magdalene & Yeshua, has a Violet Flame Temple in Glastonbury which was activated from a seed planted by Sarah in one of her past lives.

'Sarah's White Flame of Divinity'

https://rachels-school-df9d.thinkific.com/courses/sarah-s-white-flame-of-divinity

Sarah's Flame is coming upon the Earth! Sarah, daughter of the Magdalene, holds the Divine Template for the New Earth and is here as teacher, mentor, guide. We are Ready!!

'Sowing the Seeds of Sarayei'

https://rachels-school-df9d.thinkific.com/courses/sowing-the-seeds-of-sarayei

A Cosmic Transmission from Ascended Master Sarah! Sarah invites you to come on a journey to the Heart of the Tor in Glastonbury. Cosmic Star Child, Sarah represents a new way forward - the Divine Feminine & Divine Masculine come into Oneness & sows her Seeds of Sarayei directly into your heart. A first step to becoming an Earth priest/ess of Sarah.

Bibliography

'Braiding Sweetgrass: Indigenous Wisdom, Scientific Knowledge, and the Teaching of Plants' (2020), Robin Wall Kimmerer, Penguin.

'Mary Magdalene Revealed' (2021), Meggan Watterson, Hayhouse UK.

'Mary Magdalene, Bride in Exile' (2005), Margaret Starbird, Bear & Company.

'Mary Magdalene Beckons: Join the River of Love', (2012), Mercedes Kirkel, Into the Heart Creations.

'Sarah's little book of Healing', (2nd edition 2020), Rachel Goodwin, published on Amazon Worldwide.

'Sarah's little book of Chants, Prayers and Practices' – will be published in 2022/23

'Sophia - New Revised Edition: Goddess of Wisdom, Bride of God', (2001), Caitlin Matthews, Quest Books.

'St. Mary Magdalene: The Gnostic Tradition of the Holy Bride', (2006), Tau Malachi, Llewellyn Publications.

'The Dangerous Old Woman', (Audio Series), Clarissa Pinkola Estés, Sounds True.

About the Author

RACHEL GOODWIN is a British channel and healer, living in Denmark, who has been working with Sarah, daughter of the Magdalene since 2005. She is an initiated Priestess of Sophia, the Shekinah, and the Goddess.

Rachel was born in 1970 in a small town on the southern coast of England, and after being nominally educated at an all girls grammar school, left to try and find her way in the world. After unsuccessful attempts as a bank clerk, and then in the Royal Air Force, Rachel finally settled down as a mental health nurse, only to be launched onto a spiritual path after her mother died when Rachel was 26. In the years after this, Rachel learnt how to be a healer, channel, psychic, priestess and shamanic practitioner.

Rachel lives in the sacred town of Roskilde in Denmark, with her Danish husband and son, and can often be seen around the town happily talking to trees and communing with land energies. You can see more about Rachel and her work at https://www.rachelgoodwin.dk/

Printed in Great Britain
by Amazon